# THE NATURE OF GRE

G. S. Kirk is Emeritus Professor of Greek at Cambridge and Fellow of Trinity College; and was previously a professor at Yale, Bristol and Cambridge. He was born in Nottingham in 1921 and was educated at Rossall School and Clare College, Cambridge. His publications include *Heraclitus* (1954), *The Presocratic Philosophers* (with J. E. Raven, 1957), *The Songs of Homer* (1962), *Myth, its Meaning and Functions in Ancient and Other Cultures* (1970), *Euripides, Bacchae* (1970), *Homer and The Oral Tradition* (1977) and two volumes (Vol. 1. 1985, Vol. 2. 1990) of a commentary on *The Iliad*.

# G. S. KIRK

# THE NATURE OF GREEK MYTHS

PENGUIN BOOKS

PENGUIN BOOKS

Published by the Penguin Group
Penguin Books Ltd, 27 Wrights Lane, London W8 5TZ, England
Penguin Books USA Inc., 375 Hudson Street, New York, New York 10014, USA
Penguin Books Australia Ltd, Ringwood, Victoria, Australia
Penguin Books Canada Ltd, 10 Alcorn Avenue, Toronto, Ontario, Canada M4V 3B2
Penguin Books (NZ) Ltd, 182–190 Wairau Road, Auckland 10, New Zealand

Penguin Books Ltd, Registered Offices: Harmondsworth, Middlesex, England

First published in Pelican Books 1974
Reprinted in Penguin Books 1990
7 9 10 8 6

Printed in England by Clays Ltd, St Ives plc
Set in Monotype Bembo

For
Hugh Lloyd-Jones

# CONTENTS

# PREFACE

THIS study of the nature of Greek myths is intended, among other things, to complement my earlier *Myth, its Meaning and Functions in Ancient and Other Cultures* (Berkeley and Cambridge, 1970). At certain points, especially in Part I, it inevitably follows the same general lines; but for the most part it carries the earlier work further, within the limits of a book written for a wider audience. I have made only slight reference to Brian Vickers's *Towards Greek Tragedy* (Longman, 1973), which is critical of my emphasis on the schematic quality of surviving Greek myths. This is partly because Professor Vickers's work appeared when my own book was in page proof, but mainly because his views, although vigorously stated, do not generally strike me as being well founded.

The spelling of Greek names is sometimes inconsistent: roughly speaking, familiar names are kept in their familiar Latinized forms (e.g. Oedipus, Achilles), whereas less familiar ones (e.g. Ouranos, Lykaon) are directly transliterated. All translations from Greek are by myself.

I am most grateful to Professor Hugh Lloyd-Jones and Dr Christopher Gill for generously reading the work in typescript and making many corrections and suggestions, almost all of which were adopted. For the closing chapter I drew in addition on philosophical resources in Bristol, in the shape of Professor Stephan Körner, Dr Thomas Szlezák and Dr Christopher Rowe. Grace Nevard, a former Classics student at Bristol, gave valuable help as a research assistant. Rachel Lee typed successive drafts with persistent efficiency and tolerance. To all of these, who are innocent of my own faults, heartfelt thanks.

*March* 1974                                                      G.S.K.

# PART I

*

# THE NATURE OF
# MYTHS

# CHAPTER I

# PROBLEMS OF DEFINITION

*The Nature of Greek Myths*: it looks like the usual kind of catch-all title, but it means what it says. That is, the book's main purpose will be to discuss the sort of things that Greek myths are and are not, their functions and limitations and possible development, rather than merely to describe their contents. Plenty of other books do that; the trouble is, they usually do little else, beyond perhaps setting the myths in the broadest of cultural contexts. If they add anything at all in the way of interpretation it tends to be arbitrary and intuitive – in other words, valueless. Interpreting a myth is difficult, sometimes unexciting, and many myths, for different reasons, lie beyond interpretation. The hard truth is that before offering a reasoned interpretation of any single myth one has to make a systematic investigation of the complex nature of myths as a whole. From which the reader will see that these pages will not lead him directly to the deeper understanding of specific Greek tales, but will involve him first in a broader consideration of myths in general.

Books about 'Greek mythology' that consist mainly of paraphrases, with or without random interpretation, are all very well in their way, but they tend to leave the reader with a sense of disappointment and anti-climax. The myths seem more pedestrian, when presented that way, than we remembered or hoped them to be. The only paraphrases that satisfy are of the *Tanglewood Tales* kind. They are spare, simple, slightly emotional, and intended for children. Unfortunately they can *only* satisfy children or the childlike. Not because myths themselves are necessarily childish and innocent, or have come down from 'the childhood of the race'; rather their narrative charm survives better in a bare and evocative outline than in a detailed account that lacks the colour of the original language and literary form. That is not just a consequence of the difficulties of translating from one language to another; to some extent the same problems face even those who can read Greek and Latin. The vital fact is that myths in Greek literature exist for the most part only in brief allusions. With certain exceptions, notably the sub-epic poet Hesiod, the lyric poets Stesichorus, Simonides and Bacchylides, and the tragedians, classical Greek authors simply refer to one or other aspect of a myth – and they do so constantly – without setting it out in full. The myths were so well known that formal exposition was unnecessary, and in the high classical period, at least, it was felt to be provincial. This changed in the Hellenistic world after the conquests of Alexander the Great. Callimachus and Apollonius retold certain myths at length, and were imitated by Roman poets like Propertius and Ovid; but their exposition was artificial in tone, and their interests were concentrated on special aspects like minor aetiology or the physical transformations of heroes and heroines into trees, rivers or stars.

The consequence is that modern paraphrases are closest, not to the inspired poets of the classical age, but to the stolid encyclopedists and grammarians of the Greco-Roman era. Paraphrasts, both ancient and modern, have been in danger of transforming Greek myths into a very prosaic affair. Myths are of their nature allusive, their mode of reference is tangential. They do not aim at completeness or logical sequence, and when they are reduced to learned exposition they lose much of their charm. That, together with the tendency of Greek poets to take the main mythical plots for granted, means that a myth cannot often be presented through the continuous words of a Homer, a Pindar or a Sophocles. I shall use poetical accounts where possible, but the content of many myths will inevitably have to be reported in prosaic terms, either in a concise modern version or in the words of ancient mythographers (the best of them being Apollodorus, the author of the *Library*, who wrote probably in the second century A.D.). In order to avoid a surfeit of paraphrase and leave room for other discussions I shall deal only with myths that seem typical or most significant.

Largely as a result of the taste for paraphrase and a consequent indifference to niceties of interpretation, there is a severe shortage of books that treat Greek myths in an acceptably critical manner. That would be a rash remark if it were not supported by agonized complaints from all who have tried to teach 'Greek mythology' to students at any level above kindergarten. H. J. Rose's *Handbook of Greek Mythology* has been through several editions since its appearance in 1928, and has been translated into German, but it remains a book of paraphrases, although a good one. Robert Graves's two volumes in the Penguin series consist of extensive paraphrases adorned by interpretations of unusual idiosyncrasy. There are sundry mythological dictionaries, including an immense German one edited by Wilhelm Roscher; they too tend to be erratic over questions of interpretation, and strongly preoccupied with the literary variations of myths in the classical period itself. The best handbook is the German one by Preller and Robert (especially the part of it rewritten by the latter), but even this tells us little about the nature of myths, and in any case it is not available in English.

Much of the critical work on Greek myths written in English during this century has been done by the so-called 'Cambridge School', consisting of Jane Harrison, Gilbert Murray (an Oxford Australian), A. B. Cook and F. M. Cornford. They responded with enthusiasm to J. G. Frazer's *The Golden Bough* and to the new school of French sociologists headed by Émile Durkheim. They believed, after Robertson Smith, that all myths were closely dependent on rituals, and they rightly perceived that Greek myths are not utterly removed from savage ones as a kind of superior species. But their interpretations were one-sided and often far-fetched, and by the early 1930s classical scholars were sated with mythical theory. Certain important generalizations, together with a good deal of sheer falsehood, had been absorbed, but the general reaction seems to have been that the work of the Cambridge School, what with Jane Harrison's *Prolegomena* and *Themis* and A. B. Cook's enormous *Zeus*, was enough to last for several generations. More recently the Swedish scholar Martin Nilsson established himself as a far more critical judge of Greek myths, but his main concern, apart from the remarkable if incomplete discovery summed up in the title of his book *The Mycenaean Origin of Greek Mythology*, was with religion.

Greek scholars (I say 'Greek' rather than 'classical' because *classical* myths are to all intents and purposes *Greek* ones) have been content until recently to leave the theoretical discussion of the nature and meanings of myths to others: to anthropologists in particular, but also to psychologists and historians of religion. The results have been not altogether satisfactory. Anthropologists, as I shall show later, have become embroiled in some very extreme theories about the nature of society, and that has distorted their approach to the myths that are one of the primary manifestations of non-literate culture. Despite this, Franz Boas's *Tsimshian Mythology* of 1916 and Bronislaw Malinowski's *Myth in Primitive Psychology* of 1926 have proved to be landmarks. Recently, too, in the four volumes grouped under the general title of *Mythologiques*, the French anthropologist Claude Lévi-Strauss has advanced a new structural theory which has its own special value; but its opacity is likely to defer still further the essential clarification of basic issues and definitions. Meanwhile historians of religion have continued to concentrate on the relations between myths and rituals, an important problem which will be quite fully investigated in Chapter 10, whereas psychology continues to trim, in no very inspired fashion, the theories of the mythical unconscious outlined by Freud and Jung.

In short, it would not be unfair to say that the nature of myths is still, in spite of the millions of printed words devoted to it, a confused topic. The state of Greek myths, in particular, is only better in so far as classical scholars and the general literary public have been content to let most of the theoretical discussion wash over their heads, concentrating meanwhile either on new contributions to the paraphrase industry, sometimes with pictures, or on specialized research into literary variants.

Certain negative gains have, it is true, been recorded. Some of the wilder speculations of the past have been cut down to size; the theory, for example, that all myths are allegories of nature or of meteorological events. It seems incredible now that many of the best minds in nineteenth-century Europe could envisage myths only as encoded descriptions of clouds passing over the sun or torrents sweeping down hill-sides. But that was the case, and we owe it largely to Andrew Lang, the journalist, folklorist and teller of fairy-tales, that this strange exaggeration was eventually laid to rest. He himself put another universal theory in its place, namely that all myths are a kind of primitive science.[1] That view still has its modern adherents, and a well-known classical scholar wrote as recently as 1969: 'True myth is an explanation of some natural process made in a period when such explanations were religious and magical rather than scientific.'[2] These and other theories have their positive sides, which will be considered in Chapters 3 and 4. Meanwhile they still play their part in compendious and sometimes puzzling modern opinions, like that of an expert on Nordic myths that mythology 'is the comment of the men of one particular age or civilization on the mysteries of human existence and the human mind, their model for social behaviour, and their attempt to define in stories of gods and demons their perception of the inner realities.'[3]

One could marshal scores of generalizations like this, each inconsistent with most of the rest, each purporting to offer a definition of the underlying essence of all myths everywhere. What is wrong with such attempts is not merely their arbitrary quality and lack of supporting evidence, but also, and even more serious, their unspoken assumption that myths are all of one kind, that there can and must be some universal explanation of the nature and purpose of all myths whatsoever. It does not seem to have occurred to most scholars that the thousands of particular stories to which the name 'myth' is commonly applied cover an enormous spectrum of subject, style and feeling; so that it is *a priori* probable that their essential nature, their function, their purpose and their origin will also vary.

Consider how different are the following: the myth of the castration of Ouranos, Sky, by his son Kronos the father of Zeus; the myth of Adam and Eve; the myth of Noah and the Ark; the myth of the making of Pandora, and then of her release of evils from the Jar; the myth of Oedipus, his solving of the Sphinx's riddle and discovery of his own parricide and incest; the myth of the Minotaur in the Labyrinth; the myth of Zeus transforming himself into a bull or a shower of gold to make love to Europa or Danaë; the myth of the Labours of Heracles; the myth of the birth of the god Apollo and his sister Artemis on the island of Delos; the Myth of Er in the tenth book of Plato's *Republic*, in which Er gained a vision of the whole structure of heaven and earth; the myth of the death of the Gods, or Ragnarøk, in the Scandinavian *Edda*; the myth of the creative Rainbow Snake in many parts of Aboriginal Australia. All these are myths – they do not include equivocal 'folktales' or 'legends', to be discussed shortly – and one only has to consider a few of them to understand what profound differences they imply. One main result of our inquiry is bound to be the emphatic assertion, against all the universalistic theories of myth to be surveyed in Chapters 3 and 4 (including recent recruits like Lévi-Strauss's structural theory), that there can be no common definition, no monolithic theory, no simple and radiant answer to all the problems and uncertainties concerning myths. In this respect Greek myths go with the rest.

The first requirement is to develop a workable system of primary categories and definitions. Again, one might expect all this to have been done ages ago, if not by those who have dared to envisage a 'science of mythology' (and they range from the classicist K. O. Müller in 1825 to Kerényi and Jung) then by the anthropologists and others who have developed universal and quasi-scientific theories of myth. At the risk of seeming permanently querulous I must reveal the strange truth that the preliminary logical clarifications have not been completed and have only rarely been even attempted. Most writers have been content to accept the loose and clumsy definitions of the past, or to amend them by adding arbitrary and inadequately argued concepts of their own. What is meant by the term 'myth' itself, and how is it related to 'legend', 'saga', 'folktale' or 'fairy-tale'? What is implied by 'mythology' as distinct from 'myth' or 'myths'? Even these basic words are used in vague and indistinct ways, and no agreed set of concepts to which they might appropriately refer has ever been established.

A glance at articles on 'myth' in the encyclopedias (whether general ones or special encyclopedias of religion, philosophy, psychology, classics or the social sciences) reveals how confused the situation really is. Nor is it much better with words and concepts associated with myths in their purposive and functional aspects: 'aetiological', 'naturalistic', 'speculative', 'charter-type', and so on. One might reasonably expect historians and philosophers of religion to have established a viable language for describing the relations between religion and myths, but it is not so. 'Religion' itself is a notoriously fluid concept, but the different senses and categories of 'ritual' might have been worked out without too much difficulty. Yet most anthropological and religious writers do not even recognize any complexity in the term, and refuse to allow for the existence of different types of ritual with correspondingly different implications for their relation to myths. The situation of 'sacred', which will be examined later in considering the view that myths are sacred tales, is little better. A few writers have tried, albeit unsuccessfully, to clear up one or two of these uncertainties, and the implications of 'sacred', at least, have been the subject of copious if unrigorous debate. Yet the truth remains that there has been no sustained attempt on the part of the relevant disciplines to agree on the basic use of terms or on the avoidance or limitation of ambiguity. It may seem presumptuous to try to alter such a hallowed state of confusion, especially within the limits of a single unpretentious volume; but that is what anyone writing about Greek or any other myths in 1974 is obliged to do.

What is a myth? That, I suggest, is the proper form of the question, and not 'What is Myth?' (with a capital M), still less 'What is mythology?' (or 'Mythology'). Even 'myth' *as a collective term* is suspect. All these forms misleadingly imply that what one should be defining is some absolute essence of all myths, some Platonic Idea of 'that which is truly mythic'. They suggest that one can go straight for the essence without first consciously considering and delimiting the instances. That is one sort of defining process, but not one to which we can resort in the case of myths. It might be possible so to approach, say, the character of red-headed girls, because at least there is no doubt (if we ignore the problem of marginal cases) about what red-headed girls are and which are the red-headed ones. In the case of myths we do not know that to begin with. What we need, in fact, is some agreement about the kind of phenomena we may properly class as myths, on the basis of which we can proceed to infer more general qualities. Myths are a vague and uncertain category, and one man's myth is another man's legend, or saga, or folktale, or oral tradition. What we need to decide is the sort of thing to which the term 'a myth' can be applied by general consent; and that will entail separating off instances for which those other terms are preferable descriptions. What remains may turn out to be a class of phenomena grouped rather formally, for example by the possession of a particular narrative quality or a tendency to be expressed on special kinds of occasion, rather than by something essential to the concept of 'myth' itself.

'Mythology', even when deprived of its capital letter, is a particularly ambiguous term. It can mean two different things: the study of myths, or a set of myths. In the first use it is parallel to 'entomology', 'astrology', and the like – words that imply theorizing about or studying insects, heavenly bodies, and so on. The second use, which has become the commoner of the two, is a loose and misleading extension of the first. Statements like 'I am interested in mythology' (that is, the study of myths) are taken to imply 'I like myths as such', and as a further step 'the myths of Greece and Rome' are described as 'classical mythology'. 'Mythology' in this loose sense refers to a particular set or ethnic group of myths. *The Mythologies of the Ancient World*, for instance, is the title of a useful book, edited by S. N. Kramer, about the *myths* of the Sumerians, Egyptians, Greeks and so on. On the whole this extension of the proper application of 'mythology' is a nuisance. The only additional meaning carried by the compound word, as compared with the simple plural 'myths', is an implication of comprehensiveness or grandeur. Many people feel they can enjoy myths without wanting to study them in the analytical manner in which an entomologist studies insects. In that case what they like is not mythology but myths. Of course, I began by arguing that you have to do some *mythology*, in the correct sense, in order to enjoy *myths*; nevertheless, from now on I propose where possible to eschew the use of 'mythology' in any sense, simply to avoid misunderstandings, and to write about 'myths', 'a myth', 'sets of myths', 'the study of myths' and so on. The semantic ambiguity has no basis in ancient usage, and for Plato (the first writer known to have used the word) *muthologia* meant 'talking about, or telling, stories'. Later confusions may well have helped determine the rather muted reactions of classical scholars to the important problems still raised by myths. Has 'talking about myths' in the sense of retelling them come to be regarded as somehow tantamount to their analytical study? That is debatable, and other diversionary factors, notably the need for special attention to literary and artistic variants, have certainly played their part. Yet it remains true that 'mythology' is a highsounding name that lends a spurious quasi-philosophical glamour to what may be a very simple interest.

The etymology of 'myth' reveals, from one point of view, very little. From another, it discloses what may turn out to be a crucial, if apparently banal, fact. In Greek, *muthos* basically means 'utterance', something one says. It came to mean something one says in the form of a tale, a story. That led to still narrower applications; for example it is Aristotle's word in the *Poetics* for the plot of a play. In a different development of its meaning *muthos* was sometimes contrasted with *logos*. This latter term, which forms one element of the compound *mutho-logia*, 'mythology', implies something like 'analytical statement' or even 'theory'. From this contrast arose the exaggerated sense of 'myth' as 'untruth', a sense that can be forgotten from now on – which is not to deny that myths are predominantly fictional, imaginative creations rather than factual records. *Muthoi*, at all events, came to connote 'stories' rather than 'statements', and when the Greeks themselves talked about *muthoi* they most often meant, just as we might, the traditional tales of gods and heroes. They did not intend to imply anything in particular about the accuracy or falsehood of those tales, some of which were regarded as containing important elements of truth at least until the time of Plato.

Etymology and ancient usage suggest that myths are stories, and that does not contradict modern practice. Not all stories are myths, of course; novels are not myths, short-stories are not myths, tales improvised for children are not myths. By 'myths' we commonly mean, as the ancient Greeks did, *traditional* stories. Once again, however, not all traditional stories are myths. Many of them concern historical events and persons of the past, and, although these can take on qualities that would often be counted as mythical, they are not themselves usually classed as myths. The traditional stories about King Alfred burning the cakes or George Washington cutting down the cherry-tree are not myths in most people's vocabulary. They are not entirely historical, but they are too much caught up with history and pragmatic reality to count as myths. It is safer to give such semi-historical traditions a separate name and describe them as 'legends', since they are not useful for defining myths, except at the margins. Many Greek tales, especially those known from Homer's *Iliad* and concerned with the Trojan War, are historical or historicizing in this way. According to the present argument they are better counted as legends; yet they tend to occur in the mythological handbooks, where the proceedings at Troy usually fill a substantial chapter. Most people would probably say that Achilles, Hector and Diomedes are figures of myth, part of 'Greek mythology', but I shall argue later that they should at least be distinguished from definitely non-historical personages like Apollo, Perseus or Medea. In the initial process of definition and limitation it is better to concentrate on primary and simple instances and leave the quasi-historical tales on one side.

Can it then be said that all non-historical traditional tales are myths? Not really, because animal fables, for instance, are both tales and traditional, and yet they would not usually be described as myths. Neither would other kinds of moral or cautionary tales, which are often passed down by mouth from generation to generation and are therefore traditional. A larger category that many would hesitate to class as truly mythical comprises what are called 'folktales' – simple tales of adventure, intrigue and ingenuity, sometimes with giants or other supernatural components. Grimm's tales are of this kind; they were collected from European peasant communities, but virtually every society has its folktales. Ingenious devices or evasions, the solution of simple dilemmas, wish-fulfilment adventures involving the slaying of monsters and the winning of princesses: these are more prominent characteristics of folktales than fantasy, profundity or other-worldliness, the qualities we most expect to find in myths. Yet there is no rigid distinction. 'Folktale' qualities are found in some myths, 'mythic' qualities in some folktales. Greek myths like those about Perseus are replete with folktale elements: the dangerous quest for the Gorgon's head, the villainous king who promotes it, the magical instruments that help the hero, the tricks by which he deceives the old women and avoids Medusa's fatal glance. Even the Oedipus story is developed around incidents that are redolent of folktale: the child's discovery by the herdsman, his growing up in ignorance of his true parents, the tensions over kinship and marriage. Clearly the distinction is a complex one, and it will be elaborated in the next chapter. Meanwhile folktales contribute another large class of traditional tales that do not accord with what most people mean by myths, or at least are not central and typical representatives of the genre.

Am I perhaps being too free with phrases like 'what most people consider as myths', and with the idea that a popular view of myths forms a reasonable basis for further definition? After all, the equation of 'myth' with 'lie' is popular enough, yet it is useless for our purposes. But that is a particularized application, almost a metaphorical use. A broader view about what kind of tales should be called 'myths' may be more helpful. 'Myth' is such a general term, and its etymology and early applications are so unspecific, that one is compelled to take *some* notice of contemporary usage. Modern philosophers as well as Aristotle have started from popular opinions about indefinite subjects like goodness and the nature of Being. Provided long-standing usage is regarded as indicating no more than a broad area of probable relevance, general opinions on the range of a term and the limits of a corresponding concept can be a valuable starting-point.

'Most people' assume that myths are a special *kind* of traditional tale, and that the qualities that make them special are those that distinguish them as profound, imaginative, other-worldly, universal or larger-than-life. In fact many critics have been prepared to name some single quality that does all these things – although they naturally do not agree on what this quality might be. Anthropologists, for example, have convinced themselves that all myths are sacred tales in some sense; the most prolific living expositor of myths and religions, Mircea Eliade, feels that all myths reproduce the creative era, the time before history when things were developed and set in order. Thus it is because myths are concerned with profound subjects, with the 'sacred' or supernatural origins of things, that they possess their special aura.

That is an interesting idea which will be further explored in Chapter 3. At present it is relevant to observe merely that some agreed myths do indeed possess a quality that might be loosely described as sacred, or as evoking the possible events of a creative past, but that many others do nothing of the kind. Even Greek myths provide obvious exceptions, and they, as we shall see, are relatively restricted in their subjects. Myths about the births of the gods and goddesses and the development of the present order of things can be called sacred in one sense; some of them are extraordinarily secular in feeling (the castration of Ouranos by Kronos, for example, or the birth and precocious infancy of Hermes), but at least they are formally concerned with divine beings. The hero-myths, on the other hand, are for the most part entirely secular, and are not even placed in a strongly creative era. Some of the heroes are admittedly aided or persecuted by a god or goddess, as Jason is helped by Athena or Heracles is thwarted by Hera; and according to the strictest definition a hero has one divine parent – although that is not the case with many accepted heroes, like Oedipus or Bellerophon. Yet the dominant tone of these heroic tales is not noticeably sacred or otherworldly, not even, sometimes, especially imaginative. At some points that is because they come close to being folktales rather than myths; the Perseus cycle, as already noted, is specially dense in folktale elements. Indeed it has often been debated whether the heroic tales should be counted as true myths. More often still it has simply been assumed without discussion that what is loosely called 'Greek mythology' should be divided into 'divine myths' and 'heroic sagas'. Now the Scandinavian word 'saga' denotes a historically-based tale, and that is certainly inappropriate to many Greek hero-tales that contain virtually no historical reference whatever. Moreover most people would certainly place the heroic tales within the limits of what they mean by myths. If asked to give an example of a Greek myth they would be as likely to name Heracles and the apples of the Hesperides, or Jason and the Golden Fleece, as divine tales like those of the births of Aphrodite or Dionysus. Finally, and most important, some of the most imaginative and otherworldly Greek myths have no concern with the gods, the sacred, or any specifically creative era: the myth of the Labyrinth, for instance, or the wise Centaur Cheiron, or Talos the bronze giant of Crete.

Greek myths are strangely limited in their themes, and that is the result, as will be seen, of a long history of development and conscious organization. In particular they are substantially lacking in that obsession with the rules of social organization that is conspicuous in the myths of savage cultures. In that kind of myth, for example the Amazonian tale of Geriguiaguiatugo outlined on p. 183 f. there is no strongly sacred tone, and although the actions take place in a creative epoch it is not this that gives the myth and its variants the quality of underlying seriousness. Rather it is the tale's ability to deal with matters of lively concern to those who pass it down from one generation to the next, matters like the relation of man-made rules about incest to the instincts implanted by nature and exemplified among animals. The consequence is that non-Greek myths, although they may fit the 'creative era' idea better than most Greek ones, often depend on quite different and more practical qualities for their imaginative and evocative power.

On the whole I feel that the attempt to isolate some central specific quality of myths is misdirected. There are too many obvious exceptions. It is probably better, and less methodologically constricting at an early stage of the inquiry, to accept that several different kinds of traditional tale (with certain obvious exceptions like moralizing fables and historical tales) come under the heading of 'myth'. This accords with the impression of enormous diversity given by known sets of myths, and by the comparison of one ethnic set with another. All that it is prudent to accept as a basic and general definition is 'traditional tale'. Further examination of that apparently banal phrase is rewarding. First, it emphasizes that a myth is a story, a narrative with a dramatic structure and a climax – as Aristotle said, a beginning, a middle and an end. Myth-making is a form of story-telling. Second, 'traditional' is significant because it implies, not only that myths are stories that are told especially in traditional types of society (which means above all in non-literate societies), but also that they have *succeeded* in becoming traditional. Not every tale, even in a story-telling and non-literate society, becomes traditional – is found attractive or important enough to be passed from generation to generation. A tale must have some special characteristic for this to happen, some enduring quality that separates it from the general run of transient stories.

There is obviously not just one such characteristic, like sacredness in some sense, but a whole range of possibilities. A tale may establish itself because of its narrative force or charm. If it has no particular quality beyond that, it is probably no more than a folktale. Often, however, a tale has both narrative power and some additional interest, for example in offering an explanation for some important phenomenon or custom, palliating in some way a recurring social dilemma, recording and establishing a useful institution, or expressing an emotion in a way that satisfies some need in the individual. Then, too, it might reinforce a religious feeling or act as powerful support or precedent for an established ritual or cult practice; in that case it is 'sacred' in a clearer sense. In short, many tales that implant themselves in a society so strongly as to become traditional have to possess both exceptional narrative power and clear functional relevance to some important aspect of life beyond mere entertainment. Frequently, because transmission by a non-literate or oral society presupposes acceptance by the whole group (or at least a prominent part of it like the adult males), the important aspect of life to which the tale refers is a communal or social one. It is this social function of some but not all myths that persuaded 'functionalist' anthropologists of the Radcliffe-Brown school (on which see pp. 32, 66 f.) to argue that myths are exclusively concerned with society – that they are one aspect of its machine-like operation. That is an exaggeration, and the position has been moderated by contemporary British anthropologists. Some myths, like the wish-fulfilment ones stressed by Freud or those that deal with death as an individual prospect, obviously relate to persons rather than groups, even if they achieve permanence *through* the group in tribally organized and traditional cultures.

The position at which we have arrived is that myths are on the one hand good stories, on the other hand bearers of important messages about life in general and life-within-society in particular. In a non-literate and highly traditional culture tales are a primary form not only of entertainment but also of communication and instruction – communication between co-evals and also between older and younger, and therefore between generations. It is difficult for us, living as we do in an age of super-literacy, but also dominated by the 'media' and by advertising, to envisage a way of life in which the only forms of mass-communication (as distinct from practical communication between individuals) are ritual on the one hand, story-telling on the other. Yet it was from that kind of life that myths emerged and passed down through the tradition until they were finally recorded in writing by ethnologists, grammarians or missionaries. Development in that kind of society over several generations gave myths their characteristic density and complexity, their imaginative depth and their universal appeal. At the same time they tend to have a limited range of themes, which are made to perform multiple functions and reflect different interests. That is why global theories of myth are so peculiarly disastrous. Not only do they fail to account for many individual myths; they distort those that they do partially explain by implying that only one kind of interpretation is relevant, and that the parts of the myths that do not respond to it are arbitrary and extraneous. Myth-making societies use tales to comment on every aspect of life, and they cram into them reflections of a variety of interests and preoccupations. Myths are not uniform, logical and internally consistent; they are multiform, imaginative and loose in their details. Moreover their emphases can change from one year, or generation, to the next.

# CHAPTER 2

# THE RELATION OF MYTHS TO FOLKTALES

MYTHS are tales, and tales are a primary form of expression and communication in a traditional society. Yet tales told by story-tellers, or in less formal ways, have no absolutely fixed outline in a non-literate culture. The central themes remain fairly constant, but the details and emphases change with the interests of teller and audience. Much the same seems to have happened in ancient Greece with the oral heroic songs that became the basis of Homer's epics; and a similar variation could still be seen a few years back among the *guslars* or heroic singers of rural Yugoslavia, where literacy has only recently gained the upper hand over oral tradition.

The evidence for change in the emphases of orally transmitted myths is provided mainly by anthropologists, because it is they who have most closely studied non-literate societies in action. One of the best treatments of the flexibility of myths and tales was published some sixty years ago by the great American ethnologist Franz Boas in his monumental *Tsimshian Mythology*.[1] There he recorded many of the traditional tales of this Indian tribe from the Pacific coast of Canada. His methods of gathering versions were a bit casual by modern standards, but the scope of the work and the perceptiveness of many of its conclusions are still impressive. He was particularly interested in the way story-themes are transmitted from one tribal group to another, and discovered that there is a gradual unification of themes and tales as the tradition lengthens and cultural contacts broaden. European folktales, he concluded, are far more uniform in their contents than those of the North American Indians. This is the result of a background of ethnic and social stability lacked by the Indian tribes, which have been involved in constant upheavals and migrations over the last thousand years.

Boas refused to draw any absolute distinction between folktales and myths. One might make rather firmer typological definitions than he did, but his main argument remains valid: that there is a persistent seepage from one kind of tale to the other – from 'serious' to 'entertainment' tales, by a naïve definition, and the other way about. 'The facts', he wrote, 'that are brought out most clearly from a careful analysis of the myths and folktales of an area like the north-west coast of America are that the contents of folktales and myths are largely the same, that the data show a continual flow of material from mythology to folktale and vice versa, and that neither group can claim priority.'[2] The Tsimshian distinguished between, and had different names for, historical or historicizing tales (which I prefer to call legends) and those set in the prehistoric or 'mythical' era when animals and humans were intermixed. Yet even here there is no complete separation, and animals find their way into the historical tales just as legendary details intrude into the timeless ambience of the creative ones. Boas's pupil Ruth Benedict made the same point a little differently, at the same time as adding the debatable refinement that myths are religious and associated with ritual: 'A story passes in and out of the religious complex with ease,' she wrote, 'and plots which are told as secular tales over two continents become locally the myths which explain the creation of the people and the origins of customs and may be dramatized in religious rituals.'[3]

Boas and Benedict made surprisingly little impact on the theoretical study of myths, mainly because of a new anthropological theory propounded in the early 1920s by Bronislaw Malinowski. Malinowski had been penned up in the Trobriand Islands, off the south-east coast of New Guinea, by the war, and was able to observe at leisure how closely the traditional tales were connected with every aspect of Trobriand social life. Myths, he concluded, are not a reflection of cosmic events or of mysterious impulses in the human soul, but rather a 'charter' (as he called it) for social institutions and actions, a validation of traditional customs, beliefs and attitudes.[4] That was all very well, and a refreshing correction of armchair theories, but it tended to obscure Boas's important observation that myths bear some essential relation to folktales. Malinowski distinguished three categories of Trobriand tales, each with its own native name; they correspond roughly with serious myths, historicizing legends and tales told just for entertainment. Unlike Boas and Benedict, he did not emphasize that themes passed freely from one type to the other, that yesterday's folktale can be tomorrow's myth. Moreover his idea that the 'serious' uses of myths are neither emotional nor reflective, but rather are connected with the mechanical functioning of social life, became the core of the exaggerated theory known as 'functionalism' that developed into orthodoxy in the circle of A. R. Radcliffe-Brown.

According to this theory, as we saw, myths like rituals are part of the complex social mechanism, and so are developed solely in response to the structural requirements of the organic group. In his *Political Systems of Highland Burma* (1954, reprinted with corrections 1964) E. R. Leach, one of Malinowski's most distinguished pupils, could still assert: 'Myths for me are one way of describing certain types of human behaviour ... ritual action and belief are alike to be understood as symbolic statements about the social order.'[5] At the same time he argued against orthodox functionalists that society is a dynamic and not a static organism. That at least concedes the point that myths can alter in their emphasis, and indeed he himself demonstrates this clearly enough in his study of Kachin myths. Yet the essential relation between the myth as a social or religious phenomenon, and the popular tale as a mode of communication about several different aspects of human experience, was overlaid by this whole grandiose and ultimately unreal exercise in sociological theorizing.

More recently still anthropologists, especially those who have worked in Africa where the folktale tradition is exceptionally strong, have begun to value the tale as a thing in itself rather than as a cog in a social machine. E. E. Evans-Pritchard, the doyen of British social anthropologists, admitted in *The Zande Trickster* that 'generally speaking, anthropologists during the last few decades have ignored the folk-lore of the peoples they have studied . . . I have myself erred in this respect and this volume is an act of penance.' Moreover he echoed Boas when he wrote that 'no very clear distinction can be made between myth and folktale.'[6] Much the same position is taken by Ruth Finnegan in her *Limba Stories and Storytelling*; she refuses to use the term 'myth' for Limba stories about the gods and the origins of things, because 'the Limba themselves do not make any clear differentiation between these stories and others; nor is it altogether easy to force such a distinction on them from outside.'[7] Her own view of what constitutes a myth is perhaps rather simplistic (she thinks that a myth is 'systematic', 'associated with ritual' and repeated in an unchanging form), but that does not invalidate her testimony about the overlap between different kinds of traditional tale. Moreover she notes that the basic plots of stories are common to many different tribal groups, but that the Limba alter and adapt them in accordance with their 'present way of life, current interests and literary conventions'.

Perhaps the conclusion to be drawn from the Boas position, which recent anthropologists are inclining (often almost unconsciously) to revive, is that there is *no* viable distinction between myths and folktales. Yet it is still useful, I believe, even in the absence of any hard-and-fast dividing line, to identify certain kinds of motif, plot and treatment as belonging to a folktale tradition rather than to what most people mean by myths. Folktales are concerned essentially with the life, problems and aspirations of ordinary people, the folk. They are not aristocratic in tone. Greek myths, on the other hand, when they are not about gods, are about 'heroes', aristocratic figures far removed by birth and context from the ordinary people. Indeed it was this aristocratic colouring of the content of Greek myths, especially as presented by class-conscious poets like Pindar, that caused the tales of European peasants, once they were noticed in the early nineteenth century as having an interest of their own, to be labelled as 'folktales' or 'household tales' rather than myths – by which people of those days meant the exalted deeds of Theseus, Heracles, Zeus, Athena and the rest. Folktales are not concerned with large problems like the inevitability of death or institutional matters like the justification of kingship. Their social pre-occupations are restricted to the family. Difficulties with step-mothers or jealous sisters are folktale topics, worries over incest and the limits of permissible sexual encounter are not. Supernatural elements in folktales encompass giants, monsters, witches, fairy godmothers, magical equipment or spells; they do not extend to gods in any full sense, to questions of how the world or society was formed, or to matters of religion. Folktales tend to be realistic but at the same time impersonal; they are set not in the timeless past, as myths often are, but in specific but anonymous time and place, and their characters usually have generic names. These tales are designed for the people, for Everyman, and they are kept as general and uni-versal as possible. Ingenuity and unexpected success: these are the qualities that bring amusement and excitement into ordinary lives, and they are applied to ideal people in ideal landscapes simply because nothing quite like that ever happens at home.

Finally, folktales tend to be told in special ways, to be rich in simple narrative devices for introducing surprise or climax. One of their common subjects is a test or quest; the hero has to perform some difficult and dangerous act in order to survive, win a prize or defeat a wicked enemy. Often the quest is three-fold, each stage being more challenging than the one before. That is almost a cliché of this kind of adventure, and it occurs even in Greek hero tales. Bellerophon is exiled because the queen falls in love with him and falsely accuses him of trying to seduce her; that is a universal ingenuity motif, the 'Potiphar's wife' theme that occurs in other Greek myths too, for example the stories of Phaedra and Hippolytus or Peleus and the wife of Acastus. Then Bellerophon is set three tasks, one after the other: first he has to kill the monstrous Chimaera, then he defeats the fierce tribe of the Solymi, finally he is exposed to those dangerous female warriors the Amazons. Another typical narrative motif is that of the 'single survivor'. When the Thebans send an ambush against Tydeus, father of Diomedes, he kills all of them except one, who carries back the bad news; and when the fifty daughters of Danaus are bidden to kill their persistent cousin-suitors they all do so – save one, Hypermnestra, who falls in love with her cousin Lynceus and marries him instead.

Actually Bellerophon surprisingly fails to exemplify this particular motif, because when after his threefold triumph the Lycian king sends a force to finish him off he responds by killing every last one of them: 'against him on his return the king wove another deceit,' sang Homer at *Iliad* VI, 187 ff.; 'he chose the best men from broad Lycia and sent them as an ambush; but those men returned not home again, for blameless Bellerophontes slew every one.' An oversight, perhaps; but Homer makes up for it with another typical folktale ploy whereby the king finally abandons his wrath and gives Bellerophon the princess as bride and, just as the fairy-tales say, 'half his kingdom'. As Homer puts it, 'he gave him his daughter, and half of all his kingly honour also; and the Lycians cut off for him a parcel of land better than all others, fair orchard and ploughland for him to work as his own.'

Is there a degree of inconsistency here? On the one hand I

am urging that there *is* a useful working distinction between folktales and myths; on the other hand folktale-type elements seem to turn up even in Greek tales that I persist in calling myths. But there is no real contradiction if one accepts the Boas–Benedict position about the interplay between folktales and myths, and especially if one believes that in an oral society every kind of tale tends to evolve with the passage of time and circumstance. The Bellerophon story is a complex entity, a concretion of different themes and motifs; that is so, at least, with the version we know from Homer. It has undeniable folktale elements: the tricky but familiar sexual situation, the token whose dangerous message is unknown to the bearer (for Bellerophon was dispatched to the king of Lycia with 'baneful signs' that told the king to destroy him), the threefold quest, the royal reward. But Bellerophon is more than a folktale character. His association with the winged horse Pegasus is more than a routine magical aid, and he comes to grief in a manner unknown to folktale heroes, by aspiring to ride up to heaven – in other words to cross the borderline between men and gods. That is the stuff of myths, of more complex and more deeply imaginative tales.

The truth is that these folktale elements are part of the whole business of story-telling; therefore they find their way even into tales that reflect deeper preoccupations, and do not primarily depend for their traditional status on sheer narrative and dramatic value. To put it in another way, all tales rely to some extent on well-tried narrative devices and dramatic turns of events. Folktales, in which these elements are stronger than intellectual and imaginative ones, are particularly rich in such devices (which is why one refers to 'folktale motifs' and the like); but even the subtler and more complex tales, or myths, cannot avoid them altogether. Sometimes, indeed, narrative qualities take over from the others in one part of a myth, as happens predominantly with Perseus and to some extent with Bellerophon. Even the most obviously 'serious'

Greek myths, including divine ones, reveal the occasional folktale touch. Hera, a venerable figure in many respects, is also the typical nagging wife who makes Zeus' social life a misery and forces him into ingenious transformations (a bull, a bear, a golden shower) that equally possess a certain folktale quality. Kronos is chosen by Gaia, mother Earth, to be her champion because he is the youngest and bravest of her children. That is a typical folktale idea, as is the father–son conflict itself; and Kronos' severing of Ouranos' genitals (those of the sky-god who would not desist from mating with his wife the earth) has something of the ingenious-solution quality that is also common in the traditional narratives of the people.

It should now be reasonably clear what I mean by 'folktale', 'folktale motif', and so forth, even if the nature of myths remains, as it must, still rather nebulous. The alternative to all this straining after working categories is to abandon 'myth' and 'folktale' altogether; to conclude that what we are dealing with is simply various kinds of tale, and to write merely about 'Greek traditional tales'. That would present its own difficulties and limitations, and is, I believe, needlessly severe. Yet I can see well enough what one perceptive critic had in mind when he wrote in relation to an earlier book of mine that 'his major problem is one that he shares with many recent writers, namely that "myth" does not turn out to be an analytic category of any great usefulness.'[8]

# CHAPTER 3

# FIVE MONOLITHIC THEORIES

ONE of the basic truths about myths, which cannot be repeated too often, is that they are traditional tales. Such tales develop manifold implications and meanings according to the character, wishes and circumstances of their tellers and audiences. Therefore they are likely to vary in their qualities and functions. The main fault in the modern study of myths is that it has consisted so largely of a series of supposedly universal and mutually exclusive theories, each of which can be easily disproved by marshalling scores of agreed instances that do not accord with it. Yet most of these theories have seemed to illuminate *some* myths at least; for example those of a particular form, or those associated with a particular kind of community or culture. After all, a theory could never begin to establish itself if there were not certain phenomena to which it seemed more or less relevant. My own conviction, nevertheless, is that there can be no single and comprehensive theory of myths – except, perhaps, the theory that all such theories are necessarily wrong. The only exception would be a theory so simple as hardly to deserve the name (like that implied by the 'traditional tale' definition); or so complicated, and containing so many qualifications and alternatives, as not to be a single theory at all.

Myths, in short, constitute an enormously complex and at the same time indefinite category, and one must be free to apply to them any of a whole set of possible forms of analysis and classification. Not all myths, in any event, are susceptible of explanation. Folktales, for example, if we include them under myths in their widest sense, are hardly 'explicable'; or rather their explanation would consist primarily in a series of stylistic and ethnological observations, little more. In the case of the remainder, each of the established theories may have its possible value. Yet even that implies seeing individual myths as simple and uniform, whereas I argued that traditional tales in general are liable to undergo changes corresponding, among other things, to their social and historical setting. Those changes do not occur instantaneously, and even a myth that has one simple point in an earlier form (and many are liable to have more than one) can develop confusing ambiguities as that emphasis gradually merges into others. Myths, therefore, are often multifunctional, and consequently different hearers can value a myth for different reasons. Like any tale, a myth may have different emphases or levels of meaning; if these are especially abstract, then the area of ambivalence is increased still further. The consequence is that analysis of a myth should not stop when one particular theoretical explanation has been applied and found productive. Other kinds of explanation may also be valid. Just as a human action can in psychological jargon be 'overdetermined', or have more than one motive, so can a tale about human actions contain more than a single aspect and implication.

The multifunctionalism of myths was usefully emphasized by Dr Percy S. Cohen in the 1970 Malinowski Memorial Lecture.[1] In a sense his contribution is a refinement of the point made by Franz Boas and described in Chapter 2, although strictly that applied only to the interplay between 'serious' myths and folktales. In any case the idea of multifunctionalism is not intended as an all-embracing theory (since it would be untrue to say that all myths are multifunctional), but rather as a loose generalization about many myths on the one hand, a contribution to methodology on the other. Even so, there is a danger that the generalization will be abused. 'Multifunction-alism' and 'overdetermination' can be made the excuse for wilful and imprecise analysis, for pressing some special interpretation of a myth that can be more simply accounted for. Yet different types of causation do undoubtedly co-exist; a myth might have, for instance, a specific social implication (for example that incest is socially dangerous) as well as a psychological one (for example that forbidden relationships are attractive). To identify the social concern is not necessarily to dismiss the psychological intuition. As I stated before, every kind of possible analysis should be applied to a myth before one is satisfied that it has been adequately examined and, to some degree, 'explained' – or recognized as inexplicable.

Two criticisms are likely to be levelled at the kind of methodological statement I have just made, one of them trivial, the other more serious. The first is that using the old theories of myth, and one or two new ones as well, as a kind of litmus test, with the expectation that one or more may prove positive, is eclectic and therefore despicable. Yet eclecticism surely has a good and a bad sense? In the good sense it implies no more than considering all possible approaches to a problem and then selecting those that seem most promising. These are merged with other attitudes and observations into a fresh view, one that does not utterly discount all previous insights. In the bad sense the selection of previous views is a more or less mechanical affair, and the conclusion an unwieldy concoction of discordant bits and pieces.

Obviously the various monolithic theories of myth must not be used indiscriminately, yet many of them have their legitimate applications. One of the more extreme theories, as we saw, was to the effect that all myths are about natural phenomena, the sun, moon, winds and so on. That is in itself absurd, yet it is obvious that *some* myths are concerned with such matters. Poseidon is quite undoubtedly associated with the sea, underground springs and earthquakes, and when he and Athena were competing with gifts to win possession of Athens it was a fountain of water he offered by striking the Acropolis with his trident. That is one sort of nature myth. A more obvious instance is the myth of Ouranos, sky, being forcibly separated from Gaia, earth, so that the world might exist between them. Or again Helios, who sees everything that happens on earth, is the Sun, and his return each night in a golden bowl round the northern stream of Okeanos is a perfectly intelligible, if mythical, reflection on a fact of nature, namely that the sun sinks in the west and rises in the east. It is not, therefore, 'eclectic' in any malign sense to admit such correspondences, while rejecting the wilder excesses of the nature-myth school. Those who make this feeble rebuke are presumably still wedded to the idea that there must be a single explanation of all myths, and therefore that any complex account is automatically vicious.

The second and more serious criticism is that in describing the possibilities of various functions, and in referring to different planes of reference and so on, one might be implying that myths are always determinable given the right methods; whereas we all know that 'mythical' implies a poetic or mystical essence that is not to be analysed in logical and concrete terms. One might go some way towards meeting this criticism by regularly considering the poetical and mystical aspects, among others, in the course of the flexible approach I have been urging. Yet that would not be enough, because the point of the criticism is that such aspects are simply not identifiable by the analytical methods under discussion. How far that is really true remains to be considered; it *looks* unobjectionable to say that myths work on a level beyond reason, but it may not be quite so true as it looks. It would be rash to deny that some myths have hidden symbolic meanings, that they are in some ways akin to dreams, and that elements in them are derived from unconscious rather than conscious attitudes; yet these may be less important components than is often assumed. Certainly they do not reveal themselves as crucial elements of most Greek myths, although we have seen that there may be special reasons for that, and that Greek myths are not really typical. But in any event myths are not all, or even predominantly, mysterious and illogical; that they are stories sees to that. Many aspects remain for which analytical approaches can be valid and productive. Indeed, even poetical truth, symbolism and unconscious meaning are susceptible to certain kinds of analysis; it is simply that the assumptions on which the analysis needs to be based are not straightforward, that allowances have to be made for connections and relations not covered by western logic. The days when E. B. Tylor and Lucien Lévy-Bruhl could write about a special kind of 'primitive mentality' in which there was no system whatever, and according to which phenomena were connected by 'mystical participation' and so on, are long past.[2] That may have been a necessary stage in the discovery and rehabilitation of the savage cultures, but it neglected the obvious truth that most natives are not at all stupid, and indeed are moderately practical in determining causes and effects in daily life.

It was the myths, above all, that seemed to defy rational analysis and to give rise to the idea that their makers were rambling around in a kind of mystical fog. Yet closer observation, and the whole tendency of anthropologists to treat tribal peoples with increasing respect, have shown that most of the apparently illogical connections in 'primitive' myths are not really so. Rather, the logical systems involved are different from those standardized in western cultures. Lévi-Strauss showed in *La Pensée sauvage*[3] that many simple societies, far from having no category structure at all, have systems of immense range and complexity. That is fact; yet one has to guard against sentimentality at this point, for it is all too easy to add (as many now do) that these alternative logical structures are 'just as good' as the ones we happen to use. After all, they say, even Aristotelian logic has had to be replaced by different kinds in certain conditions, much as the Euclidean system, which once seemed the essence of logical geometry, is now recognized as too restricted for study of the world at large. But the truth is that for many purposes Aristotelian logic, which has established simple and consistent rules of cause and effect, is greatly superior to alternative systems depending on loose grades of symbolic association. Some aspects of myths can be appreciated more fully by these alternative systems, but there are also elements and qualities to which discursive analysis can properly be applied, at least as a preliminary stage. Such rational techniques certainly have their place in the consideration of the five monolithic theories that now follows.

The first universal theory has already been touched upon: it maintains that all myths are *nature myths*, that is, they refer to meteorological and cosmological phenomena. Originally a German obsession, it spread to England and reached its climax under Max Müller, a distinguished philologist who became professor at Oxford. Müller thought that myths were often formed through a misunderstanding of names, especially those attached to celestial objects; they were, he suggested in a phrase that became notorious, 'a disease of language'. At least that was a variant on the commoner idea according to which tales about a hero defeating a monster must always refer, by some mysterious code, to dawn overcoming the darkness of night or the heat of noonday dispelling the mists of an autumn morning. None of the scholars who propounded such remarkable ideas were able to say (or much interested in saying) just why myth-makers had gone to such enormous lengths simply to propound allegorical statements about obvious natural phenomena. There are occasions, of course, on which the personification of such events can be useful. Burning a snowman to represent the end of winter, or envisaging lightning as the weapon of a god who can be placated by sacrifices, are obvious and intelligible devices. But how do the wedding of Peleus and Thetis, Heracles' enslavement to the Lydian queen Omphale, Pasiphaë's unnatural love for the Cretan bull, Hermes' theft of the cattle of Apollo or Zeus' displacement of his father Kronos come under this heading? Or a hundred more?

Other sets of myths point the same way. Odhinn and Thor may be nature gods in Nordic myths, but what about Balder and Freyja? Certain actions by Mesopotamian gods are concerned with the separation of primeval waters, with irrigation, and matters of that kind, but many others are related rather to social, political or theological developments. Gilgamesh, the nearest thing to a Mesopotamian mythical hero-figure, is certainly no sort of disguise for the sun, the moon, a wind or a thunderstorm. Amerindian myths, again, sometimes describe figures that descend from the sky and are married to the daughter of the sun, for instance; natural objects and cosmic events are not excluded, but the main concern is with the imaginative prehistory of local customs and the immediate environment, as well as with problems and contradictions in human circumstances. The obvious truth is that there *are* such things as nature myths, but that not all or even most myths are of this kind. No one in his right mind has thought so since Andrew Lang finally lost patience eighty years ago and exploded the whole elephantine theory.

All the same, the embodiment of aspects of nature in myths and cult is an important topic, and the excesses of the nature-myth school have meant, if anything, that it has been too little considered in any serious way. Raffaele Pettazzoni, admittedly, has demonstrated that most known myth-making cultures assign the primary position to a sky god or weather god, and that he then becomes the guardian of order and society. The Greeks accord perfectly with this idea, because Zeus, their chief god, is a derivative of the Indo-European sky god Dyaus (the genitive of Zeus in Greek is *Dios*). He is imagined as dwelling in the sky, or at least on a high mountain-top reaching into *aither*, the pure upper air, and his weapons are lightning and the thunderbolt; he is the protector of strangers and suppliants, and guardian of oaths. It is Zeus, too, who makes rain from the clouds; one of his standard epithets is 'cloud-gatherer'; his Latin equivalent is Jupiter Pluvius (Jupiter of rain), 'Ju-piter' being closely related to the Sanskrit *Dyaus-pitar* as well as to Zeus 'father of gods and men' in Homer's phrase. In Hesiod's *Theogony* the final challenges to Zeus' supreme power come from the older gods, the Titans (whom he blasts with lightning-flashes that burn up the void between earth and sky), and then from the storm-monster Typhoeus. In all this he behaves like a typical weather god. He resembles Sumerian Enlil, lord of air and winds, and Babylonian Marduk who replaced Enlil in the Akkadian 'Epic of Creation', in which the monstrous Tiamat is split by Marduk so that her upper half becomes sky and her lower half earth. The Hurrians, too, who dominated northern Syria and much of Asia Minor in the second millennium B.C., worshipped a powerful weather god, and his son Telepinu was associated with the fertility of the earth – when he ran off in a rage there was a great drought, and even the gods began to suffer.

Telepinu's disappearance exemplifies an essential connection between one category of nature deity, namely the sky, rain and weather gods, and another kind that dwells in the earth and represents the fertility of plants and indirectly of animals and human beings. Zeus himself is not a 'chthonian' god – one that operates from beneath the surface of the earth – but his brother Hades and his sister (and at one time consort) Demeter are, and so is her daughter Kore, the Maiden, also known as Persephone. Persephone was abducted by Hades, lord of the underworld, as she picked flowers one day, and the consequences were exactly like those in the Hurrian myth of the disappearance of Telepinu. There was a great famine and the corn died. The gods were alarmed, and in the end Zeus had to command Hades to release his new bride. But Persephone still goes down to him for a third of each year, because he gave her a pomegranate seed to eat and therefore bound part of her to his realm.

Zeus has links, therefore, with the underworld, although he remains explicitly the god of sky and upper air. In the division of the world that he made after establishing his supremacy, his brother Poseidon was awarded the sea, his other brother, Hades, the kingdom under the earth. The earth's surface was to be shared among all three, but in practice Zeus was supreme there too. This connection between sky, the place from which rain comes, and the earth that is fertilized by it also appears in Zeus' ancestry. The primordial pair of gods, still half-envisaged as great world-masses, were Ouranos and Gaia, sky and earth; and sky lay upon earth and made love to her without cease. The myth can be seen as a symbolic representation of the interplay between rain and soil that makes plants come to life and grow. Aeschylus wrote in his lost *Danaids* that 'the holy sky passionately desires to penetrate the earth . . . rain falls and impregnates earth, and she brings forth pasturage for flocks and Demeter's life-giving corn'; and according to an admittedly late source the initiates at the Eleusinian mysteries looked at the sky and called out 'Rain!', then looked down at the earth and called 'Conceive!'.

According to Hesiod's *Theogony*, 'First of all, *chaos* came to be.'[4] *Chaos* in archaic Greek means 'gap' rather than 'disorder', and the Hesiodic account resembles many myths from all over the world (as well as the Akkadian creation myth that was probably its particular prototype) in which sky and earth had to be forcibly prised asunder before the world of men could come into being. Specifically it is Kronos, one of Gaia's children trapped within her womb, who castrates his father Ouranos as he enters the earth in yet another fertilization act (see p. 113 ff.). Kronos can now be born, together with his brothers and sisters the Titans; he in his turn behaves abominably to his children, among whom is Zeus. Zeus' father, then, is an elusive figure; but the one thing known about his cult, as distinct from the details of this complex succession myth and his paradoxical association with the Golden Age (see p. 132–6), is that he was some kind of fertility god, for the feast called Kronia in his honour was a festival of tilling and harvest (see p. 233). His wife and Zeus' mother, Rhea, is even more colourless in the accounts that survive, but at least it can now be seen that Zeus is son of a fertility god as well as grandson of sky and earth in a constantly fertile relation. He becomes sole master of the sky, but in his nature there lies the vitality of the earth as well.

Tales about gods that represent or control the sky, the earth, rain and the weather are only one category of nature myths, even apart from the complex stories about disappearing deities of fertility. There are also, for example, sun gods and moon gods. Mesopotamian myths are especially rich in such figures, and Shamash is the great sun god who observes everything that happens among men and is consequently arbiter of oaths and justice. Helios, his Greek equivalent, has similar properties, and the interesting thing is that this kind of nature god tends not to be fully anthropomorphized. Greek poets like Stesichorus and the elegist Mimnermus could write about the wife and children of Helios, to whom he returns each night when he sinks in the west, as a detail in the story of Heracles who returned from his western adventures by borrowing the sun-god's bowl; but we hear little else about these relatives, and they are not very concretely imagined.[5] In a Sumerian myth Enlil behaves rather scandalously with the lovely Ninlil, who is a minor, and is followed by her to the underworld.[6] The other gods are outraged, not least because they know that she is shortly to give birth to Nanna-Sin, one of the gods associated with the moon, and a moon god belongs in Enlil's realm of the upper air and should not be born in the 'house of dust' – which is what the Sumerians and Akkadians called the underworld, the world of the dead. But again the moon god himself remains rather abstract.

No less important than the myths of sun and moon are those about the sea. In·Egypt the primeval water was Nūn, out of which a conical bit of land thrust itself up; it became the earth – pyramids recall its shape – and the primal waters receded and became the Nile and the outer seas. For the Akkadians, Enki, lord of sweet waters and wisdom (because he is flexible and devious like water trickling through the irrigation channels?), was one of the 'younger gods' who overthrew Tiamat, the serpent-deity of primeval water who was split in two, leaking rain from the sky and sending up springs from beneath the earth. In Greek myths Poseidon rides the waves in his chariot ('and the sea-beasts rejoiced to see their lord', as Homer sang) or dwells in his underwater palace at Aegae, but his cosmological functions are less conspicuous. Thetis and Eurynome, however, are sea goddesses who have strange associations with the original creation of the world in minority versions.

Winds, too, are personified and become the subject of traditional tales. Typhoeus (in his alternative form Typhon the origin of 'typhoon') succumbed to Zeus, but in a later epoch Boreas, the north wind, snatched away Oreithyia, daughter of Erechtheus King of Athens, much as Hades had ravished Kore-Persephone. Boreas took her to his palace in Thrace, because that is the region to the north of the Aegean from which the north wind blows upon civilized Greeks, and she gave birth to Zetes and Calais who were lesser wind gods. The north wind is a potent factor in Greek life: the shrill Etesians blow in summer and make or mar the sailing season, and across in the Adriatic the 'Bora', as it is now called, is a constant menace. It was the north wind that disrupted the Persian fleet at Salamis, and the Athenians started a cult to commemorate it; not too long afterwards Socrates provided a classic instance of trivial rationalizing when, according to Plato in the *Phaedrus*, he proposed that the rape of Oreithyia by Boreas was based on an Athenian princess who happened to be blown over a cliff.[7]

Not only winds but rivers, headlands, mountains and springs all acquired their local deity, nymph or spirit – what the

Greeks called a 'daemon' – and tales grew up about them that were usually obvious in their localized aetiological intent and automatic in their use of recurrent motifs. They barely qualify as myths, and yet were the product of one of the most important assumptions behind myths in general: that the natural world is permeated by forces somehow envisaged in human terms. Animism, personification, anthropomorphism, the 'pathetic fallacy' – all these are overlapping tendencies that underlie the idea of nature gods and myths about the physical world.

It is tempting to dogmatize about such attitudes, to reduce them to formulas such as that primitive man (whoever *he* is) envisaged the world as a 'thou'; that he thought of it, and talked to it, as another person. This is an interpretation urged in respect of Egyptian myths by H. and H. A. Frankfort, editors of an important book in the Pelican series called *Before Philosophy*. Yet exactly how and why the earliest myth-makers thought about the world as they did, and what particular kind of anthropocentric and symbolic motives persuaded them to imagine gods in the form of the sky, or sky as behaving in some respects like a man, must remain unknown. One can assert that certain aspects of nature, like thunder or storms at sea, were terrifying and that men domesticated them by treating them as subject to quasi-human motives, so that they calm down in the end or are bought off by gifts and assuaged by prayer or flattery. One can also suggest that at a certain stage of development men are so self-centred that they see the whole of their outward experience as like themselves. One can argue that the reverence they feel in the face of nature is compared to the reverence they felt for their own fathers, so that the weather god in particular is treated like a superhuman parent.

All these are possibilities, and there are several others; the origins of anthropomorphism must in any event be quite complex. Yet E. E. Evans-Pritchard had emphasized in

*Theories of Primitive Religion* that speculation on the 'precise' origin of religion is a learned waste of time; and it is equally impossible to reach back to the origins of personification. Our sophisticated and literate intuitions on this topic are apt to be totally misleading. What is more fruitful is to distinguish carefully between different classes of anthropomorphic creation: between, for instance, the personified representations of major aspects of the natural world, like sky or sea, and more random associations of complex mythical figures with natural phenomena, such as Apollo with the sun and Heracles with hot springs; or between both these types and nature-spirits like nymphs and satyrs, which often seem to arise from a distinct kind of rustic imagination.

Two points remain to be made about Greek nature myths. The first is that 'nature' for the Greeks did not conspicuously include animals. There is no shortage, of course, of animal characters: Io turns into a cow and Zeus into a bull; Cerberus who guards the entrance to Hades is a many-headed dog; there are famous monsters like the Calydonian boar or the Nemean lion, and half-serpentine figures like Echidna and Typhoeus, or even Cecrops the first mythical king of Athens. Bellerophon rides on the winged horse Pegasus, Arion on a dolphin; Zeus' special bird is the eagle and Athena's the owl. But there is no real confusion in the Greek mythical world between men and animals as such. Yet that is a property of myths in many regions, especially the Americas and Africa. Greece has its trickster figures, but they are men like Sisyphus, Autolycus or Odysseus, or anthropomorphic gods like Hermes or Prometheus. For the Plains Indians of North America, on the other hand, the trickster is Coyote or Crow, and for numerous African tribes he is Spider. They are half men, these creatures; Coyote in the Winnebago trickster cycle has a huge penis that he has to carry in a box slung over his shoulder. Their status is truly ambivalent: usually they look like men or women but have the character of animals, but sometimes they mix with the animals and become almost identical with them.

The common assumption behind these sets of myths is that animals once possessed the earth, and in many creation stories, for example of how the sky was first lifted up, it is a bird or animal that performs the crucial act. Then, when the earth takes on its present form, the animals gradually engender human beings, and after the intermediate stage represented in many non-Greek myths they lapse into their present forms. The ancient Egyptians worshipped gods in animal shape almost exclusively in the pre-dynastic period before about 3000 B.C., and right down to classical times their gods had animal heads or other animal characteristics, as Horus resembles a hawk or Anubis a jackal. Some people believe the Greeks once thought the same, and that the formular epithets for Athena and Hera, literally 'owl-faced' and 'cow-faced', are proof of it. Other gods have animal characteristics, too: for example Artemis is closely associated with Callisto who turned into a bear, and was served in her cult at Brauron in Attica by little girls in yellow dresses who were also known as 'bears', and Poseidon and Demeter were worshipped in horse-headed form in Arcadia.

Such theriomorphic tendencies, if they are as much as that, are the exception rather than the rule. The situation is quite different from that of so many 'savage' myths; the Greeks envisaged no period in the past when animals ruled the earth or animals and men were intermixed. Their anthropomorphism was severe. They missed something thereby, I believe, but the reason for it may be obvious: they no longer lived in a world dominated by animals, by the need to hunt and trap them and keep them at bay, in the way that many simple tribal communities did and do. Admittedly their remote ancestors, long before they came down into Greece shortly before 2000 B.C., had been prehistoric hunters; the habits and mentality of bears and bison must have been among their main preoccupations. The Swiss scholar Karl Meuli argued that certain hunting attitudes persisted in the historical practice of sacrifice, but at the least the animals slipped into secondary roles in their myths.[8] Already by the early Neolithic age, say 5000 B.C., the ancestors of the Greeks were abandoning the life of a hunting community; they had domesticated some animals and had little to fear from the rest. Animals became tools, not masters, and the proto-Greeks started on that long process of humanism, of placing man at the centre of the universe, that distinguished them from the Egyptians with their interminable tradition of dreary crocodile-gods and the like.

The second point about nature in Greek myths is that it came to be treated in a rather desultory way. The great early succession myth, with Sky and a supposedly flat Earth separated at the horizon by Okeanos (the surrounding fresh-water river) remained as a fixed component of the pre-scientific world picture. But in less obvious respects the mythical account of the natural world became surprisingly vague. Where and what is Olympus, home of the gods? Is it a mountain or the sky itself? At times the Greeks were clear that it was Mount Olympus in Thessaly, the highest mountain in Greece, and when Hermes descends from the gods in the *Odyssey* he crosses Pieria close to its foot. On other occasions the Olympians were envisaged as dwelling in the sky itself; whereas at *Odyssey* 6, 44 ff. Olympus is described by a compromise as 'neither shaken by winds nor drenched by rain, nor does snow fall upon it, but bright cloudless air is spread all about it'. Such indecision reflects, no doubt, the difficulty of insisting on a literal mountain-top, a bare and often hostile place, as site of the golden halls of Zeus; but it also testifies to a decreasing interest in relating the gods of myth to the world of nature. About half of the Greek pantheon (Hera, Athena, Ares, Dionysus, Aphrodite and Hermes at least) have no connection with the cosmological or meteorological side of nature, and the associations of some of the others, as of Apollo with the sun and Artemis with the moon, are relatively late. The late-Greek interest in astrology and in tales of the transformation of mortals into stars arrested and even reversed the process, but back in Hesiod's time the cosmological aspects of the birth and development of the gods were thin. In Homer, too, they were little emphasized, and Iris, goddess of the rainbow and messenger of the gods in the *Iliad*, is quietly replaced in the *Odyssey* by Hermes, who was no sort of natural phenomenon but a renowned traveller and escort.

Second among the great all-embracing theories is the one loosely covered by the term *aetiological*; it implies that all myths offer a cause or explanation of something in the real world. When Andrew Lang dismissed the nature-myth theory, he tried to put in its place the idea of myths as constituting a kind of proto-science.[9] In short, he was not merely objecting that many myths are clearly not about nature; he was arguing that even those that are, are more than just pretty allegorical conceits – that they are explanatory in some way. This, he claimed, rather than any concern with specific subjects like natural events or human society, is their central characteristic. Unfortunately the idea of myths as a kind of primitive science is not in itself particularly helpful. It suggests that myths were a kind of halting advance on the road to epistemological maturity. That is a very Aristotelian formulation; indeed the 'proto-science' view of myths is quite similar to what Aristotle felt about the early Greek physicists (the 'Presocratic philosophers' from Thales downwards) as representing a first step towards the reasoned truth disclosed by himself. Yet Aristotle and the Presocratics were at least talking about the same kind of thing, the nature of the physical world. Myths, on the other hand, are obviously not concerned just with that; they plainly encompass such things as the emotional valuation of many aspects of personal life. In the final chapter I shall be dealing with the transition in Greece from myth-making to the discursive uses of reason; meanwhile it is worth observing that the two categories are neither polar opposites nor successive and mutually exclusive phases in the attack on a common set of problems. It was natural for Lang, living in the heyday of Victorian science, to make that kind of mistake, but we should be able to avoid it.

'Aetiology' is in any case an unsatisfactory term.[10] It is still much used, probably because it sounds important in the same way as 'mythology' does. It means, presumably, 'the study of causes'; for *aition* simply means 'cause' in Greek. In practice, however, the statement that myths are aetiological means no more than that they offer causes. That seems a fairly clear and harmless statement, except that it is plainly false in respect of many myths. Even apart from legendary and folktale types there are obvious counter-examples from the range of other traditional tales. The Golden Fleece, for example: that does not explain or offer a cause for anything, unless perhaps for the feeling that one should not become entangled with foreign enchantresses like Medea. But that is not an accurate use of 'cause', and one would have to stretch the word in a similar way to predicate 'aetiological' of Oedipus or Theseus or most of the myths associated with Heracles. Even the divine myths are often non-explanatory. Aphrodite is born from the sea fertilized by the severed member of Ouranos, and that has been thought to recall the foam-like appearance of sperm; but this would not *explain* anything, it would merely be a picturesque reference to the sphere of human activity she is known to control. Zeus, again, fights the Titans, just as Enlil, Enki and the rest fought the 'older gods' in Mesopotamia, as a stage in the evolution of more specific gods out of vaguer ones, or, in a more abstract sense, of order out of disorder. That admittedly reflects a certain view of the world and its development. Here we are approaching closer to a 'cause', an *aition*: a causation of how the world came to be as it is now. Yet even this is a loose use of the term, and it would be less misleading to say that Zeus and the Titans may represent a particular attitude to the problems of organization and chaos.

There are, nonetheless, many unambiguously explanatory myths. Yet here again there is a difficulty; for they are explanatory in such different ways and on such distinct levels that it becomes misleading to assign 'explanation', just like that, as their common function. Some tales offer trivial and concrete explanations of details in our environment or of the names of familiar objects or creatures. They are 'just so' stories, and the cause they offer is arbitrary, if neat and entertaining. Why is Hephaestus, the smith-god, a cripple? Factually, perhaps, because the smith's was a craft that lame men could pursue; mythically, because Zeus once threw him out of heaven and he fell with a crash on the island of Lemnos. Why is the Hellespont so called? Because it was named after young Helle, who fell off the ram with the golden fleece when she was fleeing on its back with her brother Phrixus. Why are only fireless sacrifices offered at the altar of Athena on the acropolis of Lindos in Rhodes? Because when the altar was inaugurated someone forgot the matches.

The Australian Aborigines have many such myths. Why are there black patches on the land near the Daly River, and why do dogs eat their food raw? Because once upon a time, in the 'Dreaming Era', Chicken Hawk, Big Hawk and Dog had some yams to eat; they tried to make fire with firesticks but could not, so Chicken Hawk stole fire from some women nearby; on the way back he dropped embers that made the black patches, and by the time he returned Dog had grown impatient and eaten his yams raw.[11] Every natural feature on the route across country and between water-holes has some simple aetiological tale attached to it: such-and-such an ancestor stopped there for a rest, or gave it its name when he passed that way in the Dreaming Era. Hundreds of myths of American Indian tribes are of the same simple kind, although, as with the Australians, there are also more complex ones that operate on a deeper level.

Often a single tale includes several separate *aitia*, some trivial and some more serious. In the Tsimshian tale of Asdiwal, collected in several versions by Boas and subjected to an elaborate structural analysis by Lévi-Strauss, Asdiwal undergoes various adventures that are closely associated with three successive wives, one of them divine, as well as with the typical annual movements of his tribe up and down the salmon rivers.[12] In the end he is turned to stone on a mountain, and (according to a variant version ostensibly about his son Waux) the pieces of fat with which his wife was stuffing herself become the conspicuous greasy-looking flints that still lie in that particular valley. Apart from the trivial aetiology of the flints, there is a reflection – rather than an explanation, since that depends on the behaviour of the fish and is obvious – of annual tribal movements, also a pointed consideration of the consequences of different kinds of marriage, which themselves depend upon tribal rules about relations with brothers-in-law. I have not mentioned the various folktale-type motifs and episodes that additionally enliven this complex myth, which it would be highly misleading to describe simply as 'aetiological'.

Sometimes the relation between apparently trivial aetiology and profound exploration of problems is quite subtle. Myths of many different peoples concern themselves with the origin of, and reason for, death; usually they seem superficial, like the Australian Maung tale about Moon and Possum, who were once men who quarrelled. Moon killed Possum, and he said as he was dying, 'After me men will die for ever'; but if Moon had spoken first men would not die, since Moon is continually reborn as the new moon.[13] It is a widely held idea that mortality is due to some such trivial accident or mistake. In the ancient Akkadian tale of Adapa, the hero is a priest who makes the mistake of cursing the god of the south wind; summoned up to the sky and offered a choice between the food of life and the food of death by the great god Enlil, he makes the wrong choice, apparently because he has been mis-led, accidentally or not, by Enki the god of wisdom.[14] The particular application is not a Greek one, for the Greeks seem to have accepted that men are mortal and in this respect quite different from the gods. They hated death, but did not find it helpful to make up tales explaining it away or showing it as somehow inevitable. Yet the tale of Prometheus and the sacrifices is a variant of the Adapa motif. Prometheus, acting on behalf of men, offers the great god Zeus a choice of flesh or bones; Zeus is deceived, or pretends to be, by the outer wrapping of fat, and chooses the bones. From that time on men have kept for themselves the flesh of sacrificial animals and have burned the inedible bits for the gods (see p. 137 ff.). The roles have been reversed vis-à-vis Adapa, and the issue is the nature of sacrifice rather than of death. The common element may be in itself no more than a folktale-type in-genuity motif, but it is similarly applied in order to set up an ambivalent situation about a matter of basic human concern.

It is surely no accident, and not simply the result of a re-current taste for a neat idea about making someone choose the worse of two alternatives, that death is often seen as due to a simple mistake or an act of human folly. There *is* something contradictory about our attitude to death; in one way death seems inevitable, yet we have a sneaking feeling that it need not always have been so. Here, then, myths are working to counteract an inconvenient and confusing biological urge. The situation over sacrifices in the Prometheus myth is not too different, because sacrifice is both a crucial part of Greek life and manners and a key to the relation between men and gods, mortals and immortals.

There is one kind of *aition* that looks trivial but may not, in the ancient world at least, have been so; once again it differs entirely in its mode of operation from much that is included under the heading 'aetiological'. I refer to the assignment of causes on the basis of the apparent meaning of a word or name. There are frequent etymological details in the literary versions of Greek myths, since the taste for significant etymology occurred relatively early. The poets of the Homeric tradition were already intrigued by the resemblance of the name 'Odysseus' to the verb *odussomai*, 'I am angry'. By the time the *Hymn to Apollo* was composed, probably late in the seventh century B.C., the taste shows itself more crudely. Pytho, the old name for Delphi, is derived from the serpent destroyed there by Apollo and allowed to rot, *puthein*. The priests installed in his sanctuary are Cretan sailors, diverted there by the god himself who appeared to them as a dolphin – because there was an old cult of Apollo Delphinios in Crete.[15] This combines etymology with the learned interpretation of cult epithets by the construction of banal mythical precedents; the two are related but not identical. In the early classical era the interest in etymology took a new turn. Heraclitus the Presocratic philosopher found it significant that one word for a bow resembled the word for 'life' (*biós* and *bíos*), and Aeschylus related the name of Helen to the idea that she 'took the ships' (*hele-naus*), that of Apollo to *apollunai*, 'destroy', and that of Zeus to *zēn*, 'live'.[16]

We might be disposed to count these occasional Greek instances as mere *jeux d'esprit*, were it not for the much more widespread Egyptian and Mesopotamian occurrences. A text inscribed in two pyramids at Heliopolis in Egypt in the 24th century B.C. addresses the sun god Atum in these words: 'thou didst arise as the *ben*-bird of the *ben*-stone in the *Ben*-house in Heliopolis; thou didst spit out what was Shu, thou didst sputter out what was Tefnut.'[17] This refers to the creation of the world and depends on several different etymologies. The meaning of *ben* is uncertain (although the bird, at least, later came to be identified with the mythical phoenix), but there is a significant pun on the word 'arise' (*weben*) just before. Shu is the air god, and he is spat out because his name vaguely resembles the word for 'spit' (*ishesh*), whereas Tefnut,

the goddess of moisture, resembles *tef* meaning 'sputter'. Air
and moisture force the sky apart from the earth, and in this
particular cosmogony they are envisaged as blown out by
the sun god because their names suggest a primordial sneeze.
(At the lower level of folk-magic, the Egyptians wrote the
names of their enemies on bowls which they then ritually
smashed.) Not dissimilarly in the important Sumerian myth of
Enki and Ninhursag, Enki the god of fresh water becomes sick
and is placed in the vulva of Ninhursag, goddess of the primeval stone-heap. He is diseased in eight of his organs, and the
earth-goddess gives birth to eight deities whose names somehow resemble the names of those organs.[18]

Primarily, this last myth seems to be about the extension of
irrigation into the desert and its relation to human sexual
rules, but the miscellaneous group of lesser deities is connected
with the central situation between Enki and Ninhursag solely
by an exercise in etymology. Learned Sumerian priests have
undoubtedly put their fingers in this particular mythical pie,
but the result is something more than trivial word-play, for
it was evidently believed that names revealed part of the true
essence of the things or persons to which they were attached.
Plato's dialogue *Cratylus* was still concerned with this possibility some thirteen hundred years after the Enki myth was
inscribed on a tablet at Nippur – and much of the myth itself
is older.

Malinowski objected to the theory that myths are explanatory almost as strongly as Lang had objected to the theory that
they are allegories of nature. He proposed instead (and this is
our third monolithic theory) that they should be considered
as *charters* for customs, institutions or beliefs.[19] By that he
meant something close to 'explanations' in a loose sense, but
devoid of theoretical quality. His study of the Trobriand
islanders of the western Pacific had convinced him that their
myths always had strongly practical ends, that they bore no
resemblance to science and were not created in response to

any demand for knowledge. These emphases seem rather banal nowadays, but were justified by the extravagant terms in which Lang and others had written of myths as predominantly speculative. Similarly Malinowski's insistence that the only person qualified to pronounce on myths was not the classical scholar (he was thinking especially of Sir James Frazer) or the armchair philosopher, but the practical anthropologist 'who has the myth-maker at his elbow', made more sense then than now.[20] Today, rather, one might feel tempted to implore the anthropologist to desist from theorizing and do a little more observing. Even so, I concede that Malinowski was right in stressing the need for observing myths in action; certainly his own observations made an important difference to the study of myths, even apart from the rightness or otherwise of his 'charter' theory. And the truth must be that the proper study of myths requires the careful attention of a whole group of disciplines, comparative religion as well as psychology and anthropology. Classical scholars intrude themselves here almost by courtesy – at least, once it is conceded that surviving Greek myths are atypical.

What the charter theory implies is that in a traditional society every custom and institution tends to be validated or confirmed by a myth, which states a precedent for it but does not seek to explain it in any logical or philosophical sense. Why does the king always belong to that particular clan? Because the first king, whose name was such and such, did so. That instance could be historical as much as mythical, but others are not. Why does that clan possess lands in the richest part of the island? What is the justification for it? Because the clan-ancestors emerged from beneath the earth in that particular region. Even such accounts as this are pseudo-historical. They purport to offer a historical event as the reason for a present state of affairs, although the event is often imaginary, or at least of a different order from events in our direct experience. Now it is plain that such validations are 'aetiological' in one sense; the tale told to account for the practice of fireless sacrifices at Lindos was exactly of this kind. Almost any *aition* will do, provided it shows how the debatable custom or practice might once have happened for the first time. Plausibility in historical or realistic terms is unimportant. Indeed, the validation is a myth, a tale, and it must be striking and entertaining apart from anything else. Plausible or common-sense validations (like 'one family settled in the region and then its descendants gradually spread and took over more of the land') are too banal to be memorable, and therefore are not often accepted as charters in traditional and non-literate societies, or at least have to take their place beside the more exotic and memorable accounts that become myths.

The charter idea is undoubtedly right for some myths; it is undoubtedly wrong for many others. Moreover Malinowski allowed his feeling that myths have nothing to do with philosophy to run away with him. Even the myths he recorded in the Trobriand group sometimes have speculative implications that escaped him. Many of them are practical, and some are concerned with simple magic to ensure the fertility of the gardens or the seaworthiness of the boats. Others, however, are more complex. Those that deal with the origins of the *kula* system (an extraordinary convention whereby ceremonial bracelets are traded round the ring of islands in one direction, ceremonial necklaces in the other) often have important implications; they reflect basic preoccupations with respect to subjects like youth and age (since good looks are a factor in favourable *kula*-bargains) or the relation of garden-fertility to social status.[21]

The consideration of other sets of myths makes the matter still clearer. Lévi-Strauss has proved that many of the myths of the American Indians are in a way concerned with problems. They set up artificial (mythical) situations that are unconsciously framed to establish some kind of mediation of these problems, which often present themselves as simple antitheses. Mesopotamian myths are likewise sometimes speculative; the curious inverted relationship between Gilgamesh and his friend Enkidu in the Akkadian Gilgamesh-epic is a case in point. Even Greek myths, in which the speculative element has been eroded in the course of a long literate or quasi-literate tradition, contain important examples. The Prometheus tale does not merely state a precedent for the division of sacrificial meats. By the trickery involved, and by Zeus' immediate retaliation in withdrawing fire from men's use, the whole transaction is transformed into a debatable moral issue or something like one. The myth that immediately follows in Hesiod concerns the first woman, or Pandora, and it continues the same tendency. She is created as a fresh punishment for mortals when Prometheus has stolen back fire; but once again an implied contradiction at the heart of the situation gives the simple folktale motif of the extravagant or inquisitive wife a speculative reference, for women are revealed as both alluring and wasteful, as tricky but necessary.

A similar conflict of attitudes shows itself in the range of developed goddesses. Artemis and Aphrodite stand at opposite poles, most clearly so in Euripides' *Hippolytus* where the pure devotee of Artemis who rejects sex is literally torn apart for his obsession. It is true that in her earlier, Asiatic form Artemis is also a mother-figure, and her cult-statue in the temple of Ephesus ('great is Diana of the Ephesians') was multimammary, covered with breasts. The Greeks did some simplification here, but it resulted in the intriguing polarity between her and Aphrodite. Among heroic myths one has to look harder for theoretical overtones, but Cheiron the good Centaur provides them, and so does Bellerophon with his presumptuous trip heavenward on Pegasus, Heracles in his dealings with the underworld or with women (Queen Omphale whom he served as a slave, sometimes in female dress, or his wife Megara whose children he murdered in a fit of madness), Peleus in his ultimately unsatisfactory marriage with the sea-goddess Thetis, and Oedipus in his dilemma of ignorance. These instances are by themselves sufficient to dispose of the theory that all myths are non-theoretical charters. By admitting that there can be charters for 'beliefs' Malinowski himself indicated the internal contradictions of his theory, for myths concerned with abstractions like the limits of mortality or just behaviour are not mere arbitrary fairy-tales to put a stop to anxiety or dispute. They are part of an (often unconscious) argument. Even on concrete matters like the validation of social institutions the charter theory is too complacent, implying as it does that society is a static machine. Malinowski's pupil E. R. Leach was surely right when he emphasized that 'myth and ritual is a language of signs in terms of which claims to rights and status are expressed, *but it is a language of argument, not a chorus of harmony*' (my italics).[22]

In one way Australian myths can be interpreted as providing strong support for the charter theory; as the Berndts put it: 'Myths, then, may be used to explain or account for certain rites, or to show why various actions are performed: why a certain tribe practises circumcision, or why it does not while its neighbours do. The answer may be that some mythical character gave the order for this, or set the fashion for it.'[23] Seen in a slightly different light, however, Australian myths lend support to a somewhat different theory, the fourth in our selection, which is really a subtle development of Malinowski's charter idea.

Mircea Eliade has written numerous books to show that the purpose of all myths is to evoke, or actually to re-establish in some sense, the *creative era*.[24] The intention, he thinks, is not simply nostalgic, although there is an element of Golden-Age wistfulness in it. It is also practical, even magical in a sense, since by reconstituting that era one can also revive some of its unique creative power. Telling how Demeter found her daughter Persephone, with the result that the corn sprouted once more, is effective in increasing the power of the crops as they thrust their way out of the soil each year. Any tale that restores for a time the mythical past is helping the world to maintain the order it formerly achieved, and helping humans to share in the power of the divine actions *in illo tempore* (as Eliade puts it in a catch-phrase). Australian myths are especially relevant here, since it is a common Aboriginal idea that the beings that existed at the beginnings of the world still exist. They live on in a disembodied form in what is called by some tribes the 'Dreaming Era' or 'Eternal Dreamtime' – the implication being that they appear to us as in dreams, that they actually 'happen' just as dreams do. They are not identical with the ancestors who also appear in myths, but it is they who gave rise – as Rainbow Snake, or the Two Men, or the Djanggawul brother and sisters, or the trickster known in north-east Arnhem Land as Namaranganin, or many others – to human capacities like childbirth and to actual human ancestors. As a result of this conception myths and rituals, which in Australia are rather closely linked, can be said to actualize these beings and to bring the Dreamtime into the present with potent and fruitful results.

Eliade generalizes this conception without subjecting it to the stringent test of applying it to the majority of myths in many different cultures. He simply reiterates. For example: 'Periodically, the most important events were re-enacted, and so re-lived; thus, one recited the cosmogony, repeated the exemplary gestures of the gods, the deeds that founded civilization. There was a nostalgia for the *origins*; in some cases one could even speak of a nostalgia for the primordial Paradise.'[25] But the truth seems to be that many myths of many societies are not of this kind and do not respond to any such interpretation. The idea of the Dreamtime is a unique conception; other myths cannot necessarily be seen in this light. Amerindian myths, for example, are not evocative or nostalgic in tone, but tend to be detailed and severely practical. Many are about animals who acted as inventors or 'culture heroes' in a mythical epoch that was, admittedly, the time when things were put in order. But since then the animals have turned into men, and the distinction between men and animals has become a firm one. That in itself reduces the effectiveness of myth-telling as a reconstitution of primordial power. Moreover many Amerindian myths manifestly have other and quite different functions; I am thinking particularly of the Amazonian myths considered in detail by Lévi-Strauss and of the North-west coast myths collected by Boas, which contain foundation and charter acts, folktale motifs, trivial aetiologies, serious structural implications of the kind outlined by Lévi-Strauss for the myth of Asdiwal, reflections of religion, and so on.

Greek myths, too, utterly fail to support Eliade's universal theory. The whole range of Greek heroic myths lies outside any true 'creative' era. Heracles and Cadmus found cities, and Heracles great festivals like the Olympic games; the earth is cleared, to some extent, of monsters (which are purely local menaces), but re-telling this kind of myth does not evoke a strongly creative past. The Golden Age is gone forever – a nostalgic dream, perhaps, but not a practical one. Perhaps the divine myths provide better support? On the whole, no. Zeus triumphs over his enemies, divides the world among the gods and establishes Dikē, Justice or the proper order of things, over mortals, but that does not constitute a creative era of the kind Eliade had in mind. Indeed, Greek myths are silent about the invention of many human functions and social institutions. Childbearing, for example, is no longer the object of mythical curiosity as it was for so many other people. Pandora just appears, and even before her men seem to have been born. Greek myths, as we shall see in Chapter 11, were vague and ambivalent about the creation of mankind. Basic social institutions like marriage, inheritance or kingship are simply taken for granted; that raises other problems, but it provides poor support for the idea that all myths have this function of reviving a specifically creative era. The study of other sets of myths would lead to the same result: that Eliade's idea is a valuable perception about certain myths, not a guide to the proper understanding of all of them.

The fifth universal theory is also one of the most long-lived and important. It proclaims that all myths are closely associated with *rituals*. In its extreme form it asserts that myths are actually derived from rituals, which in the course of time seem pointless and obscure and therefore give rise to aetiological tales that purport to explain them in some sense. That was the remarkable intuition of a famous late-Victorian Old Testament scholar, W. Robertson Smith. His *Lectures on the Religion of the Semites* (1894) might easily have passed into obsolescence within a generation or so, but the idea expressed there that myths are derived from rituals achieved near-immortality when it was adopted by his friend and admirer J. G. Frazer and became the basic presupposition of *The Golden Bough*. The 'Cambridge School' of Jane Harrison, Gilbert Murray, A. B. Cook and F. M. Cornford delighted in the thought that the apparently refined Greek culture might actually depend on primitive rituals, a thought that seemed to give life to the otherwise rather literary phenomenon of Greek religion. Biblical scholars, too, drew support from the apparent applicability of Robertson Smith's theory to certain Greek myths, and in their turn encouraged classical scholars by providing favourable Oriental instances. Even apart from the Bible itself, the ancient Near East appeared rich in supporting evidence. Akkadian rituals, in particular, were well-documented, and it was undeniable that ritual had played an important part in the life of the Mesopotamian peoples from at least 2500 B.C. onwards.

The study of the Australian aborigines initiated by Spencer and Gillen at the end of the last century added further confirmation that myths and rituals could be closely associated in the lives of some peoples. Out of this perception, among others, there now arose the anthropological theory of functionalism, developed in an extreme form by A. R. Radcliffe-Brown (who began as a student of Australian anthropology) and his pupils in the Malinowski tradition.[26] Functionalists saw society as a tight and complex mechanism, every aspect of which was related to basic social ends (marriage, property, the rules of kinship). Rituals were a prominent aspect of savage societies among others; myths therefore must be fitted into the same pattern, and since they were often apparently subordinate to rituals the Robertson Smith-J. G. Frazer theory was accepted with only minor adaptation. E. R. Leach, as we saw earlier, corrected the emphasis on society as a static structure, but even he could assert that 'myth implies ritual, ritual implies myth, they are one and the same.'[27]

That is just one specific form of what is surely an exaggerated and one-sided theory. It is simply not true that myths are always associated with rituals, let alone identical with them in some curious way. Societies differ enormously in the amount of ritual in their life, and they differ too, even in highly traditional groups, in the range and importance of their myths. Even where both rituals and myths are prominent, as among the Australian Aborigines, many myths are independent of rituals. That is not always easy to discern from anthropological accounts, for they have been dominated by the idea that over the whole range of story-telling only those tales that are overtly connected with rituals can bear the full title of myths. Yet that is obviously not so by any reasonable standard for defining what we mean by a myth. It takes some ingenuity on the part of the Berndts, for example, to deny the title of 'myth' to tales like that cited on p. 56 about the origin of death; or to a Pitjandjara tale of how the Two Men were once travelling near the south coast: one of them had the water-bag and refused to give it to the other, who pierced it so that the water came out and drowned them, becoming the sea; or to another tale of the same tribe about how Tulina, an old spirit-man, caught and cooked a Mamu (evil spirit) child.[28] His wife recognized a hand in the stew and disappeared: Tulina grew breasts and suckled the other children, then went in search of a second Mamu child that had, although lamed, escaped him. The Mamu then attacked Tulina, milked him, cut off his parts and gave them to the lame child who was made whole.

This tale has no ritual connection, although it is obviously a myth. It also has no stated social reference, although one probably lies concealed. Lévi-Strauss has demonstrated the reflection of social and other preoccupations in many Amazonian myths of apparently similar inconsequentiality. These are not just casual tales thought up by some transient character and then forgotten; they are traditional, and they are important. So too in ancient Mesopotamia many of the most striking myths to have survived contain no known ritual reference whatever: Inanna's Descent to the Underworld, for example, or Enki and Ninhursag, or most of the Gilgamesh-epic. Norse myths, another major group, likewise bear only slight and tangential reference to ritual practices.

Greek myths will be considered more closely from this point of view in Chapter 10; meanwhile the following observations may be of interest. The great theogonical succession myth has no known ritual implications; the ancient Greeks did not carry out actions designed to imitate or reproduce the separation of sky and earth, Kronos castrating his father or Zeus displacing Kronos. These crucial ideas belonged to myths and not ritual. The cult of the gods sometimes included allusions to the myths of their birth, but through the recital of the tale itself rather than the performance of an associated ritual. As for the major heroic myths, one finds virtually nothing in the way of ritual corresponding to the deeds of Perseus, Heracles, Jason, Oedipus, Bellerophon, Orpheus, Peleus, and a mass of others. In general, Greek myths as they survive seem singularly devoid of ritual connections. Certain counter-instances will be discussed later, but in the meantime it looks as though this were one more universal theory that is better discarded.

# CHAPTER 4

# MYTHS AS PRODUCTS OF THE PSYCHE

THE theories considered in the last chapter proposed that myths refer primarily to the world of nature or to men as involved in society or worshipping gods. Their inner reference, that is, is supposed to be to the objective environment or to the human view of the outside world. It is now time to review a group of interpretations that claims to find the ultimate reality of myths in the individual psyche itself. If myths have a purpose and a reference outside their surface meaning as narratives – and according to these interpretations they have – then they are held to be primarily concerned not with society or the outside world, but with the feelings of the individual. They may become traditional through communal performance and be supported by the customs and attitudes of the group, but their essential appeal is to each separate person in his endeavour to come to terms with himself rather than with community or environment as such. The distinction between individual interests and those of individuals grouped in a society is often a fine one, especially with traditional or totalitarian communities in which collective interest is ostensibly paramount. Yet clearly there is a difference between one's enjoyment of a tale that justifies a certain custom, or fits a piece of the natural environment into place, and the satisfaction gained by identifying oneself with the hero of fantastic and ultimately successful adventures. Most of the theories to be considered would hold that even the objective functions of charter and the rest are really secondary to the psychological needs of the individual.

The psychological uses of myths can themselves be divided

into different categories representing distinct functions; for example a myth might be important because it expresses something that otherwise lies repressed or dormant in the individual, or alternatively because it seems to fulfil some wish or create a desirable emotional condition. The first function would be analogous to Aristotle's idea that watching tragic drama brings about a *catharsis*, a kind of purgation, of pity and fear. The myth of the monster at the heart of the Labyrinth, on his interpretation, would express and so relieve the fear of unknown horrors; and if it is true that we have a hidden terror of killing our own fathers, then the story of Oedipus and Laius at least brings it into the open. The effect is quite different from that of the second category, in which a myth provides a kind of emotional consummation. 'Wish-fulfilment fantasy' was the Freudian formulation of the tendency to imagine ourselves winning fame, wealth or beautiful companions. Day-dreams of that kind are often consoling, and the kind of myth or folktale in which the hero overcomes terrible dangers to perform the quest and win the prize can be seen as a generalized fantasy in which the hero represents the individual listener, who imagines his own problems and frustrations as running parallel to the larger and more concrete ventures of the tale.

That some myths have this sort of effect, and depend on it for their power to attract audiences, is beyond dispute. One of the reasons for enjoying the tale of Theseus and the Minotaur is that Theseus escapes from danger by killing the beast and escaping from the Labyrinth – with the aid, of course, of a beautiful princess. After horror, fulfilment: the two kinds of psychological effect are not mutually exclusive, in fact they often complement one another. Further discrimination needs to be made within each category, and I have obviously only presented the crudest outline. Psychologists and others can take the matter further, and no doubt have done so *en passant*. Yet for the most part they remain wrapped up in great psychological theories that are both more complex and less plausible than these simple discriminations.

The 'great' psychological theories of myth are those connected with Sigmund Freud and Carl Jung, to which must be added the elaborate and less widely-known ideas of Ernst Cassirer, much of whose voluminous *The Philosophy of Symbolic Forms* is about myths as one of the primary forces of cultural expression. I have also held over to this chapter the structural theory of myths advanced quite recently by Claude Lévi-Strauss. This is not in all essentials a psychological theory; it makes use of elaborate analyses of anthropological materials and concedes that myths are primarily concerned with problems and contradictions in society rather than directly with the individual psyche. Yet its ultimate foundation is the assumption that the human mind (what Lévi-Strauss calls the *esprit*) always works in roughly the same way – and that myths and society are the products of mind and reflect, with almost scientific accuracy, its common structure. The theory is much concerned, therefore, with the psychological and mental origins of myths, although its brilliant author prefers to say little about the processes themselves but rather to map the indirect evidence for their operations. Finally I shall consider in more general terms the fantasy-producing dislocations of ordinary consequence and logic that are characteristic of many myths and are implicit in Freud's theory of dreams.

Not many of Freud's special theories are widely accepted today. His fame depends on the general concept of the unconscious mind, and his emphasis on infantile sexuality, in particular, is seen to be exaggerated. Yet *The Interpretation of Dreams*, first published in 1900, is still regarded by many admirers as his masterpiece. In it Freud recognized that myths and dreams often work in the same way; a general connection had already been asserted by E. B. Tylor, but Freud went far beyond him in relating the symbols of myths to those of dreams. There is, indeed, an obvious connection, and we do not need mechanistic theories about unconscious dream processes to convince us of that. It is a commonplace among several tribal societies, especially among Australian Aborigines with their 'Dreaming Era', that myths and dreams evince a similar insight into reality. Many of the Indian tribes of the American South-west agree in spite of other cultural differences that myths are dreamed, and are created in that way. They are of great importance, being closely connected with the complex rituals on which the life of the Pueblo Indians, in particular, is centred.

Freud, then, carried further this kind of view of the relation of myths and dreams, and emphasized the part that both may play in the life of the unconscious mind. His particular intuitions about the 'dream-work' (in which the mind rearranges experiences and emotions so as to repress potential anxiety and so protect sleep), and his reduction of this work of the unconscious to the three functions of *condensing* the material of daytime experience, *displacing* its elements, and *representing* it in symbols and images, are deeply suggestive, even if they are too formal and mechanical to be convincing in detail. Something like these processes may have taken place in the evolution of myths; that is Freud's implication, and it could be correct for certain types. It is probable, for instance, that many myths are *symbolic* in that they represent a hidden attitude or preoccupation indirectly, by means of concrete actions in an overtly different sphere; and we shall see that their fantastic quality often depends on their *dislocation* of everyday connections, a process close to what Freud called 'displacement'.

Quite apart from the correctness or otherwise of Freud's ideas about dreams, I feel that there certainly are important connections between the two phenomena. It would admittedly be wrong to regard a myth simply as a product of some kind of unconscious mentality, and its quality of traditional tale shows that to be an over-simplification. Yet the manipulation of emotions and experiences, at a less than fully conscious level, does seem to be implied in those myths that plainly bear on social and personal preoccupations. At present it is hard to say more than that. Continuing studies of the nature of dreaming should ultimately be helpful; unfortunately it is much harder to examine the processes of myth-making, since the last traditional societies, those that remain untouched by literature and the values of western society, are being rapidly and almost systematically exterminated.

One particular Freudian theory in this field has been less helpful: the idea that myths are in some sense 'the dream-thinking of the people', that they preserve the unconscious preoccupations of the infancy of the race. Freud's followers Karl Abraham and Otto Rank had a hand in formulating this misleading conception in its extreme version. The former wrote in his *Dreams and Myths* (1909, translated into English in 1913) that a myth is 'a fragment preserved from the infantile psychic life of the race, and dreams are the myths of the individual' (p. 72). Freud himself had asserted at about the same time that 'myths . . . are the distorted vestiges of the wish-phantasies of whole nations – the age-long dreams of young humanity.'[1] Freud's statement includes the additional idea that myths are 'wish-fulfilment fantasies', which is clearly right for some myths but not for all. Now the idea that myths are the dream-relics of society in its infancy appealed to Freud and his followers because it seemed to fit so neatly with the idea that man is determined by infantile emotions, that his adult psyche is conditioned by the relics of infantile wishes, repressions and experiences. Yet it is, of course, nonsensical, if only because a race, or human society in general, is quite different from an individual who grows from infancy to adulthood. To conceive it as such is to be guilty of an absurd kind of genetic fallacy. Our general thinking is deeply infected by this anthropomorphic metaphor, but there is no need to import it into subjects like the study of myths.

In so far as they are truly traditional, myths derive from an oral stage of culture; most of them retain elements from a period many generations earlier than their first recording in writing. Yet that hardly places them in an inchoate stage of human development that might correspond with the 'infancy' of the race, even if we accepted the metaphor, so the idea is misleading there too. Many of the problems on which myths concentrate are perennial ones like those of nature and culture or life and death, and the palliations they suggest are by no means 'infantile', not even necessarily innocent. They are remarkably similar to those that are still offered, under slightly different guises, by religion or popular morality. Finally the concept of myths as an emanation of a kind of racial unconscious distorts the degree of collective authorship that can reasonably be assigned even to traditional tales.

A similar difficulty arises with the theories of Jung and, to a certain extent, Lévi-Strauss, but it was the philosopher-sociologist Émile Durkheim who, with his idea of religion as an amalgam of 'collective representations' (by which he meant collective *ideas*), came closest to the Freudian fallacy. Yet Durkheim at least conceded that ideas shared by a group come in the first instance from individual minds; and with myths, too, individual imagination combined with the contemporary interests and preconceptions of the social unit. Behind this assumption of a collective mind that reveals itself in the formation of myths and religious ideas there lies that other conception, both romantic and condescending, of the 'primitive mentality' of the savage – the conception developed by E. B. Tylor and Lucien Lévy-Bruhl whereby pre-literate man moves not in a world of reason or individual decision but as a prey to strange emotions and mystical associations. 'Collective' mind is the only sort these unfortunate and truly mythical creatures could really lay claim to. We now know that this is not how even the most primitive of men behave; they have minds, and reasons, of their own.

Even less persuasive than the 'infancy of the race' idea is

Freud's view that certain unconscious tendencies descend from prehistoric father-son competition in the 'primal horde'. That instincts for survival develop in line with the cultural evolution of mankind is plausible enough, but Freud used an inadequate study of animal behaviour to support an adventurous intuition about humans. His 'Oedipus complex' has not, in the end, won many converts, and its interest from the point of view of specifically Greek myths is surprisingly slight. That is, Freud hit upon the Oedipus myth to provide a title for a complex condition that he thought he detected in his Viennese patients. It was an obvious choice in one way, since Oedipus in the mythical accounts killed his father and married his mother. But he did so by accident (or in accordance with divine decree), and there is no suggestion, not even in Sophocles' *Oedipus Tyrannus* (980–82), that he was responding to some unconscious desire or exemplifying a universal propensity.

The significance of the unconscious mind, its working in myths as in dreams, the special effects of repressed emotions, the need to fulfil certain desires if only in imagination – these, from our point of view, are Freud's great discoveries. His followers have made further refinements, and many of the myth-interpretations offered so blithely by modern writers are vaguely Freudian in feeling. One influential example has been a paper by the distinguished American anthropologist Clyde Kluckhohn, called 'Myth and Ritual: a General Theory'.[2] It starts from the assumption that myths and rituals are essentially connected. Myths do not depend on rituals, rather they are an alternative form of expression of a single psychological state. Both represent 'adjustive responses' to anxiety-producing situations and provide gratification by 'anxiety reduction'; in other words they distract our attention from unpleasant things in life, and meet specific worries by supposedly effective forms of ritual behaviour or consolatory tale. Another of their functions, according to Kluckhohn, is to achieve a 'sublimation of anti-social tendencies', the 'discharge of emotion of individuals in socially accepted channels'. Myths about murder or incest, that is, purge us of an unhealthy preoccupation with these things, whereas ritual bloodshed directs our sadistic desires into a socially acceptable, even a useful, form.

In this kind of interpretation, more clearly than with Freud himself, we see the familiar tendency to impose a universal motive on all myths. The fallacy is obvious. Many myths are patently concerned with other things than the reduction of anxiety or the sublimation of our baser instincts: charter-type myths, myths of creation, and so on. Similarly many kinds of ritual have other purposes: for example, those that maintain the cult of a god, perhaps by a formalized cleansing of the divine apparatus as in the Athenian festival of the Plynteria, in which Athena's robe was annually carried down to the sea in procession and washed. A taste for ceremony is a different kind of ritual motive, just as the love of neat tales provides a distinct motive for myths. The two phenomena are not, in any case, anything like co-extensive (as I shall show in Chapter 10), and many of their forms presuppose quite separate intentions, psychological or otherwise. We can thank Kluckhohn for reminding us that some myths tend to reconcile us to the human condition, although we knew that already. The sublimation of anti-social tendencies is a more specific idea, already canvassed by A. M. Hocart and others, but its ultimate ancestry is Aristotle's purgation of fear and pity. That may be an essential aspect of some tales, although the idea needs further consideration. In any case there are other psychological functions of myths that are totally excluded by Kluckhohn's one-sided theory, and some of them emerge from the different interpretations now to be considered.

Carl Jung became a member of the Freudian circle but broke away from it. In some respects his ideas show Freudian ancestry, in others he drastically amended the presuppositions of the master. Like him, he saw that myths and dreams can each reveal certain configurations of the unconscious mind; but instead of vestiges of wishes and concerns from the 'infancy of the race' he saw them as revelations of what he called the 'collective unconscious', an inherited and continuing involvement of mankind with certain key symbols.[3] The importance for the practising psychologist of the 'archetypes' (a confusing Jungian term that refers either to these universal symbols themselves or to a disposition to form them) is that their particular deployment by the individual, as in dreams, is the index of an unconscious psychic drama that produces mental health or illness. Myths, on the other hand, reveal the normative psychic tendencies of society – tendencies that include a preoccupation with contradictions and problems, both social and personal. Nothing in myths is 'infantile'; on the contrary they reveal the unconscious urges and phobias of modern as well as ancient societies, and their expression eases the complexities even of present-day living. One of Jung's strongest intuitions is that men depend on these ancient and traditional forms of expression, ritual and religion as well as myths, no less now than before; consigning them to the sphere of historical curiosities has merely increased the neurotic malady of modern man. With that general idea that myths are a crucial element in the psychic, let alone the social, balance of the group we may well agree. Unfortunately many of Jung's more specific intuitions are less acceptable.

Most dubious of all is the very idea of 'archetypes': the earth-mother, the divine child, the wise old man, the sun, god, the self, the animus and anima (the female idea of man, man's idea of woman), even certain shapes like the mandala and the cross, and also the number four. Jung asserts that these images recur time and time again in myths, dreams and other manifestations of the popular consciousness. But is that really so? Is it true in any form specific enough to be significant? Jung's disciples have been content to accept his repeated assertion that this *is* the case, and to fall back on the instances from a few myths, and from the history of art and medieval mysticism, that most impressed Jung himself and are used and reused in his prolific writings. What is needed is obviously a statistical survey of mythical motifs (of recurrent figures rather than typical events), and that is something that his surviving followers seem to find both unnecessary and spiritually repugnant.

I have suggested in an earlier book that wise old man, earthmother, divine child and so on are not, in fact, recurrent figures of many sets of myths: not, specifically, of Greek myths.[4] The 'old man of the sea', Phorcys or Nereus, is a typical prophet figure, and the wisdom of age is incarnated in Nestor, who lived for three generations of men and whose advice is constantly sought by Agamemnon according to Homer's *Iliad*. Demeter undoubtedly symbolizes the fruitfulness of the earth, and the loss of her daughter Persephone is one of the most ancient and poignant of Greek myths. The divine child might conceivably be represented in tales about the youth of Dionysus, Hermes or even Heracles. But these themes are not universal or even particularly common in Greek myths, and the concepts they embody cannot truthfully be said to predominate over many others. But, in any case, are Jung's collective symbols more than basic human ideas necessarily involved in human physiology and social circumstance? An infallible male parent is a factor in the psychic development of most of us who have known our fathers; the sun is important, that goes without saying; the idea of god crops up in one form or another in every human society; 'earth-mothers' are a common conception, and the Greeks were obsessed by the Asiatic Cybele and prototypes of Artemis as well as by Demeter. Naturally some of these common ideas reveal themselves in myths; it would be strange if they did not. But does that tell us anything beyond the fact that myths sometimes refer to common human ideas and generalizations? Do we have to posit a 'collective unconscious' that goes beyond the universal interests of humanity to account for them? Do we have to use confusing terms like 'archetype'? Do we have to believe, as Jung and his follower Karl Kerényi did, that there can be an actual *science* of mythology, by which certain symbols can be accorded specific values and their uses assigned a place on a chart of psychic normality?

A more intriguing idea of Jung's is that certain concepts can be inherited no less than biological behaviour patterns. That remains to be proved or disproved; its attraction for the study of myths is that it might account for the occurrence of quite detailed mythical themes in apparently independent cultures. The battle between 'evolutionists' and 'diffusionists' has rather died down at present; it used to be a great source of scholarly contention whether an apparently similar idea had evolved independently (because of common elements in human circumstance) or was the result of cultural contact. It is useful to point out, through 'Kon Tiki' experiments and the like, that diffusion may be wider than at first appears; but certain mythical ideas, notably that one of the first creative acts was the separation of the sky from the earth, or the 'earthdiver' motif whereby a creator figure dives to the bottom of the primordial ocean and brings up a speck of earth that turns into the dry land, occur in such distant and unlikely places that the operation of imagination after an instinctual pattern has its aetiological attraction. Against this whole possibility of inherited ideas is the view of mental functions associated with Jean Piaget, whose studies of child development suggest that apparently *a priori* concepts like number, space and causation are developed experimentally in the first few years of life.

One of the weak points in the whole discussion of myths as a form of expression has been an ambiguity in the meaning of the term 'symbol'. It is a difficulty that arises in Ernst Cassirer's view of the nature of myths. Cassirer undertook the enormous task of composing a philosophy of culture; the result is

Kantian, eclectic, ultimately unconvincing, but admirable for its occasional flashes of insight. Myth is seen as one of the main 'symbolic forms' of expression, language itself and science being the others.[5] A myth, he asserts, cannot be evaluated intellectually, because it is not allegorical but tautegorical – a form of expression in its own right, in which the spirit opposes an image world of its own to the factual world of experience: pure expression as opposed to derivative impression. In so far as this requires us to treat myths as the products of emotion rather than reason, it is a salutary corrective of intellectualizing theories of myths of the 'proto-science' kind. But beyond that, what does it all mean? In the end it transpires that the 'mythical consciousness', which comes into operation when the external world 'overcomes a man in sheer immediacy' so that 'the subjective excitement becomes objectified and confronts the mind as a god or a demon', is little more than the capacity for religious awe.[6]

For Cassirer, myth and religion are continuous – but that should not make us forget that many myths are quite unlike religion, that *their* genesis at least must be quite distinct from that of feelings about gods or cult. Moreover Cassirer is vague about what precisely is 'expressed' by this emotional contact with the outside world; at times it is a 'god or demon', at others a symbol. But a symbol of what? Once again we confront the difficulty that a symbol, even if it is not allegorical, an item in a rational code, must have emotional content at least. For Cassirer it seems at times that this content is simple, a kind of feeling of divine presence. (But is that really what most myths are about?) At other times, however, he writes about 'basic mythical configurations' that possess 'factual unity' because of an 'underlying *structural* form'.[7] These symbols, at least, are complex, more detailed than mere feelings of godhead and the like, and in fact their 'basic configurations' resemble the Jungian archetypes, just as their common structure prefigures the ideas of Lévi-Strauss. Certainly Cassirer was not unsympathetic to Jung, if only because Jung abandoned the Freudian concentration on sexual motivation that seemed to Cassirer a degradation of human culture. But like Jung he remained indecisive about the nature and operation of mythical symbols; and one suspects that both alike are conditioned by the essentially Freudian idea of fixed correlations between certain symbols and certain kinds of feeling or preoccupation, notably between phallic or womb-like objects and sexual obsession or repression.

On the whole Cassirer has little to add to the simple thought that lies beneath the metaphysical theorizing of Jung: that there are certain basic human concerns whose expression in myths enhances the integration of the individual with his social and physical situation. That thought is important for Lévi-Strauss, too, but his theory of myths is more interesting, not least because it offers detailed analyses of how myths mirror the inner tendencies of man.[8] The theory depends, as I wrote earlier, on the basic assumption that the human *esprit* is structurally similar at every period and in every kind of society. It also accepts most of the 'functionalist' position that society is a machine, every part of which is involved in the operation of the whole. For Lévi-Strauss the structural unity of the social machine is effected by the consistent structure of the minds that ultimately determine its forms. Myths, like rituals, are part of the machine and fulfil specific roles in making it work; therefore they, too, are ultimately determined by the structure of the mind. Lévi-Strauss can even tell us one of the main characteristics of this structure: a tendency to polarize experience, to divide it for the purposes of understanding into sets of opposites, much as a binary computer does.

It is true that many kinds of society are known in which the classificatory system is binary in character. Simple societies are often arranged in moieties, that is, in two groups each of which selects marriage-partners from the other, although

Lévi-Strauss himself has shown that such apparent systems are often in reality more complex than that. In other societies, too, one can frequently detect a disposition to make binary (as opposed to ternary and so on) divisions of the objects of experience; we shall see that the Greeks showed such a tendency. There are, of course, objective factors that encourage this way of looking at things. There are two sexes to impose the division on some of the most important facets of social life, those concerned with mating and the continuance of the tribe. Moreover the contrast between subjective and objective, oneself and the world outside, reinforces a tendency to see things in terms of contraries: desirable and undesirable, his and mine, black and white, friend and enemy. Human individuality as well as human physiology encourages us to divide our world into pairs, and that tendency is undeniably reflected in some aspects of social organization. Yet it would surely be truer to say that inevitable binary aspects of human and social organization impose themselves on the mind, than that a purely mental structure determines every product of human behaviour. Nothing yet known about the brain suggests that it must function like a binary computer, yet structuralism unmistakably implies that it does so.

Turning to myths, we observe that their quasi-binary quality for Lévi-Strauss is their function (as he sees it) of *mediating contradictions*. That is, men are faced with all sorts of problems in their lives, some of them general ones that do not depend on individual circumstances: problems like how to reconcile one's own interests and ambitions with those of the group, how to endure the thought of death when all our instincts are for life, how to temper natural greed and lust with discretion. Most of these general problems present themselves in the form of contradictions: between desire and reality, the attainable and unattainable, the individual and society. The function of myths, then, is to make such contradictions bearable, not so much by embodying wish-fulfilment fantasies or releasing inhibitions as by setting up pseudo-logical models by which the contradictions are resolved, or rather palliated.

One of the clearest instances of what Lévi-Strauss has in mind is his analysis of the Pueblo Indian myth of creation, in which hunting is interposed as a means of subsistence between agriculture on the one hand, warfare on the other.[9] In another part of the same myth-cycle the polar categorizing of animals into *grazing* and *predatory* is amended by the observation that *carrion-eating* animals intervene between the two other types, for they eat dead food but do not kill to get it. The contradiction mediated by this myth is precisely that between life and death, and is achieved by pointing out that, in specific spheres of food-production and the instinctual behaviour of animals, there is no simple opposition between living and dead but that there are intervening stages between the two. That raises a doubt, but no more, about the finality of our own death. Myths do not set out to give philosophical proofs, but rather to effect an altered emotional response to an aspect of our experience.

Lévi-Strauss's main body of evidence comprises the myths of related tribes of Indians in Brazil and Paraguay, and is particularly valuable because these myths have been recorded over hundreds of years by missionaries of a comparatively sophisticated kind. Their records of mythical variants have enabled Lévi-Strauss to show that what tend to change in a myth, as time passes, are the specific personnel or individual events; what remains constant is the relationship between one character or event and another, in short, the whole structure of the tale. It makes little difference whether a myth is overtly about a young girl disobeying her mother or a grandmother poisoning her grandson – the structure remains unchanged and is related to a conflict between generations, ultimately to its mythical resolution.

There are difficulties about the theory in the extreme form in which its author presents it. In maintaining that what myths are really concerned with is a sort of algebra, an abstract structural affinity between mind and environment that transcends specific social problems and preoccupations, he is certainly pressing the structural intuition too far. But the idea that myths are especially concerned with mediating contradictions, and that they do so by showing how 'empirical categories . . . can serve as conceptual tools for disengaging abstract notions', is a productive one.[10] It does not, as it happens, work with such dramatic success with Greek myths (and other western ones) as with those of the Bororo Indians and their neighbours, but that is probably for two reasons: that the former have been distorted by a literary tradition, and that in any case their structural emphases, in the absence of a reasonable number of variants, lie concealed. Structuralists, however, find any dilution of the theory repellent. The idea that a mythical structure can be altered in the course of transmission is in itself objectionable to them, because in their view the human mind, which always asserts its structure in the same way, should ensure continuity; and since all myths are the product of mind and society, they should all be equally susceptible to structural analysis. At this point I can only disagree, and point to the influence on any narrative tradition of accident, human weakness, changing social background and arbitrary personal choice.[11] The whole Lévi-Strauss concept, like so many other anthropological theories, has become absurd in its stringency. Society is *not* a machine, although it has its machine-like aspects; the human mind is *not* utterly rigid in its analytical functions; myths are *not* all alike in their structure and purpose, even at the most abstract level.

Those perceptions, that admission of the less-than-total rigidity of mental acts and social arrangements, enable us to make use of the possibility that a myth is suggesting some kind of mediation, along with other possibilities such as those already considered – that it may be a charter, offer an explanation, have a primarily dramatic value, and so on. That some myths are concerned with problems, especially with major causes of anxiety like the nature of death, is in any case obvious. What a modified structural interpretation can offer is the special insight that underlying relationships rather than overt subjects (even when interpreted symbolically) may be the significant factor, together with the idea that problems tend to take the form of contradictions, and that contradictions may be eased by revealing a *tertium quid*, even sometimes a fictitious one.

One of the basic oppositions discovered by Lévi-Strauss in the life and myths of his South American Indians is between Nature and Culture, often symbolized in their myths by the difference between the raw and the cooked. Greek myths, too, seem preoccupied with the contradiction between natural and human law, between force and restraint, barbarism and civilization; and Lévi-Strauss's work may help us to realize the paramount position of this general contradiction, which I shall explore further in Chapter 8 in relation to Heracles. But there are other signs, too, that the 'polar' way of looking at things is endemic in Greek thought from an early stage. Artificial constructions like the Centaurs (half man, half horse) and Cyclopes (one-eyed giants) are developed in ways that seem unconsciously to emphasize the interlocking virtues and vices of Nature and Culture. The Centaurs are powerful and often savage, as when they get drunk and break loose at the wedding of Hippodameia, the Lapith princess who is their neighbour in the lands bordering Mount Pelion. They try to rape her and the other girls, and for that they are driven away by King Peirithous and pursued by Heracles himself. But chief of all the Centaurs is Cheiron, who remains aloof from these disgraceful events and leads a supremely civilized and exemplary life, the paradigm of Culture, in his paradoxical mountain cavern. That kind of duality is less clearly seen in the Cyclopes. If we remember only Polyphemus in the *Odyssey* we retain a terrifying picture of bestiality and cannibalism, but the truth is that the Cyclopes as a whole are related to the gods, that they live peacefully enough, and that Polyphemus is something of an outsider. The rest of them, indeed, were envisaged as having built the giant walls of Tiryns and Mycenae after manufacturing for Zeus the thunderbolts with which he established his supremacy and the rule of law.

Again, in their conception of the three great world-masses of fire, earth and sea (or water) the Greeks included contradictory strands that the myths help to bind together. Fire is both sacred and profane, beneficial and destructive. It comes in the form of lightning from the *aither*, the bright sky or pure upper air that is the natural place of the gods; it purifies all evil, burns it away like chaff; it is the gift of the gods to men, and the means whereby men not only cook their food but also burn sacrifices and so maintain their link with the divine; it is the essential medium of pottery and metalwork, the crafts presided over by deities like Athena and Hephaestus. In its contrary aspect, however, it is the means of divine punishment and fiery destruction: Zeus' thunderbolt and lightning-flash. Water, too, is both life-giving and, in the form of disastrous floods like that from which Deucalion and Pyrrha were sole survivors, associated with death. Earth is clearest of all, since it is both the birth-place of the corn, partner to the fertilizing rain that falls from the sky, and receptacle of corpses, the place where the stricken souls of the dead descend to the realm of Hades. In other respects, too, the Greeks tended to stress the contradictions at the heart of things. Women are seen as a glory and an evil, love as daemonic and divine, old age as bringing both wisdom and foolishness. Sometimes the myths suggest a mediation (Prometheus in the case of fire, Persephone of earth), but often they do not, and in general it is important to concede that many elements of the Greek world-view, for instance in the list of divine functions themselves, are not polar in kind.

That is getting some distance from myths as a psychological

phenomenon; the digression arose out of the supposed link between the polar structure of myths and the structure of the mind. The Lévi-Straussian theory is clearly founded on a particular view of the *esprit*, which presumably includes the psyche; but it turns out that what is valuable in the theory does not really depend on its presuppositions about mind. Mediation implies a polarizing tendency that is in a sense mental in origin, but even so this structural evaluation belongs to the intellectual interpretation of myths rather than the psychological.

It must be admitted that the total harvest on the psychological side (to return to that) is rather thin, especially in view of the confidence with which psychologists have propounded their views and the respect with which they have been received. Myths, of course, are only one aspect of the products of the unconscious mind; but Rank, Abraham and Jung, as well as Cassirer, devoted special attention to them. There are, moreover, specific details of psychological studies that throw light on certain mythical themes, independently of the universal theories. Modern investigations have shown that dreams about flying are surprisingly common; their implication is arguable, but they help to show why the myths of Icarus flying towards the sun or Bellerophon on Pegasus are especially haunting. That is, their main theme coincides with one that is both common and mysterious in dreams. I am more doubtful about the Freudian explanation of floating-on-water myths as an unconscious reference to the embryo surrounded by its fluids, and the association of paradise myths with unconscious reminiscences of the happiness of childhood is surely arbitrary, since there are many other possible explanations. Other motifs will be referred to appropriate psychic possibilities as they arise, but in general no reason has yet been revealed why myths are psychologically satisfying *as such*, why they should constitute a unique form of expression (as opposed to other forms of narrative) that elicits a special kind of imaginative response. Their traditional quality reveals more about their special kinds of subject and imagination than any determinable relation to the human psyche, and it is in their particular themes rather than their aetiology as an expressive mode that they lay claim to more than casual psychological interest.

And yet one should not give up so easily. There *is* some imaginative quality about many myths, at least, that elicits a very particular kind of response, an empathy at an almost visceral level akin to the impact of great music or poetry. Such feelings are not confined to a few especially evocative themes (although it may be there, I suggested, that specific psychological theories make their contribution). Perhaps the quality that elicits them should be associated not with a special mode of mythical expression but with the overall subject-matter of myths, or even the special circumstances in which they are told. The first possibility takes us back to Mircea Eliade's theory that myths reconstitute the aura of a creative epoch in the past, an epoch of mysterious power. We noted that this may be true of some myths, but that there are many to which it does not apply. A survey of Greek myths does little to support Eliade's intuition. The cosmogonical ones (for example the succession of Ouranos, Kronos and Zeus) have a certain imaginative brutality, but creativity that can be turned to human use is hardly yet in question. Prometheus' activities on behalf of men are more pointed, but their effect is intellectual rather than emotional. The birth of the various gods and their acquisition of functions, not unlike the deeds of the heroes (even when they entail journeys above or below the earth), are too pragmatic in tone to accord with the theory. Despite the rationalizing organization to which they were subjected, Greek myths as a whole still possess a certain imaginative power, but it is not of the kind posited by Eliade. Mesopotamian myths are in many ways more striking than Greek, but again they lack forceful nostalgia directed to paradigmatic events '*in illo tempore*'.

A different suggestion is made by the anthropologist V. W. Turner, that myths are 'liminal' – which means that they are told in 'threshold' or transitional situations.[12] The idea is an extension of the famous identification by A. van Gennep of a kind of ritual known as *rites de passage*, whose function is to effect the passage from one vital or social status to another: at birth, at puberty and initiation, at marriage, old age and death. Such rituals tend to be performed at unusual times and places (at night, in the bush or desert, naked or in strange clothing) so as to remove the participants from normal space and time. They interpose a sacred interval in the flux of profane experience in order to facilitate the sharp transition from one condition to a totally different one. According to Turner, myths too 'are frequently told at a time or in a site that is "betwixt and between"'. The trouble is that this is probably not true of more than a small minority of myths. It is obviously not true of Greek myths in any phase that we can reconstruct, and even in tribal societies myths are very often told in informal and prosaic circumstances. Certain kinds of myths are recited ceremonially, yes – but there is no justification for thinking of these as typical of the *genre*, with the rest nowhere. Nor is it the case that ceremonial myths (which tend to be charters) are more imaginative than the rest. If, as he suggests, myths give some kind of 'total perspective', it must often be for different reasons. At this point, indeed, Turner seems to fall back on a position close to Eliade's; myths 'are felt to be high and deep mysteries which put the initiand temporarily into rapport with the primary or primordial generative power of the cosmos'.[13]

Nevertheless part of the special imaginative power of many myths is that they do in fact provide something resembling Turner's 'total perspective', at least a wider perspective than that of ordinary life. I have already mentioned the fantastic side of myths. Part of it depends, not on striking narrative motifs, but on the use of supernatural elements, whether monsters, gods or magic. The effect is not religious in kind, as implied by those who emphasize the 'sacred' as the essential mythical property. Rather it points to the coexistence in human experience of the ordinary and the extraordinary, the sacred and the profane. That is one mode of mythical fantasy. Another, related but distinct, depends on the *dislocation* of normal sequences and expectations; something that leads beyond paradoxicality to a kind of dream-like, sometimes nightmarish, other-worldliness. Freud stressed the 'displacement' of waking experience as one function of the 'dream-work'. If myths resemble dreams in their dislocation of events, as indeed they seem to do, it is not, presumably, for exactly the kinds of psychological reason (protection of sleep, repression of anti-social desires) envisaged by Freud. Rather I suggest that the dislocation of everyday life is in itself life-enhancing and liberating. It is not, according to this view, the 'liminality' of myths that gives them a 'total perspective'; rather it is their capacity to reveal fresh and otherwise unimagined possibilities of experience. That cannot be a completely unfamiliar concept to a society that enjoys surrealist art and requires a 'Theatre of the Absurd', and it seems plausible that the unconscious appeal of dislocation-fantasy might be no slighter, if different in quality, in the stratified and culture-bound circumstances of a traditional pre-literate society.

Greek myths are not strong in dislocation, and the fantasy they periodically display is more dependent on their supernatural components. The same is so for Nordic myths, and indeed for most that have been at some stage subjected to literate or quasi-literate transmission. Mesopotamian myths unexpectedly retain some of the qualities of apparent dislocation despite a long tradition of writing. Examples are Gilgamesh's dropping of precious objects through a hole into the underworld, Enkidu's fatal rush to retrieve them, or the earth-goddess Ninhursag curing Enki's eight diseases by placing him in her vagina.[14] Mechanical juxtaposition of themes and the determination of events by etymology are special factors leading to unpredictable sequences. Even so there is a genuinely fantastic residue, although it is not nearly so striking as the fantasy that permeates the myths of tribal societies among the Amerindians or Australians. According to a Pitjandjara myth from central Australia, two Spider sisters were taking food to a circumcision novice in the bush; one tried to get him to copulate with her and laid him in a pit, but he still refused; eventually she took him up to. the sky.[15] Here we detect another motive for apparent paradoxicality, for many of the details of the tale are connected with ritual practices – the pit and the sexual abstention in particular. There is, then, an allegorical level that complicates the fantasy, but the point is that it does not abolish it or render the myth less mysterious in relation to ordinary profane experience.

Classical scholars, on the whole, have found the comparative absence from Greek myths of 'horrible features' (as H. J. Rose called them) and major illogicalities to be admirable, a sign of the clear thinking for which Greeks of the classical period are rightly admired. It is true that the myths, by the time of Homer and Hesiod, had been given an organized form in which the supernatural had been assigned a definite place and from which other forms of fantasy, especially ritual crudities and other disruptions of everyday experience, had been largely extruded. That had, without doubt, its beneficial effects; perhaps it even helped the development of a rational view of the world, a matter to be discussed in the final chapter. But I suggest in all seriousness that Greek myths were not always like that; they were not always so bland, so devoid of real unexpectedness. They cannot always have lacked that crude power and ecstatic dislocation of ordinary life that may be an essential element in the formation of a truly creative culture.

# PART II

\*

# THE GREEK
# MYTHS

# CHAPTER 5

# GREEK MYTHS IN LITERATURE

GREEK myths as we know them are not the kind of traditional tales that alter their emphases according to changing interests and social pressures. On the contrary, most of them are already fixed in relatively inflexible literary forms. They have ceased to be part of an oral culture and a fully traditional kind of society. They have become a part of literature, and this is a crucial consideration whenever the temptation arises to compare them with the myths of other and simpler peoples. They still undergo changes, but the changes are of the kind determined by individual authors with unique aesthetic goals, or by the development of fresh literary techniques and new *genres*, and not primarily by the social, intellectual and emotional concerns of the community as a whole. The result is a set of myths of a very unusual kind. How did they become so, what was the precise nature of this literary development, and what are the special tastes and concerns of the main literary sources for Greek myths? It is with that kind of question that the present chapter will be concerned.

\*

Greek literature is dominated by Homer, a crucial if ambiguous figure in the transmission of the myths. He stands at the very beginning of western literary history (apart from the fragments from Mesopotamia and Egypt), and as a person we know very little about him; but then neither did the classical Greeks themselves. He lived across the Aegean, somewhere in Ionia, in one of the Greek colonies on the seaboard of what is now western Turkey, probably during the middle and latter part of the eighth century B.C. He was the man primarily responsible for the *Iliad*, a poem in over sixteen thousand hexameter verses about the wrath of Achilles and the fighting before Troy in the tenth year of the Trojan War. The second great early epic, the *Odyssey*, tells of the adventures of Odysseus on his return from the same war to his island home in Ithaca, and of how he eliminates the suitors who were laying siege to his wife and taking over his palace. Whether the composer of the *Iliad* was also responsible for the *Odyssey* has been debated from antiquity and is perhaps no longer very important. What matters is that both poems, despite minor differences, are alike in background, language and heroic values, and that they make equally heavy use of traditional narrative derived from earlier singers.

Homer came near the end of a long oral tradition.[1] He made something spectacularly new out of the poetry assimilated from his predecessors, yet the fact remains that much of his material, including much of its mythical content, goes back long before the eighth century B.C., some of it to close to the time of the Trojan War itself, and odd details to long before that. The war seems to have taken place in the middle or later part of the thirteenth century, and was one of the last great ventures of the Achaean Greeks – those that lived in the Late Bronze Age palaces and fortresses of Mycenae, Tiryns, Lacedaemon, Pylos, Corinth, Thebes, Orchomenus, Athens, Calydon, Iolcus. Much of the content of the *Iliad* and *Odyssey* is a poetical and imaginative development of those times. Whether Agamemnon and Menelaus, Achilles, Diomedes and Odysseus, Paris, Andromache and Hector were in origin actual people is infinitely debatable. On the whole it seems probable that the more important characters in political terms, Agamemnon of Mycenae and Priam of Troy at least, were historically based, the less important ones often not so. What matters for the study of myths (and this is why I called Homer 'ambiguous') is that these figures are historicizing if not actually historical: characters of legend rather than of myth in its wider sense.

Homeric references to people and events *before* the Trojan War are more cursory and allusive. The expedition known as that of the Seven against Thebes (which is also the title of one of Aeschylus' surviving plays) belonged, for the singers of the Homeric tradition, to an altogether hazier landscape; so did the deeds of Heracles and Bellerophon. Other great figures of the pre-Trojan era, like Perseus, Tantalus, Pelops, Daedalus, Athamas or Jason, are even vaguer. The tales about them were doubtless familiar, but they were not relevant to the Trojan *geste*; nevertheless they had passed down in a separate tradition for long enough to acquire the qualities of myths.

A third class of character in the Homeric poems (apart from those briefly mentioned older heroes and the newer legendary types) consists of the gods and goddesses. Here the epic tradition is altogether richer in mythical material. The poems do not concern themselves much with divine births and the development of the world, but there are frequent descriptions of gods and goddesses (especially Zeus, Poseidon, Apollo, Athena and Hera) intervening in events among mortals; these tell us a good deal about the qualities of the Olympian deities. On this subject Homer is and was the prime literary source, and one of the main genres of myth was thereby carried back into what the Greeks of the classical era regarded as an ancient and hallowed past. They were, of course, mistaken in this belief. 700 B.C., by which time the Homeric poems were more or less complete, was not even halfway back (from the point of view of a Greek living in the fifth century) to the Mycenaean age in which the events of the poems were set, and many of the gods and goddesses were formed, and their main configurations defined, earlier still. Yet Herodotus could write that it was Homer, and Hesiod who was active shortly afterwards, who established for the Greeks the birth and characteristics of their gods.[2] He was not too far out over the dates of

Homer and Hesiod themselves – 'four hundred years before my time', he wrote (i.e. about 830 B.C.) – but more seriously wrong about their originality. Homer is our earliest literary source, as well as his, with the slight exception of the Linear B tablets from Knossos and Pylos; but *we* know from archaeology, the epic language and comparative studies that much of the Homeric material is traditional and reaches back considerably further into the past.

Herodotus was not helped by another of his favourite theories, that most of the Greek gods were borrowed from Egypt, a place in which he was deeply interested. It was a brilliant intuition that much of his country's religion came from abroad, but we shall see in Chapter 11 that he got the main sphere of influence wrong. In any case Herodotus' contemporaries did not share his advanced theological views. For them the rooting of most of the divine myths in Homer was sufficient to guarantee their native origin. The *Iliad* and *Odyssey* were so famous that they became a treasury of traditional knowledge and morality. It took a critically-minded poet like Euripides or, a couple of generations earlier, the Ionian poet-sage Xenophanes to puncture the Homeric conception of the gods – to complain like Xenophanes that 'Homer and Hesiod have attributed to the gods everything that is a shame and disgrace among men, stealing and committing adultery and deceiving one another.'[3] And this kind of criticism, which looks simple but was in the circumstances highly sophisticated, made little impression on the majority of people, who continued to perform their religious duties (and incidentally to admire Homer) even when they did not believe every word about the gods in the myths.

Hesiod in the seventh century B.C. wrote a long poem called the *Theogony*, or *Generation of the Gods*, that fortunately survives. It is not a very good poem by comparison with anything in Homer, but it contains a certain rough charm and a mass of fascinating mythical and theological material, arranged so as to constitute a history of the world from its earliest stages down to the time when Zeus established himself as supreme god. Herodotus was right in thinking Hesiod himself to be responsible for much of the arrangement of this material, but, as with Homer, it is obvious that he was working on the basis of earlier sources. The myth of Kronos castrating his father the Sky is clearly older than Hesiod (whose full account of it is given in Chapter 6), and so is the corresponding episode in which Kronos is subdued by his son Zeus. On the other hand the conception of the primordial condition as 'Chaos', a great murky gap, probably owes something to the poet's own imagination.[4]

The next stage in the literary codification of myths is more heavily reproductive. A hundred years or so after Hesiod, in the sixth century B.C., cultured Greeks developed a taste for poems that were sung to elaborate music, either by a soloist or by a chorus, and were rhythmically more varied than the old epic. The Sicilian poet Stesichorus survives only in fragment, but we know that his long choral lyrics (the poem about Geryon is known to have run to a thousand verses) were relatively straightforward accounts of mythical subjects: the tales of Helen, of Europa, of Orestes, of Eriphyle, of the Calydonian boar-hunt, of several of the deeds of Heracles, of the fall of Troy. The tales he retold were of heroes, including the legendary type, rather than gods, although just as in Homer men and gods were jointly involved at many crucial points. Occasionally Stesichorus contributed a novel detail; for instance he quite certainly propagated the bizarre but moral idea that the real Helen never flitted with Paris, that what went to Troy was a wraith. That, if you like, is a kind of 'evolution' of a tale in response to fresh ethical values, but it is obviously literary in invention, and too satirical in its implications (for it is the subject of a Palinode, or song of retraction, written to avoid the danger of impiety) to be confused with the development of myths in an oral context. In any case most of his versions were straightforward ones, their embellishment literary and musical rather than interpretative or philosophical.

Much the same can be said of Simonides and Bacchylides, writers of solo lyrics who lived at the turn of the sixth and fifth centuries B.C. A charming poem by Simonides about Danaë set adrift with her baby Perseus has no pretention to altering or reinterpreting the myth; it simply takes one of the best-known traditional tales and presents part of it in a fresh poetical form and with an unfamiliar pathos.[5] Even Sappho devoted one of her songs, of which a few lines survive, to a more or less straightforward evocation of the marriage of Hector and Andromache.[6] Homer had not directly dealt with the subject, since it lay some years before the action of the *Iliad*, and perhaps one of Sappho's motives was to exploit a gap in the traditional form of the myth. In brief, for more than two hundred years after Homer, and in spite of the new personal poetry of Archilochus, Sappho and Alcaeus, the predominant poetical impulse was to present the familiar content of traditional myths, apart from those pre-empted by Homer himself, in novel poetical forms. That tells us something important about the power of the old myths as a great corpus of national culture, as well as about their possible limitations as a living mode of self-expression and communication.

The next major source of Greek myths is the Theban poet Pindar, who, like Stesichorus, wrote choral lyrics. His life spanned much of the fifth century, and his great odes, commissioned to celebrate victories in the religious Games at Olympia, Delphi, Nemea and the Isthmus of Corinth, are packed with mythical allusions, as much to heroes as to gods. The rather unimaginative conservatism of the Stesichorean tradition is at last abandoned, and Pindar becomes a violent critic of some of his rivals, perhaps including Bacchylides and Simonides, whom he dismisses as 'cackling like crows'. The poetical secret on which he prides himself is his mastery of the succinct allusion, the capacity to turn to the past for a mythical instance or precedent and then to turn back, no less rapidly, to the victor and his home and ancestors and the scene of his triumph. When Pindar boasts of his many arrows of song, of the speed of his allusions that 'speak to those that understand', of the importance of elaborating few things among many, he is referring to the power he feels in himself of using the myths to illuminate the present without the cumbersome necessity of recounting a complete action. Not that the world of myths was subsidiary and inferior: on the contrary, the 'excellence' (his word is *aretā*) that he celebrates in his victors seems to him to owe its value precisely to its heroic and divine connections, to its roots in a radiant mythical past of which the Olympic Games, above all other occasions, are seen as a rare surviving relic.

In spite of the rich concentration of his poetry Pindar was a relatively simple person, and modern attempts to discover some profound key to his use of image and myth have been a dismal failure. There is no single key; Pindar behaves like the volatile and inspired poet that he prides himself on being. Naturally there is a certain method in his poetic madness. Often there is a concrete historical reason for a mythical reference. The third Pythian ode, addressed to the powerful ruler Hieron of Syracuse, is about the mythical healers Cheiron and Asclepius, and that is because Hieron himself has fallen ill. Other odes addressed to the Sicilian dynasts depend for their brilliant effects not on developed myths (except in the case of Heracles) but on the glory and riches of the victor or on the Olympic scene of his triumph, a scene that reunites him with the heroic past of the whole of Greece. More ordinary victors, and especially those from small cities without conspicuous mythical connections, were dealt with more summarily, and even Corinth tends to receive a mere inventory of its heroic associations.

Some of Pindar's noblest songs were written for athletes from the physically inconspicuous island of Aegina near Athens. Pindar felt at home there, and it was through the heroic descendants of its mythical king Aeacus that he preferred to make delicate allusion to the ancient distinction of his own city. Yet his reaction to an Aeginetan victory is surprisingly predictable; much of the ode will be devoted to narrating parts of the imaginatively-restricted range of myths concerning the Aeacidae, the descendants of Aeacus. How is it, with his genius and passion for variety, for flitting like a bee (as he wrote) from theme to theme, that he could turn time and again to rehearsing the exploits of Telamon, Ajax, Peleus and Achilles? The answer may reveal something important not only about the poet but also about the literary uses to which myths could be put. For it was not, obviously, through any lack of inspiration that he repeats the famous deeds of the Aeacidae. On the contrary, the Aeginetan odes are in other respects, apart from the myths they include, especially brilliant, dense and allusive. The monotony of mythical reference is not the result of automatic composition or indifference, rather it arises from the poet's admiration of the island's past and his tactful perception that a victor from a land whose fortunes had drastically declined would like nothing better than to be reminded that the blood of heroes ran strongly in his veins. 'My plainest rule,' wrote Pindar, 'when I arrive in this isle, is to shower it with praises'; 'my heart tastes not of hymns without the Aeacidae.'⁷

For Pindar, at least, the myths represented a past that was of higher value than the present, that was more than halfway to a Golden Age. In resorting at every turn to the traditional myths his aim was not particularly to reinforce family or patriotic claims, and so use myths as what Malinowski called a charter. Rather it was to consolidate and where necessary recreate the nobility and vitality of the heroic past, the epoch when *aretā*, heroic excellence, flourished, when great adventures filled the earth, when men were true descendants of the gods, when their prayers evoked divine voices or direct theophanies, when the result of error was splendid ruin. To tell an

Aeginetan victor that by his actions on the race-track or in the hippodrome he has reincarnated the natural virtue of his great tribal ancestors: that is the highest compliment Pindar can pay him. In this use of myths as an active force for conserving a semi-divine past Pindar returns to a function that is more than merely literary, and reproduces in a way the evocative function of certain myths that was discussed on p. 63 ff. It is this functional vitality that gives his poetry a force that Stesichorus, Simonides and Bacchylides had lacked.

The most complete literary embodiment of the Greek myths manifests itself in tragedy, of which we possess only a small selection. Tragic drama developed out of the choral lyric, but dialogue and the impersonation of characters enabled the dramatists to subject traditional stories to new kinds of emphasis and interpretation. Variation came to be accepted for its own sake. and in certain cases – Orestes' and Electra's vengeance on their mother Clytaemnestra for the murder of Agamemnon was treated by all three great dramatists – there is a conscious development from Aeschylus to Sophocles and Euripides. The last of these, in particular, interpreted the episodes of myths in the light of a new dramatic realism and a devastating insight into what 'heroic' situations might mean in personal terms. Princess Electra, married off to a virgin peasant, became a condescending psychopathic shrew. Jason, hero of the great Argonautic expedition to win the Golden Fleece, is shown abandoning Medea for a safer, younger and less foreign bride, and Medea herself succumbs without difficulty to an insane jealousy that results in her murdering her own children. That does not prevent her from being rescued by the chariot of her grandfather the Sun – an equivocal treatment of a deity that is paralleled, for instance, by Euripides' depiction of Apollo in the *Ion*, where the oracular god of Delphi is shown making some very human errors.

Aeschylus, and especially Sophocles, did not have quite those aims, but there are other and perhaps even subtler ways in which the myths could be made to yield fresh meanings. Prometheus had been one of the most remarkable figures of the tradition, at least from the time of Hesiod and probably before that, but no one had yet had the idea of exploring through his fortunes the responsibilities of power and the obligations of culture. That is what Aeschylus does in his *Prometheus Bound* and the other two (lost) plays of the same trilogy. Even in Hesiod, Prometheus had been more than a mere trickster figure; yet in the Hesiodic contest between Zeus struggling to arrange the world and Prometheus protecting the interests of men there was no overt sign of the Aeschylean conflict between naked tyranny and the untidy liberties of civilization. That is partly a theological, partly a political dilemma. Both politics and theology had taken drastic new turnings by the middle of the fifth century, and Aeschylus uses the traditional mythical situation as background for considering these fresh problems in dramatic terms. The presentation of the myth, the drama itself, was still important, but it was given unfamiliar depths by these novel implications. In a sense that is an evolution of the tale's emphasis such as I suggested was common in oral environments. Yet there is a significant difference. The emphasis chosen by Aeschylus is only incidental to the dramatic situation itself, namely that Prometheus is being punished by Zeus by being chained to a mountain crag and having his liver devoured daily by a vulture. Zeus' violence had hardly been a factor in the Hesiodic version of the quarrel with Prometheus. Aeschylus, on the other hand, sees Zeus' struggle to establish order as a passage from physical coercion to rule by consent under the sway of his eventual helper *Dikē*, Justice; and that is a completely non-mythical conception.

The method of setting out and exploring current problems through a traditional mythical situation is shown still more clearly in Sophocles' *Antigone*, produced in 441 B.C. when the nature of Law, and the conflict between a man's conscience and the duties imposed on him by the State, were under discussion by politicians and philosophers. Antigone is a secondary character in the mythical tradition, daughter of Oedipus and sister of Eteocles and Polyneices. When Polyneices tries to win back his share of the throne and is killed in the expedition of the Seven against Thebes, his body is left for the dogs by King Creon. Antigone gives it ritual burial and is condemned to death for her defiance. That is a minor aspect of the traditional story, and may even have been a relatively recent invention; the further details involving the death of her fiancé Haemon are presumably Sophoclean. Certainly the conflict between God and Caesar is one that can be read into the basic tale, and was vaguely implicit in the general situation of two brothers fighting each other for their inheritance; but the use of the myth to develop the implication is something of a *tour de force*, and the problem explored is once again not central to the traditional narrative itself. The literate handling of traditional tales differs seriously in ways like these from oral transmission.

Even so, the conscious and non-traditional exploitation of an Antigone-type situation can sometimes throw a theoretical problem into sharper relief than can a direct and discursive treatment. Aristotle devoted some complicated chapters of his *Nicomachean Ethics* to the problem of voluntary and non-voluntary action, but the psychological complexities are far more clearly presented in the case-studies implied by Aeschylus' *Agamemnon*, in which Agamemnon had been torn apart by the apparent need to sacrifice his daughter Iphigeneia, or Euripides' *Hippolytus*, in which Phaedra struggles to suppress her passion for her stepson Hippolytus. Sometimes, too, a tragedy brings out even less obvious polarities in a mythical situation. Sophocles' *Philoctetes* is based on the story that Philoctetes was abandoned in the island of Lemnos on his way to Troy, when a snake-bite festered and became insufferable to his companions. Later the prophet Calchas revealed that

Troy could only be taken with the aid of Heracles' bow; that now belonged to Philoctetes, having been given him by Heracles in return for lighting the hero's funeral pyre and putting him out of his agony. Odysseus and Diomedes went to Lemnos to fetch Philoctetes and his bow to the Achaean camp before Troy.

That is the myth. In Sophocles' play, on the other hand, this simple, almost folktale situation is given a completely new dimension. Philoctetes becomes the examplar of unselfish generosity despite suffering; Odysseus (who had grown increasingly unpopular as the literate versions explored his qualities of cunning) is cast as the smooth and dishonest rhetorician from the city. In one way this is a contrast between inborn virtue, Pindar's *aretā*, and the acquired dexterity of pragmatism and sophistry. In another it becomes a symbolic confrontation between the unprofaned solitude of the island and the mundane ambitions of the Achaeans. Something resembling that kind of valuation of nature against culture, in a Rousseauesque sense, can appear even in oral myths, as we shall see (p. 206), but its presence in the Philoctetes story is pure Sophocles, and derives from a quite different approach, more conscious and more rationalistic than the mythical one. A distinction needs to be drawn between the instinctive use of a tale for the expression or refinement of an attitude, and the conscious choice of a familiar fictitious situation as a means of presenting a deliberate and personal analysis.

It was in poetry that the myths found their main expression in the literate era, but prose, too, played its part. The most remarkable prose users in this respect are Herodotus and Plato. They were separated in time by a mere couple of generations, yet the former was still often naïve in his attitude to myths, the latter almost ex~essively sophisticated. Herodotus used folktale themes to fill gaps in his historical knowledge – or rather, perhaps, he accepted folktale versions of real events with no particular scruple. The first book of his *Histories* provides the most striking examples of this tendency. He reports in all seriousness that Croesus king of Lydia dreamt that his son and heir, Atys, would be killed by an iron spear-point. After tremendous precautions he nevertheless gave way to the young man's request to join an expedition to hunt down a monstrous boar; during the hunt Atys was accidentally killed by the spear of his special mentor Adrastus, who had been purged of an earlier blood-guilt by Croesus himself.[8] This is myth, or folk-tale, and not history; so is the fabulous account of Croesus' own narrow escape from death on the pyre, to be described in Chapter 7.

This last story was known by many others apart from Herodotus, but that he specialized in such things is shown by his account of Astyages, king of the Medes.[9] Astyages dreamt that his daughter Mandane urinated so profusely as to flood the whole of Asia; he married her off to the Persian Cambyses, but then dreamt of a vine growing out of her private parts and encompassing Asia. That was interpreted to mean that her son would depose him, so he ordered his vizier Harpagus to kill the baby. Harpagus passed on the distasteful task to a cowherd, who substituted his own dead child; Mandane's boy grew up and was recognized by Astyages, who then punished Harpagus by serving up Harpagus' own son to him for dinner.

All this is quite clearly a tissue of folktale motifs: the grand-child destined by an oracle or dream to succeed the king, the king's attempt to kill him, the herdsman who saves the child, the serving up of a man's own child as an act of revenge, his horror at the involuntary cannibalism, the inevitable fulfilment of the dream or oracle. The tales of Oedipus, of Atreus and Thyestes, of Tantalus, and of Lykaon are merely the most obvious of several close mythical parallels that spring to mind. Herodotus can rationalize myths when he wants to; here he is doing the opposite, and seems content to accept peasant embroiderings of historical events along the lines of traditional narrative patterns. Nor is this confined to the history of foreign peoples, for at VI, 61–2 he tells how King Ariston of Sparta, only shortly before his own time, had gained legal possession of a friend's attractive wife by setting up one of those oath-that-goes-wrong situations beloved of myth. He persuaded his friend to agree on oath that each should give the other whatever single possession he might ask for. Ariston was king, and much the richer; also he was already married, so the friend thought he was safe. Others, as well as Herodotus, may have had a hand in shaping the tale along traditional lines, but that merely confirms that myths were still a dominant aspect of culture, for ordinary men as well as for historians, in the middle of the fifth century B.C.

By Plato's time, or even that of his master Socrates late in the fifth century, things had changed. It is always difficult to tell in the earlier Platonic dialogues which ideas belong to Socrates and which to Plato, but probably the habit of falling back on myths as an emotive form of persuasion belonged to Socrates himself. He is shown in Plato's *Phaedo*, for example, as crowning some rather inadequate proofs of the soul's immortality by a lyrical myth about the jewel-studded landscapes of the after-life. The proofs were partly Plato's, but the myth may have been Socrates' own. In any case Plato does not disdain to develop the tendency in other eschatological visions in the *Gorgias*, the *Phaedrus* and the last book of the *Republic*. Some may feel (as I do) that Plato might have done better to work a bit harder on the philosophical arguments before resorting to the traditional device of the persuasive myth; but that is what he tended to do, and he was thereby succumbing to an almost irresistible force in Greek culture – to what he himself called 'poetry' (including myth) as the natural enemy of philosophy.

In all these purely literary sources, poetry as well as prose, the myths tend to be treated as something special, as a kind of self-contained wisdom received from the past. Admittedly they provided a great store of typical examples; they could be used to illustrate, or argue for, most of the situations of ordinary experience. They could also be varied and adapted so as to produce obvious novelties or sensational effects. Yet all that is subtly different from the kind of organic change that tends to be undergone by myths in an oral society. In a way they have already become ossified by the time we first see them in Greek literature. Homer recounts pre-Trojan myths as a conscious diversion, or otherwise in a purely exemplary sense; Hesiod simplifies and reorganizes the theogonical tales but treats them, already, as sacred literature. Such major changes as are made are usually, by narrative standards, for the worse. Racial and political interference is only to be expected; the Athenians tried to tamper with the text of the *Iliad* to bolster their claims to the island of Salamis;[10] the Dorians, who infiltrated the Peloponnese from the north-west at the end of the Bronze Age, appropriated Heracles as a kind of tribal hero; the Athenians, again, tried to promote Theseus into a national cynosure by assigning him feats and adventures closely modelled on Heracles. Not only heroes but also gods were liable to this kind of exploitation. Apollo started his Greek career as an explicitly Ionian god, but when the oracle at Delphi gained Panhellenic influence it was this oracular aspect of him that became conspicuous in myth and cult; and when Delphi favoured Dorian Sparta rather than Ionian Athens at the time of the Peloponnesian War, Euripides retouched some of the Apolline myths to show the god in a highly unflattering light.

Such drastic political and religious reinterpretations usually presuppose a literate culture, both in Greece and elsewhere. The variations in status of the sun god Re in different periods and parts of Egypt, or the dramatic spread of the cult and myth of Osiris, were made possible by a literate priesthood; and it is hard to imagine the kind of adjustment that took place in second-millenium B.C. Mesopotamia (where the ascendancy of Babylon was probably accompanied by the recasting of the widespread creation-myth in favour of her city god Marduk) as happening in a simple oral context. Conversely the situation in Australia, where broadly diffused mythical figures like the Two Men or the Djanggawul Sisters developed seriously different functions in different regions, is improbable in a literate milieu. Literacy is opposed to that kind of inconsistency. With the concept of the fixed text comes the concept of the correct text, and incongruous versions are gradually eroded. Admittedly Greek myths, in spite of their high degree of organization, still reveal a few regional differences and inconsistencies, and there are confusions even about primitive events like the great Flood or the creation of the first man. Yet such inconsistencies are often concerned with topics not deeply rooted in the myths, or borrowed from abroad (as Chapter 11 will show) like the idea of the Flood. Other variants, especially where they relate to details like the names of minor characters and places, are the result of late and scholarly 'improvements' or clumsy bookish attempts to claim a mythical tale for one's own city.

It is their consistency and complexity, rather than their profundity, that have made Greek myths seem so superior to others, together with the extraordinary literary qualities of the classical works they pervade. And yet that kind of fertile complexity existed even before the classical age, although it was undoubtedly extended by the scholarly and encyclopedic operations that became fashionable as early as 600 B.C. Indeed it is already present in the *Iliad* and *Odyssey*, and cannot therefore be a purely literary phenomenon. I refer not only to Homer's organizing of the relatively new heroes of the fighting around Troy, although even here the numbers of those engaged and the individuality with which they are described are quite striking. But the background of earlier heroic events, too, is assumed to be familiar, and allusive references to it show both the poet and his audience to be aware of an extraordinary mass of episode and nomenclature.

When Achaean Diomedes and Lycian Glaucus meet in the sixth book of the *Iliad* Diomedes does not recognize his adversary and considers whether he might be a god in disguise; this leads him to consider in allusive detail the fate of Lycurgus, who attacked Dionysus – the passage is quoted on p. 129. Glaucus then enlightens Diomedes about his identity in terms that are no less detailed and indirect:

> 'There is a city, Ephyra, in a corner of horse-grazing Argos; there lived Sisyphus, the craftiest of men, Sisyphus the descendant of Aeolus. He begat Glaucus as son, and Glaucus begat blameless Bellerophon. To Bellerophon the gods gave beauty and lovely manhood, but Proetus devised evil against him in his heart . . .' (VI, 152–7)

There follows the story of how Proetus' wife conceived a passion for the young hero and, finding no response, denounced him falsely to her husband. This introduces the subsequent history of Bellerophon, and it transpires that he was grandfather to the Glaucus who is telling the tale. This is a not untypical digression, and no doubt Homer is summarizing some existing poem about Bellerophon and his family. But what a grasp of the whole heroic background does this demanding abbreviation presuppose in his audience!

Probably the best way to get a taste of the imposing complexity of Greek myths in their literate phase is to read the odes of Pindar, for there the allusions come thick and fast and the impression they leave is of a gorgeous and thickly peopled past that still overshadows the present. The fifth-century victors for whom Pindar writes reincarnate, in a sense, the mythical heroes of the past. The gods and goddesses are more evocative still, for they remained as objects of careful ritual till the last decline of Greek civilization. Because they too were involved in the myths, steering the destinies of heroes and constantly appearing before them – or sharing their beds – in the flesh, they seemed to carry over a kind of reality into that world from the active religious tradition in which their presence was still recognized. In the fifth century B.C., the age of Pindar, the tragedians, Pericles and Socrates, there were indeed many attacks on the gods; Euripides himself, as we saw, was not above an equivocal representation of their actions. Most people however continued to perform their private devotions and take their part in the great public festivals. Belief in the gods was far from dead, even if certain notorious myths were now rejected as literal accounts of their deeds and character. Not all or most of the tales told about them were immoral or needed to be questioned by the ethically sophisticated; and the continuity of the Olympian religion undoubtedly conferred upon the world of the myths – a world preserved and recreated by literature – a glow of actuality. The traditional myths, after all, were the dominant cultural fact of Greek life. They provided the primary subject-matter of literature (of poetry at least), they were the mainstay of education, appeal to them was constantly made by politicians and persuaders of every kind, they invaded the whole field of religion and ritual; and the Greeks were, in their curious way, a religious people.

The Greek myths, in the literary forms in which we know them, are not wholly typical of myths in general. One can criticize them on those grounds. Yet they are none the less magnificent, and if they lack, as will be seen, some of the fantasy of other myths, yet they make up for it by their sheer scope, their rich texture and their involvement with an attractive religion and a remarkable literature. Full treatment of those aspects is outside the scope of this book. But it is worth remembering, as one moves on to the consideration of detailed instances, that even in the developed and sometimes artificial forms of the high classical age Greek myths possess remarkable virtues of their own.[11]

# CHAPTER 6

# MYTHS OF THE GODS AND THE
# EARLY HISTORY OF MEN

IN considering Greek myths in detail my plan is not to attempt a complete survey, but rather to divide the myths into six categories and examine some outstanding instances in each. The first three categories are included in this chapter, the last three in Chapter 7, with Heracles and the development of hero myths held over for special treatment in Chapters 8 and 9.

The categories are as follows: first the cosmogonical myths, secondly those that describe the development of the Olympian gods. These are the divine myths as a whole. Thirdly, myths concerned with the early history of men and the fixing of their place in the world, especially in relation to the gods. The fourth category contains tales of the older heroes – the heroic myths in the fullest sense; the fifth has tales of the younger and more imitative heroes, including those of legend and the great Panhellenic sagas. These are the heroic myths as a whole. Finally, the sixth category contains later inventions of the historical period.

First come *the cosmogonical myths* about the formation of the world; they concern the initial separation of sky from earth and the replacement of the older gods of nature by Zeus and his contemporaries. Ouranos, it will be remembered, will not separate from Gaia, Earth, until the young Kronos castrates him. Kronos becomes king, but continues swallowing his own children by his sister Rhea until the infant Zeus is saved by a trick and displaces him in his turn. These events are incomparably described by Hesiod, who is also our oldest source for tales to which Homer has occasion to make only the briefest allusion. Hesiod's account in the *Theogony* is as follows:

All that were produced by Gaia and Ouranos – most dreadful of children – were hated from the beginning by their own begetter. He hid them all away, just as soon as any came into being, in an inward place of Gaia, and did not let them into the light; and Ouranos rejoiced in his evil deed. Huge Gaia groaned within, for she was crowded out, and contrived a crafty and evil device. Without delay she created the element of grey adamant and wrought a great sickle; then she addressed her dear children in encouraging tones, though troubled in her heart: 'Children of mine and of a reckless father, if you consent to do what I say, we could avenge your father's outrageous treatment; for it was he that first devised shameful deeds.' These were her words, but the children were all possessed by fear, and none of them uttered until great Kronos of crooked counsels after a while addressed his noble mother thus: 'Mother, I shall give you my promise and accomplish the deed, since I care nothing for my father of evil name; for it was he that first devised shameful deeds.' These were his words, and huge Gaia rejoiced greatly in her heart. She sent him into a hidden place of ambush, put in his hands a jagged-toothed sickle and instructed him in the whole deceit. Great Ouranos came, bringing on Night; desiring love he stretched himself on Gaia and spread all over her. And his son from his place of ambush stretched out with his left hand, and with his right hand he grasped the monstrous sickle, long and jagged-toothed, and swiftly reaped off the genitals of his dear father, and flung them behind him to be carried away. They did not escape his hand in vain, for all the bloody drops that flowed out were received by Gaia, and with the turning seasons she gave birth to the strong Furies and great Giants, gleaming in their armour and with long spears in their hands, and the Nymphs they call Ash-tree Nymphs over the boundless earth. And the genitals, once he had cut them off with the adamant, he flung away from the land into the turbulent deep; and so they were borne for a long while through the sea, and white foam rose up from the immortal flesh. In it a girl was nurtured, and first came close to sacred Cythera, then to sea-girt Cyprus . . . (154 ff.)

This, we learn was Aphrodite, and it is a typical aetiological and etymological detail, since her name can be interpreted in Greek as meaning 'she who came out of the foam' and both

Cythera and Cyprus laid claim to be the centre of her worship. Similarly Hesiod goes on to say that Ouranos called his children 'Titans' because they stretched or strove (Greek *titainein*) to do the deed.

After the birth of sundry other beings the poet returns to Kronos, now full-grown:

Rhea was subjected to Kronos and bore him glorious children: Hestia, Demeter, Hera with golden sandals, strong Hades who dwells with unrelenting heart in his halls under the earth, the loud-roaring Earthshaker [that is, Poseidon] and Zeus wise in counsel, father of gods and men, under whose thunder the broad earth quivers. These were swallowed by great Kronos as each of them came toward her knees from out of their holy mother's womb; his intention was that no other proud descendant of Ouranos should have kingly honour among the immortals. For he had learnt from Gaia and starry Ouranos that he was fated, strong as he was, to be subdued by his own son through the will of great Zeus. Therefore he kept no idle watch, but keenly observing them he swallowed down his children, and Rhea was possessed by unforgettable grief. But when she was about to give birth to Zeus, father of gods and men, then she besought her own dear parents, Gaia and starry Ouranos, to devise a plan whereby she might bear her child in secret, and repay the avenging furies of her father and of the children great crooked-counselled Kronos kept swallowing. They listened carefully to their dear daughter and did as she asked; they told her all that was fated to happen with king Kronos and his strong-hearted son. They despatched her to Lyktos, into the rich community of Crete, as she was about to give birth to her youngest child, great Zeus; and huge Gaia agreed to nurture and tend him in broad Crete. Then Rhea brought him through the swift, dark night to Lyktos first; she took him in her hands and hid him in a steep cave under the recesses of sacred earth, on thickly-wooded Mount Aigaion. To Kronos, great lord and son of Ouranos, former king of the gods, she presented a great stone that she had wrapped in swaddling-clothes. He took it in his hands and deposited it in his belly, the villain, and did not notice how his son was left behind, unconquered and carefree, in place of the stone – his son who was soon to subdue him with the might of his hands and drive him from his honoured position and reign among the immortals himself. Swiftly then did the strength and shining limbs of that lord grow, and with the turning seasons, deceived by the wise biddings of Gaia, great Kronos of crooked counsels brought up again his offspring, defeated by his son's arts and strength. First he vomited up the stone, the last to be swallowed, and Zeus set it in the broad-wayed earth in fair Pytho, under the hollows of Parnassus, to be a sign in later times, a wonder for mortal men. And he released his father's brothers, children of Ouranos, from the destructive bonds with which their father had bound them in his infatuation; and they were grateful to him for his kindness, and gave him thunder and the smoky thunderbolt and lightning – huge Gaia had hidden them before; trusting in these he rules over mortals and immortals. (453 ff.)

A few points in both passages need explanation. In the first part of the myth, where exactly is Kronos' imagined physical position? Probably within Gaia's vagina and not just sandwiched between earth and sky. Then, even before his enforced separation, Ouranos 'brings on Night', which suggests that he is already separate. Lastly it is not clear how Zeus makes Kronos vomit up the children. Some such areas of vagueness or inconsistency reflect the combination of different versions, others, the unreal fantasy that fills the two episodes. Several folktale-type motifs can be detected: the son destined to replace his father, the father's attempts to destroy him; the youngest is the bravest (Zeus has it both ways, since when his brothers and sisters are reborn he becomes the senior); swallowing a stone destroys a monster. The blood or seed of gods, if it falls on the ground, is nearly always fertile; Aphrodite's name, and the foamy appearance of both sperm and spume, suggest her as the product here, and her derivation from Mesopotamian Inanna or Ishtar, the 'Queen of Heaven', makes Ouranos or Sky the obvious male parent. Crete is suitably remote, but Zeus' removal there is mainly due to his relatively late identification with a Cretan dying-and-reborn god as well as to the prominence of Cretan cave cults. As for his uncles at the end, these are the Cyclopes and Hundred-handed Giants, and they are mentioned because they are needed as allies in his decisive fight against the Titans.

More important, this whole myth has a close Near-Eastern parallel, known from a Hittite version of a Hurrian tale of the mid-second millennium B.C. – the Hurrians being a non-Indo-European people spread across western Asia at this time.[1] Kumarbi deposes the sky god Anu by biting off his phallus; he swallows it and becomes pregnant with the all-powerful storm god, parallel to the sky and weather god Zeus. The storm god is born in an unnatural way, then in a last fling Kumarbi generates the monster Ullikummi, parallel to Greek Typhoeus, who is eventually defeated. The details are so closely similar that the Greek and Hurrian versions must be related, probably by derivation from a common west-Asiatic model. Kumarbi bites off Anu's phallus, while Kronos cuts off his father's; in both cases the blood and seed fertilize earth and produce minor gods (Aphrodite being a special detail); both Kumarbi and Kronos end up with gods inside them (the former by becoming pregnant, the latter by swallowing); these are born in peculiar ways (through the phallus, perhaps, and by vomiting); Kumarbi generates Ullikummi by copulating with a rock, while Typhoeus is born from Gaia – but according to one version Kronos smears two eggs with his seed and places them underground.

A structural analysis, emphasizing relationships rather than surface details, increases the neatness of the whole pattern as well as the similarity of the two versions. There is an unnatural retention of children within a parent, in Greek sources in the mother's womb, in Hurrian in the father's belly; they are released by violent and unnatural means, castration in the one case and pseudo-abortion in the other. In the one case sexual excess leads to castration, in the other castration leads to sexual abnormality (the male mother, the unnatural birth). Swallowing is important in both versions, but in the one case it is the fertile member, in the other living children and the sterile stone that are swallowed.

Whether these balancing relationships imply a Lévi-Straussian mediation between contradictions (for example between sexual excess and deficiency) is not clear; some kind of interest in sexual norms and functions certainly lurks beneath the surface. Freudians find the castration of the father significant, of course – but then is Kronos swallowing his children a symbol not of penis- but of uterus-envy? We must remember that the continuing sexual theme originated in the analogy between rain fertilizing the earth and a male parent fertilizing a female. Once Ouranos and Gaia are so far personified, castration becomes a plausible means of usurpation. That still leaves Ouranos' refusal to separate as a curious feature, but herein must lie a reminiscence of other and less physiological versions in which earth and sky were originally conjoined. In any case the degree of nature allegory is limited, and only extends to earth and sky and the implication of rain as seed. Zeus is a weather god, but that does not emerge naturally from the progress of the myth, for Kronos, who has no clear association with cosmology, intervenes.

Kronos (as mentioned earlier) seems to have had agrarian functions, and perhaps these mediated between sky/earth and Zeus. Otherwise his role is rather mysterious, as indeed is that of his brothers and sisters the Titans. In Hesiod's listing they include pure nonentities as well as Okeanos, the freshwater river surrounding the circular earth, and abstract ladies like Themis, Custom, and Mnemosyne, Memory. These earlier gods may be related to Asiatic 'older gods', both Hittite and Akkadian. In the Babylonian Creation Epic there is war between the older gods, led by Apsu and Tiamat (salt and sweet primeval water), and their offspring who were disturbing them, led by Ea the developed water god and by Enlil 'lord of air', later replaced by the Babylonian city god Marduk.[2] Here the younger gods irritated the older ones by behaving so rowdily that Apsu, encouraged by his vizier Mummu, planned an otherwise unprovoked attack. But these 'older gods' have clear associations with the elements, whereas most of the Greek Titans, and of course Kronos himself, do not. Possibly the Titans are unfavourably depicted in the Hesiodic version precisely because of the example of the Asiatic 'older gods'; and yet there is a strong tradition, followed by Hesiod himself in the myth of the Five Races, that Kronos was king during the Golden Age. There is undoubtedly some confusion of different mythical *schemata* at this point. Zeus is king of the gods in the present epoch, and has imposed justice and hard work upon men. Any Golden Age must have been before his time, and therefore in the reign of Kronos, for that of Ouranos was too primeval for there to be men or heroes. Kronos' association with agrarian festivals would not be inconsistent with this idea, since corn without labour was part of the Golden Age vision. From a completely different point of view, however, Zeus had to win his way to power by a struggle, and so his predecessor was also seen as an enemy of justice.

These cosmogonical myths, which certainly include themes of high antiquity, remain uneven in detail and rather mysterious. Unlike other Greek myths they have clearly withstood much of the long process of organizing and expurgation. *The other divine tales*, which form our second category, were not so fortunate. They touch mostly on the actual birth of the developed gods and goddesses and on the way they acquired their special functions and prerogatives. Apart from this they are rather thin in distinctive episodes, except where gods intervene in the actions of heroes, and even there their role tends to be secondary. The thematic variety of the heroic tales is one of the particular marks of Greek myths as a whole, and it seems plausible that in the course of development many themes originally attached to gods (for example the founding of cities and festivals, or the disposal of monsters) were displaced on to heroes. The gods, as a result, were left in majestic inactivity, comparatively speaking; nevertheless many of the tales of their birth and development are memorable enough to foster the inaccurate impression that there is a wide range of divine myths.

Zeus has defeated the Titans and established his rule among the gods, and he now embarks on a series of marriages of which the clearest account is once again Hesiod's:

> Zeus, king of the gods, made Metis his first wife, she who is most knowledgeable of gods and mortal men. But when she was about to give birth to owl-eyed goddess Athena, then he deceived Metis with a trick, and through crooked words deposited her in his belly, following the advice of Gaia and starry Ouranos. This was the advice they gave him, so that no one apart from Zeus should have kingship over the everlasting gods. From Metis, they said, it was fated that children of surpassing intelligence should be born – first the Triton-born owl-eyed maiden [that is, Athena], equalling her father in power and careful counsel, but then a child that was to be king of gods and men. But Zeus, before that could happen, deposited her in his belly . . . (924) And out of his own head he gave birth to the owl-eyed Triton-born . . . (*Theogony*, 886 ff.)

'Metis' means 'counsel', and this part of the myth is allegorical and presumably not particularly ancient: Zeus becomes wise by swallowing wisdom. But the motif also corresponds closely to that of Kronos swallowing his children. Zeus in his turn is threatened by the problem of a powerful son destined to overthrow him, and he meets it, in a repetition that is unimaginative rather than structurally significant, by swallowing the mother and so preventing the child from ever being born. Inconsistently the other child, Athena, is born from Zeus himself – not from his phallus, as Hurrian Kumarbi probably bore the storm god, but respectably and allegorically (for Athena, like Metis, is clever) from his head. The craftsman god Hephaestus is shown in many vase paintings splitting Zeus' skull with an axe to allow the fully-armed goddess to emerge; it was a famous pictorial motif. Again there is a smack of sophistication and scholarship about this piece of theogony. In fact Athena was probably a Mycenaean house-and palace-goddess, and was earlier felt to be a permanent dweller in her city of Athens; she had not been 'born' at all. Perhaps that made her available for Zeus' head; incidentally yet another god, Dionysus, was born from Zeus – snatched out of Semele's womb, when Zeus was forced to blast her with lightning, and sewed in Zeus' own thigh until the proper time for his birth.

After Metis, Zeus marries Themis, another personified quality ('custom' or 'law'), who gives birth to the Seasons and the Fates. Next he marries Eurynome, one of the many daughters of Okeanos, who bears the Graces; then, in a return to older and more concrete material, he takes his sister Demeter to his bed and she bears Persephone. Mnemosyne, 'Memory', bears him the Muses (transparent allegory here), Leto bears Apollo and Artemis, and last of all he weds Hera, who remains as his often-deceived wife from then until, presumably, eternity. These are his divine consorts; there is a long list of human mistresses too, from Semele mother of Dionysus, and Alcmena mother of Heracles, to Danaë mother of Perseus, and Europa mother of King Minos of Crete and his brother Rhadamanthys.

Zeus' daughter Athena, as protector of the royal household, became associated with the fortunes of the city as a whole, in her case Athens, which either gave her its name or derived its name from her. When Homer listed the various Achaean contingents in the second book of the *Iliad* the Athenians were described as

those who possessed Athens, the well-founded city, the community of great-hearted Erechtheus, whom once Zeus' daughter Athena reared and to whom the life-giving earth gave birth; and she set him down in Athens in her own rich temple, and there the young men of the Achaeans propitiate him with bulls and with sheep as the seasons come round . . . (*Iliad* 2, 546 ff.)

Erechtheus was one of the early legendary kings of Athens, he is 'born from the soil' because the Athenians claimed to be autochthonous, not immigrants, and Athena's temple is virtually the same as his palace on the Acropolis. That we learn from an allusion in the *Odyssey* (7, 80 f.) in which Athena left the island of Phaeacia 'and came to Marathon and broadwayed Athens, and slipped into the compact house of Erechtheus'; it is her own home too, because in a Mycenaean city the shrine of the god or goddess is set within the palace itself. Here, then, is Late Bronze Age religious realism as well as Athenian local patriotism. The tale of Athena's contest with Poseidon, in which she offers the city olive-trees and so wins its possession, elaborates the general theme. It is as Polias and Poliouchos, 'Holder of the City', that she comes to be associated with its warriors and craftsmen, especially potters and metal-workers; her protection of spinning and weaving, on the other hand, goes back to her function as goddess of the *oikos*, the household. The two contradictory sides of her are shown in the *Hymn to Aphrodite*, where she is one of those over whom the love goddess has no control:

For the works of golden Aphrodite do not please her, but rather wars and the works of Ares . . . it was she that first taught mortal joiners to make carts and chariots thick with bronze, and she too who taught shining works to the soft-skinned maidens in their halls . . . (9 ff.)

She has no consort and is not interested in love, she is Parthenos, the maiden. With Hera she was defeated by Aphrodite in the Judgement of Paris, and in a sense she is Aphrodite's antithesis, rather like Artemis in Euripides' *Hippolytus*. There is an element of reasoned symbolism here, since marriage (Hera) and the maintenance of the household (Athena) are inconsistent with love as a luxury (Aphrodite) and with countryside pursuits like hunting (Artemis). It is important to notice that, by the time this valuation originated, problems of fertility were already subordinate to those of advanced social organization.

Athena is not just an impersonal household and city goddess; from Homer onward, and probably much earlier too, she is a protector of individual heroes and intervenes in many of their pursuits. She helps Perseus, for example, to overcome the Gorgons, but it is Odysseus in the *Odyssey* that is her most obvious protégé. She meets him in disguise when he is set ashore in Ithaca by the Phaeacians:

Owl-eyed goddess Athena smiled at his words and stroked him with her hand; she was in the likeness of a woman fair and tall and accomplished in glorious works, and she spoke winged words to him and addressed him: 'He would be cunning and deceitful who could surpass you in all kinds of trickery, even if a god should come up against you. Wretch, cunning one, insatiably crafty, you were not going to desist from deceits and the lying words you love so deeply, even in your own land! But come, let us talk of this no longer. We both know how to get the better of others, since you are by far the best of mortals at giving advice and making speeches, and I am renowned among all the gods by reason of my intelligence and craftiness. Yet you did not recognize me as Pallas Athena, daughter of Zeus, who always stands by your side and guards you in every toil, and made you dear to all the Phaeacians.' (13, 287 ff.)

In this intimate scene Athena exaggerates her own reputation for cunning (which is not, usually, one of her most conspicuous qualities) in order to identify herself with Odysseus, for whom she seems to feel an almost lover-like sympathy. Odysseus in return is not above a mildly malicious ingratitude:

'It is hard, goddess, for a mortal who meets you to recognize you, even if he knows you well, because you take on all sorts of likenesses. But of this I am well aware, that in former times you were kind to me, when we sons of the Achaeans were fighting in the land of Troy; but when we had sacked Priam's steep city and were departing in our ships, and a god scattered the Achaeans, then I did not see you, daughter of Zeus, and did not notice you setting foot on my ship to keep grief away from me.' (*Odyssey* 13, 312 ff.)

I have quoted from this context not only to illustrate Athena's role as a personal protector of heroes but also to show the unusual subtlety that Homer can impose on a mythical scene. Odysseus may be a half-legendary figure, and Athena here may be doing little more than encourage him and act as informant. It is not a particularly memorable episode in narrative terms, but the description, which is leisurely and detailed and not merely allusive in the manner of so much later poetry, gives an extraordinary sense of divine epiphany and the ambivalent relationship between god and man. It is in the literary handling of mythical ideas, rather than the imaginative variety of narrative themes as such, that the Greeks as we know them were unique.

Other revealing examples of divine myths of birth and function relate to Apollo and then Dionysus, whom Nietzsche saw as symbols of opposing aspects – classical and romantic, controlled and ecstatic – of the Greek spirit. Apollo's birth on Delos is a favourite literary theme. Delos is a fascinating but arid little island, and the Greeks were evidently puzzled as to why such an important cult should have become established there in prehistoric times. The *Hymn to Apollo* is a relatively early (seventh century B.C.), if artificial, exercise in the Homeric style, compounded of two parts. The first relates how all other lands except the lowly Delos had refused to be the birthplace of the god; the second describes the foundation of his other great cult centre at Pytho (Delphi). Leto is pregnant by Zeus and has reached Delos:

When Eileithyia, goddess of the pangs of birth, set foot on Delos, then travail seized Leto and she longed to give birth. She cast her arms around the palm-tree and pressed her knees on the soft meadow, and the earth smiled beneath; and he leapt forth into the light, and all the goddesses shrieked in triumph. Then, divine Phoebus, the goddesses washed you with fair water, cleanly and purely, and wrapped you in a fine white newly woven cloth, and set a golden swaddling-band around you. His mother did not give suck to Apollo of the golden sword, but Themis with immortal hands gave him a first offering of nectar and lovely ambrosia, and Leto rejoiced at the birth of her strong archer son. (115 ff.)

The foundation of the oracle at Delphi is no less miraculous, for Apollo in the form of a dolphin leaps aboard a Cretan ship and diverts it to the bay of Crisa, where at last he reveals himself:

Strangers who dwell around many-treed Knossos – or did so formerly, but now you shall never again return to your lovely city and each to his fair home and dear wife, but here shall possess my rich temple honoured among many men: I declare to you that I am the son of Zeus; I am Apollo. I brought you here over the great gulf of the sea with no evil intent, but you shall possess here my rich temple held in much honour among all men, and shall know the counsels of the immortals and by their help be continually honoured for all your days. (475 ff.)

The Cretans are worried about their means of livelihood on this barren hillside, but the god assures them that they will be able to live off their share of the sheep that worshippers will bring for sacrifice. This mundane detail reminds us that the *Hymn*, in spite of its lyrical touches, is a priestly affair, clumsily aetiological in tone. Apollo Delphinios had an ancient cult in Crete – therefore let his priests at Delphi be of Cretan origin, and let Apollo appear to them as a dolphin. This kind of mythical detail does not appear very old, and probably developed as part of the established worship of Apollo at Delphi and Delos in historical and post-Mycenaean times.

For less cult-ridden attributes we can turn to a later source, Pindar, who for his royal patrons in the rich African colony of Cyrene sang of the nymph Cyrene and her wooing by Apollo on Mount Pelion. The god sees her wrestling with a lion and asks the Centaur Cheiron, in his nearby cave, who she is and whether he should make love to her. Cheiron replies with fitting humour and caution:

Your gentle temper has inclined you (for whom it is not lawful to touch untruth) to speak this word obliquely. You ask, lord, of the girl's family? You who know the proper end of all things, and every path? The number of leaves the earth sends forth in spring, of grains of sand in sea and rivers whirled by waves and rushing winds, and what shall come to be and whence – all this you clearly discern! But if I must contend even against one that is wise, this is my answer. You came to this glade to be her husband, and you intend to carry her overseas to the incomparable garden of Zeus; there you shall make her ruler of a city [that is, Cyrene], and shall gather an island people round her to the hill among the plains. (*Pythians* 9, 42 ff.)

Elsewhere Pindar lists the god's main functions:

It is he that assigns to men and women cures of harsh diseases; he brings them the lyre, and grants the Muse to whom he wishes, implanting in their minds a harmonious disposition that rules out warfare; and it is he that controls the oracle's hidden shrine. (*Pythians* 5, 63 ff.)

Apollo is god of prophecy and divination, of all kinds of inspiration, of poetry and music; from his oracle at Delphi he sponsors colonies like Cyrene itself. He is not always so unwarlike as Pindar implies, and in the *Iliad* is depicted as eager to defend Troy. As for his powers of healing, they probably depend on his identification with a local Cretan god called Paian. There is a shrine of Apollo Paian at Epidaurus, and a tale, again in Pindar's words, that Asclepius is really his son:

She (Coronis) had consented to another marriage, secretly from her father, when she had already lain with Phoebus of the unshorn hair and carried the god's pure seed . . . for she slept in the bed of a stranger who came from Arcadia, and did not escape the god's watching . . . and he knew then of her lying with the stranger, Ischys son of Elatus, and of her unlawful deceit, and sent his sister [that is, Artemis], rushing with irresistible might, to Lakereia . . . And many of Coronis' neighbours shared her fate and were destroyed with her . . . but when her kinsmen had placed the maid within the pyre's wooden boundary, and the fierce gleam of Hephaestus [that is, fire] ran all round, then spoke Apollo: 'I shall not, after all, endure in my heart the destruction of my own progeny by a pitiable death, at the same time as his mother's doom.' So he spoke, and with a single stride he reached the child and snatched him from the corpse, as the burning pyre made a way clear for him; and he brought the child and gave him to the Magnesian Centaur [that is, Cheiron] to be taught how to cure men's painful diseases. (*Pythians* 3, 12 ff.)

The gods do not normally tolerate the later adulteration of their seed within a mortal woman; if they do, there are twins, of which the elder is the semi-divine offspring (as Heracles was), the younger the mortal one. Apollo snatches the infant from his dead mother's body just as Zeus snatched Dionysus out of Semele, and in both cases, too, the woman is killed by the god himself. Apollo's son Asclepius grew up to be a great healer, and was worshipped both as god and hero; but he went too far (like his mother) and tried to raise a man from the dead – an impious act that earned a thunderbolt from Zeus. Apollo was annoyed at this high-handed act and took revenge, not of course on Zeus himself, but on the Cyclopes who supplied the thunderbolt.

One cannot help admiring Pindar's mythological learning and the instant recognition he expects in his audience. Allusiveness and scholarship were to become a disease in the poetry of the Alexandrian age; for the moment, given Pindar's genuine feeling for religion, they actively enrich the power of his narrative core. All the same one does not feel that the main thematic structure of these Apollo myths is necessarily very ancient. The god's omniscience, the nymph Cyrene, the Arcadian stranger Ischys, even the snatching of Asclepius from the pyre, may well be comparatively recent elaborations, marking one stage in the constant process of mythical extension. What is assuredly old is Apollo's association with healing, as Paian, and with oracles in his Pythian aspect; also of course his birth in Delos and his kinship to Artemis. There are other episodes that I have not mentioned: he shot down the giant

Aloadae that threatened to attack the gods by piling Pelion on Ossa; together with Artemis he killed the giant Tityus who tried to rape their mother Leto, and slaughtered Niobe and her children because of a foolish boast; he was servant for a year to a mortal, King Admetus, for killing the Cyclopes (the motif is similar to Heracles serving Queen Omphale to purge his killing of his own children). He had a habit of loving, but failing to win, mortal women, notably Cassandra daughter of Priam and Marpessa who preferred Idas; he was more successful with Hyakinthos at Amyclae near Sparta, but actually the beautiful boy must have been, with that name, a pre-Hellenic god whom Apollo merely absorbed into his own worship. When H. J. Rose writes that Apollo has an 'extensive mythology', this is the kind of narrative range that is actually meant; not so extensive after all, and much of it dependent on the elaboration of themes used elsewhere.

Finally Dionysus, the god who came down into Greece through Thrace, ultimately from Phrygia in Asia Minor, and became the focus of an ecstatic religion. His myths are often tales of obduracy. The Thebans refused his worship and were driven to madness and murder, and so were the daughters of King Minyas of Orchomenus and King Proetus of Argos, even perhaps Orpheus himself. Some interpreters have been tempted to take these as reflections of actual historical resistance to his cult (which reached Greece comparatively late, perhaps after 1000 B.C.), and that could be so. The myth of Pentheus at Thebes, after all, depicts a whole city at odds with the god in various ways. But there is also an individual, psychological level of meaning. Dionysus represents the irrational element in man, and his myths the conflict between reason and social convention on one side, emotion on the other. That comes out in the tale of Pentheus, to be described shortly. Homer pays little attention to Dionysus – not at all a god fit for heroes – but refers briefly to his birth from Semele and his arranging to have Ariadne killed by Artemis in Naxos once he had finished with her. His fullest reference is to another tale of resistance, one of several mythical instances of the unwisdom of opposing a god:

Nor did the son of Dryas, strong Lycurgus, last for long, because he strove against the heavenly gods. Once on a time he chased the nurses of raving Dionysus over holy Mount Nysa; and they all together cast their sacred rods on the ground, under the blows of manslaying Lycurgus' ox-goad, and Dionysus took to flight and sank into the waves of the salt sea, and Thetis received him terrified in her bosom, for strong trembling possessed him when the man threatened him. With Lycurgus the easy-living gods were afterwards enraged, and the son of Kronos made him blind; nor did he last for long once he became the enemy of all the immortal gods. (*Iliad* 6, 130 ff.)

This Lycurgus is a Thracian, and it is interesting that the opposition tales range from Thrace, in the very north-east of Greece, through Thebes and Orchomenus in its centre, to Argos in the Peloponnese. Here Dionysus is represented as a child, although his 'nurses' are also his female votaries, his Bacchants, and the rods they cast on the ground are the *thyrsi*, fennel staves with ivy bunched at the tip, that were the special implements of Dionysiac worship and ecstasy.

A number of tales show the impact of Dionysus on various Greek cities. The most famous is the tale brilliantly retold by Euripides in his *Bacchae* about the fate that befell King Pentheus of Thebes when he opposed the cult of Dionysus and his worshippers. First he tried to throw the god, disguised as a beautiful young stranger, into prison. Here is how Dionysus reports the incident to his Bacchants:

This was just the ignominy I subjected him to, that he thought he was binding me, but neither touched nor laid hands on me, but fed on empty hopes. He found a bull by the stalls where he had taken me and locked me up, and round *his* knees and hooves he cast his nooses, panting out his rage, dripping sweat from his body, setting his teeth to his lips. But close by I was peacefully sitting and watching. (*Bacchae*, 616 ff.)

No less powerful than the miracles (the palace of Pentheus was shaken by earthquake soon afterwards) are the songs sung by the chorus of Bacchants about the god they adore. They see themselves as bringing him from their native Asia Minor to Greece, and recall his miraculous birth:

> Onward Bacchants, onward Bacchants,
> bringing Dionysus,
> Bromios, god and child of a god,
> down from the Phrygian mountains
> into Hellas' spacious streets,
> Bromios the roaring one!
>
> Bearing him within her, in forced
> pangs of childbirth
> when Zeus' lightning flew
> his mother thrust him premature
> from the womb, and left her life
> at the lightning's stroke.
> Instantly into chambers of birth
> Zeus son of Kronos received him,
> and hiding him in his thigh
> confined him with golden
> pins, secret from Hera.
>
> He brought to birth, when the Fates
> accomplished the time, a bull-horned god
> and crowned him with garlands
> of snakes; for this reason the maenads
> twine in their tresses
> the beast-reared prey.

> (*Bacchae*, 83 ff.)

Dionysus is here 'the roaring one', a 'bull-horned god', because he so often manifests himself as a bull, rampant with fertility and power – which is why the deluded Pentheus had tied up a bull in mistake for the god himself. Dionysus' mother Semele, it will be remembered, was loved by Zeus and asked him to appear to her in his true form, which he did as lightning; he took the embryo from her womb as she died. The extract ends with a piece of minor cultic aetiology.

The god persuades Pentheus to dress as a Bacchant and spy on the crowds of infatuated women on Mount Cithaeron; he is instantly recognized and torn to pieces by his own mother and aunts. This is how the chorus exult, allusively as always:

> Let us dance to the Bacchic god,
> shout aloud the disaster
> of the dragon's descendant, Pentheus;
> who took female raiment
> and the fennel-rod, Hades' pledge,
> in its thyrsus-shape
> with a bull to lead him into disaster.
>
> (*Bacchae*, 1153 ff.)

Pentheus is 'the dragon's descendant' because he is descended from the Sown Men, the armed warriors who grew from the ground when Cadmus had killed the dragon that guarded the site of Thebes, and sown its teeth. The bull, again, is Dionysus himself. The disaster Pentheus suffered was a literal tearing apart, which is what the Bacchants regularly did to any young animal that fell into their hands during their crazy dances across the mountains.

The myths of Dionysus are part of his religion, and their power is derived as much from an exotic and thrilling form of worship as from their narrative themes as such. In that respect they may be unusual – although even those of Apollo, apparently more firmly rooted in Greek culture, are seen to depend for much of their apparent richness on the elaboration and nostalgic fervour of poets like Pindar.

The third category of myths is no longer divine, although it remains closely in touch with the life of the gods. It comprises tales that describe *the emergence of human beings* and the complicated acts by which their role, and in particular their exact relation to the gods, is established. Essentially it contains the myths about the Golden Age, Prometheus and the Fall of men. Hesiod once again is our main and for much of the time our only source, although the details he records (with the exception of the Five Races myth which is idiosyncratic in places) were probably familiar to many Greeks of his era.

The Greek conception of a Golden Age is rather imprecise, because it contains two separate ideas that were gradually conflated and then further complicated by later eschatologies from Italy and Sicily. The two ideas are as follows. First, there was a period in the past, often associated with the time Kronos was king of the gods, when a 'golden' race of men lived without toil and died as though in sleep after a happy life. Second, there is a distant land, called either Elysium or the Islands of the Blest, where divinely favoured humans live on instead of dying – especially the sons and daughters of one divine parent, like Peleus, Cadmus, Menelaus, Helen. They go there instead of Hades and live an eternal life of bliss, free from toil.

The first concept is represented by the golden race in Hesiod's schematic account (not an ordinary myth because it has no obvious story) of the Five Races of men:

First the immortals who have their homes on Olympus made a golden race of men; they lived in the time of Kronos, and he was king of heaven. They lived like gods with a spirit free from care, far from toils and grief; neither did vile old age come upon them, but with unwithering limbs they rejoiced in festivity, away from all evils, and died as though subdued by sleep. All good things were theirs; the life-giving earth bore its fruit freely and in abundance, and in contentment and peace they lived off their lands in prosperity. But when the earth covered this race, through the will of great Zeus they have become good daemons on earth, guardians of mortal men. (*Works and Days*, 109 f.)

The same kind of life is ascribed by Pindar to the Hyperboreans, a people especially favoured by Apollo and imagined as dwelling, as their name suggests, 'beyond the North Wind':

Everywhere are girls dancing and the noise of lyres and the shrill whirlings of flutes; with their hair bound with golden bay they feast in joyfulness. Maladies and destructive old age have no part in that sacred race, but they dwell without toils or battles, free from severe Nemesis. (*Pythians* 10, 38 ff.)

The second concept, of Elysium or the Isles of the Blest, is clearly described by Hesiod and applied to his fourth race, the race of heroes. They were killed off in the great expeditions against Thebes and Troy, and

then some of them did the end of death enclose, but to the others father Zeus, son of Kronos, gave a life and abode apart from men, and settled them at the limits of the earth; and they dwell with carefree spirit in the Isles of the Blest by the side of deep-swirling Okeanos – blissful heroes, for whom the life-giving earth thrice yearly bears its rich honey-sweet fruit. (*Works and Days*, 166 ff.)

At this point some probably non-Hesiodic verses were appended in antiquity; they claim that Kronos was king of these blessed heroes, and that Zeus had brought him up from imprisonment in Tartarus for the purpose. Obviously this is designed to reconcile the two different concepts. Pindar, too, associates Kronos with a development of the Isles-of-the-Blest conception when he takes over the traditional picture of the blessed life, laces it with 'Orphic' and Pythagorean ideas from Italy and Sicily about the rebirth of the soul, and presents the result as a reward for those who have completed just lives on earth:

But all who have endured, while remaining in each world, to keep their soul three times apart from injustice pass over the road of Zeus to the tower of Kronos, where breezes born of Okeanos blow around the Isles of the Blest, and golden flowers blaze out, some on land from glorious trees, others nurtured by the water; and they weave necklaces and wreaths from them under the just rule of Rhadamanthys, whom the great father [that is, Kronos], husband of Rhea of the all-lofty throne, keeps ever seated by his side. (*Olympians* 2, 68 ff.)

Here (Pindar goes on to say) are Peleus and Cadmus and Achilles – one more detail that belongs to the strict conception of the Isles as a kind of Valhalla for semi-divine heroes.

So we can now distinguish *three* distinct but related ideas, each of which tends to give rise to similar language (the earth bringing forth its fruits without toil, and so forth). First, there was a stage in the past when all men lived in Golden Age conditions. Second, a few privileged members of the age of heroes survive death, in similar conditions, in Elysium or the Isles of the Blest. Third, such a life is still possible for the souls of the just, as a reward after death and after judgement in Hades. The third view is certainly a later adaptation of the second, the second possibly a later adaptation of the first. Curiously, Kronos tends to be associated with all three, and at one stage Greek myths must have had far more to say about him than they do now, or at least than Hesiod chooses to reveal.

A more specific idea of a Golden Age is implied in occasional mythical allusions to men having banqueted with the gods either regularly or on certain special occasions, in particular at the marriages of mortals to immortals. It was the marriage of Peleus, father of Achilles, to the sea-nymph Thetis, and of Cadmus, founder of Thebes, to Harmonia the daughter of Ares and Aphrodite, that made the strongest mark in art and literature. Pindar uses both heroes to illustrate a moralism:

> Neither Peleus son of Aeacus nor godlike Cadmus had a life without difficulties; yet they are said to have possessed the highest blessedness of mortals, for they heard the Muses with diadems of gold singing on Mount Pelion and in seven-gated Thebes, when the one married ox-eyed Harmonia and the other Thetis, renowned daughter of Nereus the good counsellor. (*Pythians* 3, 86 ff.)

Among others who were intimate with the gods was Tantalus, the father of Pelops who later defeated King Oenomaus of Pisa for the hand of his daughter and gave his name to the Peloponnese. Pindar refuses to believe the common form of the tale, which was that Tantalus invited the gods to dinner and served up his own son Pelops, freshly cooked, to see if they could tell the difference. Demeter, still distracted by grief because of Persephone, absent-mindedly ate a shoulder, but the rest of the gods immediately detected the crime. Poseidon brought Pelops to life, gave him a beautiful ivory shoulder and was later overcome by his charms. Pindar, however, protests that 'It is impossible for me to call any of the blessed gods a glutton; I stand apart!' and implies a different reason for Tantalus' disgrace (which resulted in his being eternally tantalized by food and water that lay just out of reach). Yet the important thing at present is that Tantalus

invited the gods to the most orderly of banquets in his own dear Sipylon, offering them a return for the dinners they had given him. (*Olympians* 1, 37 ff.)

King Lykaon of Arcadia, in a thematically overlapping tale (see p. 238 ff.), invited Zeus to dine with him on Mount Lykaion and offered him human flesh. Again it is the idea of gods and mortals dining together – not always with such lurid menus – that interests us here, indicating as it does an era when gods and men were not so stringently separated as they were even in the developed age of heroes.

Somehow that era came to an end. The precise cause is not clear from the myths, and could have been the supplanting of Kronos by Zeus, or the crimes of Tantalus and Lykaon, or the general increase in impiety and bloodshed implied by Empedocles and the Orphics, of which more later. Somewhere here the flood must be fitted in (see p. 261–4); it was sent by Zeus to punish mankind, and only Deucalion and his wife Pyrrha survived it. That is the commonest version, although others talk of King Ogygus as responsible, or connect the flood with the human sacrifice initiated by Lykaon or his sons. Deucalion and Pyrrha, at any rate, recreate the human race on purely etymological principles; they do so by throwing stones over their shoulders, and the stones turn into people – but that is because the Greek word for stone (*laas*) is similar to that for people (*laos*). From such trivial ideas are myths sometimes made, more generally in Egypt and Mesopotamia than in Greece (see p. 58 f.).

At some indeterminate period after the end of the Golden Age men were poor, defenceless and weak, and a great protector came on the scene in the person of Prometheus. Prometheus was a minor god, his parents the Titan Iapetus and the Oceanid Clymene. For everything that concerns him – and he is of the highest importance for this whole third group of myths – Hesiod is once again our prime authority. This is how he describes his birth and ultimate salvation:

Iapetus led away the fair-ankled maid Clymene, daughter of Okeanos, and shared his bed with her; and she bore stubborn Atlas as her son, also renowned Menoetius and subtle Prometheus of cunning counsel and foolish Epimetheus, who from the beginning was a disaster to industrious humans; for it was he that first received the fabricated maiden from Zeus. Wide-seeing Zeus sent insolent Menoetius down into Erebus by striking him with smoky lightning . . . Atlas holds the broad sky at the ends of the earth through strong necessity . . . and Zeus bound subtle-counselled Prometheus with harsh inescapable bonds, driving them through the midst of a pillar, and sent a long-winged eagle upon him; and it used to eat his immortal liver, which grew back to its full size during the night, as much as the long-winged bird might eat during the whole day. The strong son of fair-ankled Alcmena, Heracles, slew it, and warded off cruel pain from Iapetus' son and released him from his grief, not without the will of Olympian Zeus who reigns on high . . . (*Theogony*, 507 ff.)

Menoetius is rather obscure; Atlas is well-known because he was envisaged as holding up the sky (a probably archaic concept parallel to the Egyptian idea of a sky supported on pillars); Epimetheus ('Afterthought', invented to match Prometheus which seems to mean 'Forethought') is known simply for his presumably lustful folly in receiving the first woman as a gift; but it is Prometheus who is the key figure. His imprisonment by Zeus, in the Caucasus mountains as we learn elsewhere, comes as climax to a series of clashes between the two. Prometheus begins the quarrel by trying to cheat Zeus over the division of sacrificial meats once the era of dining together had come to an end:

For when the gods and mortal men were making a settlement at Mecone, then Prometheus with eager spirit divided up a great ox and set it before him, trying to delude the mind of Zeus. For in the one lot he placed the flesh and guts, rich with fat, inside mere skin, covering them with the ox's stomach; in the other he placed the ox's white bones by an artful trick, putting them in order and covering them with shining fat. Then did the father of gods and men address him: 'Son of Iapetus, most famous of all the lords, how one-sidedly, my dear fellow, have you divided out the portions!' Thus spoke Zeus of undying cunning in rebuke, but crooked-counselled Prometheus addressed him in reply, gently smiling and not forgetting his crafts of deceit: 'Most glorious Zeus, greatest of the eternal gods, take whichever of these your heart and mind bid you.' He spoke with deceitful intent, and Zeus of undying cunning recognized and did not overlook the trick, and he devised evils in his heart for mortal men, that were destined to be fulfilled. Then with both hands he took up the white fat; he was enraged in his mind, and anger possessed his spirit, when he saw the ox's white bones as a result of the artful trick. Because of this the races of men on earth burn white bones to the immortals on their fragrant altars. Then in great wrath cloud-gathering Zeus addressed him: 'Son of Iapetus, cunning above all others, so you did not yet, my dear fellow, forget your art of deceit!' Thus did Zeus of undying cunning speak, and from this time forth, always remembering the trick, he withheld from the ash-trees the power of unwearying fire for mortal men who dwell upon earth. But the good son of Iapetus deceived him by stealing the far-seen gleam of unwearying fire in a hollow fennel-stalk, and he angered high-thundering Zeus in the depths of his spirit, and Zeus was enraged in

his heart when he saw among men the far-seen gleam of fire. Immediately he made an evil for men in return for fire; for the famous
cripple [that is, Hephaestus] moulded out of earth the likeness of a
reverent maiden through the will of Zeus. The owl-eyed goddess
Athena girded her and adorned her with a silver robe, and with her
hands she hung down from her head an embroidered veil, a marvel
to see . . . (*Theogony*, 535–75)

I consider first the deceit over the sacrifices and the theft of
fire, and continue with the creation of woman. The story of
the division at Mecone (said to be near ancient Sicyon, not
far from Corinth) is of fundamental importance, both because
it treats a crucial question of the relation between men and
gods and because it shows, more clearly than any other Greek
instance, a myth that is working towards the resolution of a
real problem. To say that it is simply aetiological in the most
superficial sense, that it offers a pretty story to divert men's
attention from the apparent anomaly that the gods are given
the worst bits at a sacrifice, is the reaction of most people and
is, I am afraid, rather inadequate. It does that, as Hesiod
indicates, but it also goes deeper. The deceptive choice offered
by a god to a mortal or vice versa is a widespread folktale
motif often used to account for the fact of death: man was
offered a choice between death and life, as in the Akkadian
tale of Adapa, and through trickery or misinformation he
made the wrong choice. The Prometheus tale is more complex. It is the mortal, or rather the defender of mortals, that
offers the choice to the supreme god, not the other way round.
Whether the god is fully conscious of the deceit remains
doubtful; Hesiod's account vacillates and suggests the conflation of different versions. Not the least interesting implication
of the myth is that the practice of making sacrifices is itself a
relic of a Golden Age when gods and privileged mortals
dined together.

Sacrifice was a crucial act of social and religious life, but
men simply had to retain the flesh and the most edible parts.

Meat was even rarer and more expensive than in Greece today'
and sacrifice was in one sense a by-product of the profession
of butchery. It was essential for the Greeks to offer *some* of
their meat to the gods, but it had to be a token. Actually it
was a perfectly logical one, since the only part that could pass
from the sacrificial burning up into the sky, where the gods
could receive it, was the smoke and savour, and that emanated
best from the fat and not the flesh. From another but no less
important point of view what was symbolically offered to the
gods was the *whole animal*; this too was best represented by
the bones, especially if they were 'put in good order' as
Hesiod says near the beginning of the text last quoted – the
intention being to reconstruct the animal symbolically.

On this occasion, then, the mythical justification of an
apparent contradiction (that the gods are given the worst bits
rather than the best) is rather inept; indeed a better defence of
the practice could have been made in rational and quasi-
philosophical terms. And yet such a defence might not in the
end have been emotionally satisfying. It could easily fail to
remove the guilt men felt over keeping the best parts of the
animal for themselves. Guilt is a cardinal feeling, and much of
the lifetime of ordinary mortals is consumed in suppressing it
by one means or another. Some such feeling demanded that
men should be made to pay for the offending practice, and
that is where the myth came in. First, Zeus withdrew fire itself, which was thought to reside above all in ash trees, a
reference to kindling from special kinds of wood. Its withdrawal was a cunning move, directly related to the practice of
sacrifice, as though Zeus had said 'All right, if you're not going
to give us gods the share of the burnt meats we deserve, there
shall be no burning at all. *We* shall be no worse off, but *you*
will have to eat your appetizing portion of flesh and innards
all raw. Just try that!'

In the later tradition Prometheus developed into a general
technological benefactor, one who brought men the arts not

only of healing, mathematics, medicine, navigation and divination, but also of mining and working metals; that view of him is best seen in Aeschylus' *Prometheus Vinctus*, 436–506. No doubt his recovery of fire was part of the same conception, but in all probability this extension of his functions is not much older than the sixth century B.C., when interest in the evolution of men from a crude and savage state – an idea that directly contradicts the mythical scheme of a decline from the Golden Age – first became prominent.

The Hesiodic account continues with Zeus' second act of revenge, the creation by various gods and goddesses of the first woman. Incidentally the Greeks seem to have had no commonly accepted myth about the creation of *man*, who undoubtedly came first. This was credited in later sources, as one might expect, to Prometheus himself, who became patron of the potters in Athens and no doubt elsewhere, and was envisaged as making men, after a common Mesopotamian pattern, out of clay. At Panopeus in central Greece visitors were shown lumps left over from the work.[3] I shall refer in Chapter 11 to some possible reasons for this apparent mythical lacuna in contrast to the specific creation stories of the Near East. Even the creation of woman exists in two versions, and Hesiod gives both, one in the *Theogony* and the other in *Works and Days*. In the former, Hephaestus completes his creation (continuing the passage quoted on p. 138), and leads her before gods and men:

from her are the destructive race and tribes of women, who dwell as a great misery among mortal men, as suitable companions not of deadly poverty but of surfeit. (*Theogony*, 591–3)

The theme of women's extravagance and ill-nature is developed in what follows. It is widespread all over the world, and its unfairness is one of the less feeble testimonies to the idea of a male conspiracy against womankind. But Hesiod, who was no fool, could see beyond the one-sided viewpoint of folktale motifs, for he added that Zeus established a complementary evil, namely that the man who refuses to marry has a dismal old age with no one to look after him and no family to inherit his possessions; while the man who happens to get a good wife (and it is eventually conceded that this is possible) has at least a mixture of good and evil.

The *Works and Days* version, on the other hand, gives a different and more familiar story. After a similar process of manufacture Hermes filled the woman with deceit,

and placed in her a voice, and named this woman Pandora (because all that have their halls on Olympus gave her a gift), a misery to industrious men. But when he had brought to perfection this drastic and irremediable deceit, the father sent the glorious slayer of Argos [that is, Hermes], swift messenger of the gods, to Epimetheus, bringing her as a gift; and Epimetheus failed to remember that Prometheus had told him never to accept a gift from Olympian Zeus, but to send it back lest it should turn out to be some evil for mortals, but accepted her and recognized the evil only when it was his. For, before that, the tribes of man lived on earth far removed from evils and hard toil and harsh diseases that bring doom to men. But the woman with her hands took the great lid from the jar and scattered them, and contrived baneful cares for mankind. Only Hope remained there in its unbreakable dwelling-place, under the lip of the jar, and did not fly out; before that could happen she replaced the lid of the jar by the will of aegis-bearing cloud-gathering Zeus. But ten thousand other banes wander among men; for the earth is full of evils, and full the sea, and diseases come upon men by day, and others of their own accord by night, bringing ills to mortals in silence, since Zeus took away their voice. (*Works and Days*, 80–104)

The aetiological details (the etymology of Pandora, literally 'all-gifts' or 'all-giving', and the silent diseases that arrive unnoticed during the night) and the rather self-conscious allegory about Hope may be relatively new embroideries, but the jar looks like a great Mycenaean or Minoan affair, and the tale as a whole is old. Once again it probably relies on an essentially folktale theme that Hesiod has suppressed, for presumably what made Pandora take the lid off was meddling curiosity. At this point the poet is even more cursory and allusive than usual. The jar is not explained, but is simply assumed to be familiar to his audience – an assumption that aided its transformation into Pandora's *box* in the Renaissance tradition.

Immediately after the myth and its moralizing conclusion that 'thus it is in no way possible to escape the intention of Zeus' comes the semi-mythical account of the Five Races, beginning with the men of the golden race (see p. 132) who were still free of all the diseases Pandora released. So Hesiod presents in his two poems an overlapping, quite complex and ultimately rather subtle picture of the Fall of Man from a condition of divine privilege and sodality to his present one of misery, disease, family trouble and old age. Some parts of the organization and a few of the details probably belong to Hesiod or his immediate sources, but most of the mythical complex, and certainly its main tendencies, seem traditional. In the end it transpires that the apparently avoidable aspects of man's condition – not death itself, for that is inevitable, but disease, painful old age, poverty and the need for unremitting toil – are the indirect result of the first quarrel between Zeus and Prometheus. The quarrel arose out of the division of the sacrifices, and that may be held to symbolize, in a way, the whole dilemma of the relation between men and gods. Ultimately it is something myths cannot explain: what they do is to suggest that things were once all right, but that men were too demanding. If they had shown self-restraint, or if Prometheus and Epimetheus had done so on their behalf, the quarrel with the gods would never have begun and women could have been accepted in a less extreme form.

Even that is pressing the myths too hard. Women are a fact of life, the human race could never have started without them. What seems to be happening is that a dilemma at the folktale level (involving the conflict between the peasant's princess-dream and his brutal assessment of actual wives by their economic value) became connected with a more basic contradiction in the human condition, that between men's immortal longings and the harsh facts of human existence. Something similar seems to have happened with the theme of the quarrel over sacrifices, since that too must once have existed independently. Yet its relevance to the question of the decline was obvious, and it became woven into the mythical texture in a way that gave a deeper and more complex meaning to the whole. Indeed the entire sequence of myths in Hesiod – Prometheus, the sacrifice, the theft of fire, the creation of women, the punishment of Prometheus, the five races of men – might be said to leave one with a feeling that things are not quite so unfair as they were, that evil is more equable than it seemed, that old age and disease are in some ways our own fault, even that things might improve if only we learned to behave better. Prometheus remains mysterious. Why he champions men is never made clear; probably he dropped into the role by the accident of being a trickster figure, one suitable to undertake the futile but engaging contest of wits with Zeus. In the end he matches Zeus – that too makes one feel that fate is not necessarily relentless, for (as we learn from Aeschylus) he knows something that Zeus does not, namely that whoever marries Thetis will have a son greater than his father. Zeus and Poseidon were both, as it happens, competing for the honour at the time, and Prometheus' secret had to be bought at the price of his release by Heracles. Even the gods have to temper the wind on occasion.

In the end it was Peleus who married the dangerous Thetis. Like all sea deities she changed her shape to avoid capture, but he ultimately caught her and their son was Achilles, greater than his father but no danger to the gods. Even this tale has its underlying relevance to the Hesiodic group, because Peleus grew old while his divine wife remained eternally young. Eventually she left him, and he ended, after much sorrow, in the Isles of the Blest. Another mortal lover, Tithonus, was not so fortunate, as the *Hymn to Aphrodite* (composed probably in the sixth century B.C.) relates:

So too golden-throned Eos [that is, Dawn] ravished god-like Tithonus of the Trojan race; and she went to ask the black-clouded son of Kronos that he should be immortal and live for all the sum of days, and Zeus nodded in approval and accomplished her prayer. Yet she was foolish, for Lady Eos did not think in her heart of asking for youth and of stripping off destructive old age. As long as lovely youth possessed him, he dwelt by the streams of Okeanos at the limits of the earth, rejoicing in early-born golden-throned Eos; but when the first grey hairs poured down from his fair head and noble chin, then did Lady Eos keep away from his bed, but cherished him still in her halls with food and ambrosia, and gave him fair raiment. But when finally hateful old age overpowered him, and he was unable to move his limbs or lift them up, this seemed to her in her heart to be the best plan: she placed him in a chamber and closed the shining doors upon him. His voice flows on unceasing, yet there is no strength in his bent limbs such as once there was. (218–38)

The Greeks were sensible about old age, passionately though they resented it, just as they were about emulating the gods or trying to become immortal. Odysseus, who rejected the chance of living on with the nymphs Circe and Calypso and insisted on returning to the admirable but ageing Penelope, was the counter-paradigm to Tithonus. The myths not only reflected that attitude to age, they even helped to define it – particularly those among them that bore directly on the relations between men and gods. It is for such reasons that I have spent so much time on them, despite Hesiod's verbose and often clumsy style. For it is here, in this relatively early but still literary form, that Greek myths come closest to the pointed functionality of their oral predecessors, a functionality that responds at times to the aetiological, structural and psychological interpretations discussed in earlier chapters. Even more important, perhaps, it is here that we are left with the strongest sense of myths as a part of life itself.

# CHAPTER 7

# THE HEROES

POWERFUL as some of the divine myths are, it is the hero myths that constitute the most prominent and varied side of Greek traditional tales as a whole. Many other ethnic collections, perhaps most, are virtually confined to divine tales and contain few heroic ones. Ancient Mesopotamia and Egypt exemplify the tendency. The Mesopotamian tales of Gilgamesh are admittedly imaginative, and important from many points of view; Egyptian heroes, on the other hand, are both few in number and predominantly legendary and realistic in character. Yet in Greece there are innumerable heroes, and they are involved in a wide variety of actions. Standard situations proliferate, but even so the total narrative complexity far outweighs that of the divine myths.

The heroes fall into an older or a younger type, according to whether their main activity is set in a timeless past long before the Trojan War, or close to the war itself. Later inventions based on definitely historical figures form another and subsidiary kind. (These three are the fourth, fifth and sixth of the myth categories proposed on p. 113.) The first two types, whose nature will become plainer as the chapter proceeds, are at some points hard to separate. Some of the 'older' heroes possess certain later characteristics, since the myths were undergoing continuous development; conversely a few of the younger and quasi-legendary ones have important older associations. Theseus is involved in historicizing and relatively recent actions, but the tale of the Labyrinth makes it eccentric not to treat him as a member of the primary group. Agamemnon on the other hand is connected through Menelaus with Helen, who seems to be descended from an ancient tree goddess; yet the story of the House of Atreus belongs for the most part to the more historicizing and younger set. Jason presents similar difficulties, but I have placed him among the older group in the first instance.

Philologists have sometimes thought that heroic names themselves may give a clue to the age of the heroes and their myths. Those ending in -*eus*, especially if they have a non-Greek stem, are thought to be among the earliest. That works well for a few less prominent heroes like Tydeus, Neleus, Salmoneus, and perhaps Orpheus. Theseus and Oineus, with Greek stems, might then be secondary developments, but Achilleus (Latinized as Achilles) would be one of the older group and not, as appears from his mythical context, a younger quasi-legendary type. His father Peleus is neutral, since his name is based on that of Mount Pelion, itself probably pre-Greek. Many of the -*eus* heroes turn out to have sons with specifically Greek compound names; for instance Aga-memnon is son of Atreus, and Neo-ptolemus of Achilleus. Several of these belong to the younger group of heroes, whereas those with names that are neither Greek nor end in -*eus*, like Kadmos (Cadmus), Bellerophon(tes) or Tantalos, tend to belong to the older. Yet on the whole this is a speculative and inadequate criterion, especially since some names, like Oedipus, Perseus, Caeneus, Jason (Iason in Greek), could be either Greek or foreign in derivation. The whole matter has been complicated by the realization that Greek was spoken in the peninsula as early as around 2100 B.C., that the Mycenaeans were thoroughly Greek, and that the Linear B tablets suggest that names of all these types were in use towards the end of the Bronze Age. Finally Heracles is beyond dispute an older hero, yet his name is completely Greek in form and means 'glory of Hera' or something similar.

Only a selection of heroes, in any case, can be discussed here. From *the older heroes* I have chosen PERSEUS, BELLEROPHON, THESEUS, CADMUS and JASON, in that order, not only because they are (or used to be) household names, but also because they illustrate several different tendencies of heroic myths. HERACLES is reserved for special treatment in Chapter 8.

This is how Apollodorus (the best of the extant mythographers, even though he wrote no earlier than the second century A.D.) tells of the birth and youth of PERSEUS:

> When Acrisius consulted the oracle about begetting male children, the god said his daughter would have a son who would kill him. As a precaution, Acrisius built a brazen underground chamber and kept Danaë under guard there. But Proetus, as some say, seduced her, and that was the cause of their quarrel. Others say that Zeus changed into gold which poured into Danaë's lap through the roof, and so had intercourse with her. Acrisius, on learning later that the child Perseus had been born from her, refused to believe that Zeus was her seducer, and so cast his daughter with her child into a chest and hurled it into the sea. The chest was carried to Seriphos, and Dictys took it up and brought up the boy. Dictys' brother Polydectes, who was king of Seriphos, fell in love with Danaë ... (2.4, 1 ff.)

Acrisius, as well as being brother of Proetus, was king of Argos, and it is there that Danaus had taken refuge from Egypt with his daughters, as described by Aeschylus in his *Suppliant Women*. That may reflect a memory of conflict between Mycenaeans and Egyptians, and Danaë too, with her similar name ('Danaans' is one of Homer's names for the Greeks), is probably a Bronze Age character. Yet the motif of the oracle must be later. It is common in Greek myths, but all the foundation legends of the great oracles (Delphi, Dodona, Didyma, and so on) point to the early Iron Age, after 1100 B.C., as their time of origin. Curiously enough there was a tale, preserved only by Aelian in the Roman period, that the mother of Sumerian Gilgamesh had been locked up for similar reasons, and that the illicit baby, thrown from her lofty prison, had been caught and rescued by an eagle. This tends to confirm that the idea of keeping one's daughter a virgin by locking her up, quite apart from the overthrow-by-grandson motif, was an ancient one; it has, of course, a marked folktale appearance. Gilgamesh's birth was said to be due to a man getting in; the Greek version is more exotic and poetical ('the son of Danaë, who we say was born from gold that flowed of its own accord' as Pindar put it – the gold being Zeus, although later rationalizers typically reduced it to a bribe given to her jailers). Two other odd details are the underground brazen house and the launching on the sea in a chest, both with parallels in other Greek myths. The house reminds one of the bronze jar that is a place of refuge for Eurystheus or imprisonment for Ares, whereas the chest is an almost traditional way of disposing of unwanted relatives or babies (for example Tenes and his sister Hemithea). It is tempting, but not especially plausible, to think of underground grain-silos or huge 'beehive' tombs as precedents for the idea of the brazen house. The floating-chest idea is less susceptible of facile interpretation, and since it is loosely paralleled in Moses and the bulrushes it seems preferable to think of it as a widely-diffused folktale idea (rather than, for instance, a Freudian memory of the embryo).

King Polydectes (his name means 'much-receiving' and resembles a title given to Hades, who receives innumerable dead into his kingdom) sent Perseus, now grown up, to get the Gorgon's head, hoping to be rid of him once and for all and so seduce Danaë without further interference. But with Athena's help the hero forced the Graiai, the old grey women, by stealing the single eye and tooth they shared between them, to tell him the way to certain nymphs. These then gave him winged sandals, the cap of invisibility and a special wallet for the Gorgon's head. Actually there were three Gorgons, Medusa being the mortal one; they were sisters of the two Graiai, and their parents were Phorcys (an old-man-of-the-sea type) and the female sea-monster Ceto. Athena guided Perseus so that he could see Medusa's reflection in his shield and so decapitate her without being turned to stone. Pindar has a pretty tale that Athena imitated the Gorgon's shrieks by playing on the flute the so-called 'many-headed tune':

> ... the art that Pallas Athena invented when she wove together the deadly dirge of the reckless Gorgons. Perseus heard it flowing in bitter agony from the monstrous snake-heads of the maidens when he put an end to one of the three sisters, bringing doom for Seriphos and its island people. Yes, he annihilated the prodigious offspring of Phorcus, and made a bitter contribution to Polydectes' feast . . . (*Pythians* 12, 6 ff.)

On the way back from the Gorgons, who lived at the ends of the earth across the stream of Okeanos, Perseus went northward to visit the Hyperboreans, and also as far south as Ethiopia or Joppa. In one of these the Andromeda adventure took place. She was daughter of King Cepheus and his silly wife Cassiopeia – silly because she boasted that she was prettier than the Nereids. The inevitable consequences followed, this time both a flood and a sea-monster. An oracle said the monster could only be sent away if given Andromeda to devour, but Perseus rescued her just in time on the promise of her hand in marriage. Cepheus' brother Phineus tried to make trouble on the grounds that Andromeda was pledged to him, but the Gorgon's head dealt with him soon enough. Then Perseus returned to Seriphos, petrified Polydectes and his supporters, left for the mainland and accidentally killed Acrisius with a discus, thus fulfilling the original oracle. He finally became king of Tiryns and founder, with Andromeda, of the Perseid dynasty.

It has long been recognized that the Perseus complex is more than usually dependent on folktale-type motifs: the escape as a baby, defending one's mother from a seducer, the meant-to-be-fatal quest, the ingenious devices (tooth-and-eye, magical gadgets for flying and invisibility, avoiding a lethal gaze), rescuing the princess, killing a relative by accident. It also exemplifies an interest in exotic lands (Ethiopia, the Hyperboreans) that is typical of test-and-quest tales. Yet this does not mean that the myth is not substantially an ancient one. Obviously it has been elaborated, as any traditional tale must be – perhaps in respect of the oracle, some of the details of Athena's help, and the magical implements; possibly in respect of the whole Andromeda episode (which must however have had a certain independent status) and some of the events after Perseus' return to Argos and Tiryns. But the birth from Danaë, the Seriphos connection and the decapitation of the Gorgon form a substantial nucleus with no special mark of later date. Homer alludes to Zeus' love of Danaë and to Perseus himself, and Hesiod adds that Chrysaor and the horse Pegasus sprang from Medusa's body as Perseus cut off her head; also that Poseidon had slept with Medusa. The location in Seriphos, an utterly unimportant island, is at first strange, but is probably aetiological in a simple way. Seriphos is notable for its rock pinnacles jutting up from the hills, and these were identified with the people turned to stone. Of serious implications there are few signs. The tale is remarkable in its own right, and the death-gazing Medusa, not to speak of the fertile golden shower, a powerful conception. There is a faint possibility, however, that underneath lies a primitive tale of an attack (by Perseus meaning 'destroyer'?) on death itself; for the Gorgons are death-dealing, and they are sisters of the Graiai who represent old age. The possible associations of Polydectes with Hades are also relevant.

Next, BELLEROPHON, who is connected with the preceding tale not only through Pegasus but also through Proetus the brother of Acrisius. Bellerophon is associated with Tiryns, but also with Ephyra which probably denotes Corinth. I mentioned earlier (see p. 35) Homer's account of his feats against the Chimaera, the Solymi and the Amazons. He first found himself in Lycia because of his innocent involvement with Proetus' voracious wife, and at the end of his successful quests was granted the daughter of the Lycian king (Iobates, according to a lost play by Sophocles) and a share of the kingdom.

But then he decides to put Pegasus – first tamed with the help of a magic bridle supplied by Athena, an incident that recalls her part in procuring magical aids for Perseus – to an impious use, no longer to rid the earth of menaces but to carry his rider to the very halls of the gods:

> If a man sets his eye on things afar, he is not tall enough to reach the brazen-floored home of the gods. Winged Pegasus threw his master, Bellerophontes, when he wished to come to the abodes of heaven and the companions of Zeus; a bitter ending awaits pleasure that lies beyond what is right. (*Isthmians* 7, 43 ff.)

Apparently Bellerophon was not killed outright, since Homer says that

> when at last he became hated by all the gods, he wandered alone over the Plain of Wandering, eating out his spirit, avoiding the steps of men. (*Iliad* 6, 200 ff.)

Bellerophon's move to Lycia may not have been a particularly early detail. It is integral to the Homeric account, but there are indications that the Chimaera may once have carried out its depredations in the region of Corinth itself. The embroilment with Proetus' wife, too, need not be organic. Like other elements in the Bellerophon complex (the magic bridle, the cryptic message that could not be understood by its bearer, the tasks designed to be fatal, the attempt at ambush, the hand of the princess as reward) it is a familiar folktale motif. In this respect, as well as in several other details, Bellerophon's deeds resemble those of his close countryman Perseus. Even the connection with Corinth may have been primarily intended to relate him to Sisyphus, whose grandson he was shown to be; Sisyphus had tried to outwit the gods by avoiding death, and that, on the most probable interpretation, is what Bellerophon was trying to do in his last ride on Pegasus. Neither in this nor in the Perseus myth are there signs of charter, political or historical overtones. On the other hand there may be an implied association between magic flight and superhuman aspiration, and the hero's eventual fate, vague but sinister, gives the myth in its developed form a distinct moral flavour.

THESEUS, by contrast, owes much of his mythical *persona* to the desire of Athenians, and especially the tyrant Peisistratus in the sixth century B.C., to make of him a great national hero. They did so in two ways: by associating him as closely as possible with Heracles, the *beau idéal*, and by ascribing to him various political and benevolent acts that were held to be the beginning of Athenian democracy. There can be no question that the myths about Theseus were enormously elaborated at a relatively recent date, particularly during the sixth and fifth centuries B.C., not only by Peisistratus and his sons, but also by the anonymous authors of more than one *Theseis*, or sub-epic poem about Theseus, and various writers of Athenian local history in the fifth century and after. Yet parts of the Theseus cycle are clearly much older, and the difficulty for the modern critic is to draw the dividing line with reasonable accuracy.

He was born at Trozen, down the coast from Athens and its ancient ally. His mother was Aethra and his father her secret lover, the Athenian King Aegeus, or even Aegeus' patron-god Poseidon himself. Aegeus left a sword and sandals under a rock as tokens, with instructions that when the boy was big enough to shift the rock he should bring them to Athens. At sixteen he did so; but instead of coming the safe way inland he took the coast road in order to dispose of several dangerous brigands – congratulating himself, it is said, that Heracles at the time was under servitude to Queen Omphale and so had left this particular bunch of villains un-molested. The lyric poet Bacchylides imagines Aegeus giving an account of these deeds:

A herald has just arrived after traversing the long road from the Isthmus, and reports the wonderful deeds of a mighty man. He has killed the lawless Sinis, strongest of mortals, child of Kronos' son the Earthshaker; he has slaughtered the man-slaying sow in the glades of

Cremmyon, and insolent Sciron too; he has gained possession of Cercyon's wrestling-place; and Procoptes, meeting a better man than himself, has thrown away Polypemon's strong hammer. (18, 16 ff.)

Bacchylides did not need to tell his audience that Sinis tied his victims to pine-trees bent together and then released; that the Cremmyonian sow was notorious for its savagery; that Sciron made travellers wash his feet and then kicked them off the cliffs into the sea, where they were finished off by a giant turtle; that Cercyon lived near Eleusis and made passers-by wrestle with him until he killed them; and that Procoptes, better known as Procrustes, 'The Smasher', caught them on the borders of Athens and by stretching or pruning made them an exact fit to his lethal bed.

Aegeus and his wife Medea, whom he married when she was thrown out by Jason, were suspicious of the stranger and tried to be rid of him by sending him after the Marathonian bull, perhaps the one that Heracles had caught in Crete and brought to the mainland. Theseus returned successful to Athens, and this time Aegeus thwarted Medea's attempt to poison his son and dismissed her. Soon afterwards Theseus disposed of the sons of Pallas, who welcomed a new heir no more than Medea had, but perhaps before that he had already engaged in his most famous exploit, the killing of the Minotaur, the 'Minos-bull'.

King Minos of Crete, in revenge for the death in Attica of his son Androgeos, had begun to exact a three-yearly tribute consisting of seven Athenian boys and seven girls; they were offered to the Minotaur, half man and half bull, offspring of Pasiphaë's union with the Cretan Bull, a union made possible by one of Daedalus' mechanical devices. This unnatural beast lives in the Labyrinth, a maze usually identified with the intricate Minoan palace at Knossos. Theseus enters the maze and kills its occupant; Minos' daughter Ariadne helps him escape, either with the famous clew or with a magic crown of light that enables him to see in the dark. The tribute is now ended.

The tale is elaborated at its beginning by a contest (also described by Bacchylides) in which Theseus dives down and visits the goddess Amphitrite in the depths of the sea, to prove his divine descent from Poseidon and so match Minos' claim to be son of Zeus. And on the way home from Crete he stops at Naxos, and there, somehow, his mistress Ariadne is left behind. Either he abandons her for another girl, or he is divinely made to forget her, or the god Dionysus desires her and takes her over, or Artemis slays her there at his behest. Theseus next calls at Delos, where he and his companions dance a special 'crane-dance' that reproduces the sinuosities of the Labyrinth. Then, as he approaches Athens he forgets to replace the black sail with the white one that was to announce a successful outcome, and his father Aegeus casts himself from the Acropolis in despair.

Theseus is now king. He wins the friendship of Peirithous King of the Lapiths, and helps defeat the lecherous Centaurs at Peirithous' wedding. Peirithous helps him in his turn in an expedition against the Amazons, modelled closely on one of Heracles' adventures, and also in repelling them when they later attack Athens to regain their queen Antiope, another victim of Theseus' manly charms. For the hero has another side to him, best represented in the curious tale of how he and Peirithous abducted Helen from Sparta when she was only twelve, to keep her in the countryside until ripe for marriage; but her brothers the Dioscuri rescued her. Later he has to help Peirithous win *his* ideal girl, no less than Persephone herself, from the underworld. They get no further than the Styx in some versions, and are then trapped in magic stone seats – although usually Theseus, but not Peirithous, is later rescued by Heracles. He returns to Athens, unifies the rural communities and performs other politic acts, then is displaced by Menestheus and takes refuge with King Lycomedes of Scyros, who treacherously throws him over the cliffs; and that (though without the turtle) is the end of Theseus.

It's a curious hotch-potch, ranging from the solemn and mysterious (the Labyrinth and Ariadne, 'Very Holy', who seems once to have been a goddess of vegetation not unlike Persephone herself) to the trivial and derivative (Helen, and especially the episode in the underworld). The politically-minded parts, with Theseus as the great democrat, are barely mythical, and the involvement with the Amazon queen, together with the subsidiary tale of his second wife Phaedra and his son Hippolytus, looks like a romantic development. The adventures modelled on Heracles, the disposal of robbers as well as the Amazon expedition as a whole, seem from the literary and artistic evidence to be substantially the creation of the seventh or sixth centuries B.C. The association with the Lapiths is unlikely to be much older, and could be the creation of the tyrant Peisistratus who had Thessalian allies. Several other points are folktale-type elements of almost any date, particularly the tale of the black and white sails on his return from Crete.

The Cretan adventure itself, however, goes back at least to the time of Homer and Hesiod and probably earlier. Indeed the later Bronze Age is plausibly reflected not only in the palace-Labyrinth (*labyrinthos* being a pre-Greek word based apparently on the term for 'double-axe', a symbol carved on several of the surviving stones of the palace) but also in the bull itself – for bull-worship and bull-games were a prominent part of Minoan culture – and in the idea of Athens as tributary to Crete, which makes sense for the Late Bronze Age but for no subsequent period. It is now known that the Achaean Greeks gained control of Crete around 1500 B.C., and the myth may reflect that, although with special emphasis on Athens. At least the island of Ceos off the Attic coast (home, incidentally, of Bacchylides) was once a Minoan colony, and conceivably parts of Attica too had come for a time under Minoan control.

Curiously enough the rape of Helen and the attempt on

Persephone are not particularly recent elements, since they figure on works of art (the throne at Amyclae and the chest of Cypselus at Olympia) described by the traveller Pausanias and belonging to the late seventh or early sixth century B.C.[1] They must already have been traditional by that date. I doubt, all the same, whether they go back as far as the Mycenaean era, although it is strange that they were not suppressed in the process of making Theseus into an august founder of the state, and this suggests an almost sacrosanct traditionality. Peirithous, too, is an ambivalent figure. He is the son of Ixion, a famous sinner who tried to rape Hera herself, and his efforts with Persephone may therefore be a narrative doublet. Yet he is traditionally associated with the Centaurs, and that part of his myth is probably quite old.

The myths of Theseus seem almost too complex for a brief treatment, yet one conclusion would remain unchanged even after a longer examination: that their main development took place during the literary period. Only the quest against Crete looks undeniably ancient, and it is rightly accepted as one of the most powerful narrative themes in Greek myths. Interestingly enough it seems to reflect, and perhaps to justify, some dimly-remembered historical event, and so provide a model for the political elaborations to which many other parts of the Theseus story owe their existence.

The fourth of our older heroes is CADMUS, an example of a mythical founder figure. Like Pelops, founder of the Pelopid dynasty at Mycenae, he came to Greece from the Near East – not, like Pelops, from Lydia, but from Phoenicia where he was one of the sons of Agenor. He and his brothers were dispatched by their father to look for their sister Europa who had disappeared; actually she had been carried off to Crete for amatory purposes by Zeus in the form of a bull, and so a Cretan bull appears indirectly in this myth as well as in those of Theseus and Heracles. Cadmus arrived in Greece and was directed by the Delphic oracle to follow a cow(!) until it lay down, and there to found the city of Thebes. Euripides tells the tale, allusively as usual, in a choral ode from his great pageant of Theban history, *The Phoenician Women*:

Cadmus of Tyre came to this land, for whom the four-legged calf sank to the ground of its own accord, so fulfilling the oracle destined to be accomplished where the divine decree announced that Cadmus should settle in the wheat-bearing plains that were to be his home, where too the fair river's moisture spreads over the lands of Dirce ... There was the murderous serpent of Ares, a savage guardian, watching the watery rivers and fertile streams with ever-wandering glances. Cadmus as he came for lustral water slew it with a rock, striking the murderous head of the deadly beast with his arm's full throw, and through the counsels of the divine unmothered goddess [that is, Athena] cast its teeth on the ground, into the deep-seeded earth; then the earth sent up a vision of men in full armour that towered over the farthest borders of the land. Iron-hearted murder joined them again with the earth that gave them birth ... (638–73)

In short, there was a spring where the cow lay down, but it was guarded by a dragon sacred to Ares; Cadmus killed it and sowed its teeth, which produced a crop of armed warriors. By throwing a stone among them he turned them against each other, but the five that stayed alive became ancestors of the chief clans of Thebes.

After a period of expiation Cadmus was allowed to marry Ares' child Harmonia, and they had four daughters: Agaue, Autonoë, Ino and Semele. They were an unfortunate group, in their lifetimes at least. Agaue tore her son Pentheus to pieces, and Autonoë, who also joined in, had a son Actaeon who had already been devoured by his own hounds. Ino was driven mad for plotting against her step-children and threw herself into the sea, whereas Semele spoiled her good fortune as Zeus' mistress by demanding that he come to her in his true shape, and being incinerated as a consequence. Cadmus and Harmonia themselves had a curious later history, predicted to Cadmus by his quasi-grandson Dionysus:

You shall be turned into a serpent, and your wife shall change into the savage form of a snake – Harmonia, Ares' daughter, whom you won though yourself a mortal. With your wife, as the oracle of Zeus declares, you shall drive an ox-cart at the head of foreigners. Many are the cities you shall overthrow with your numberless hordes; when they have ravaged the oracle of Loxias [that is, Apollo] they shall have a miserable return home, but Ares will rescue you and Harmonia and transplant your life to the land of the blessed. (Euripides, *Bacchae*, 1330 ff.)

Euripides, who had strong aetiological interests, seems to combine a number of curious legends, none of them perhaps very early except for the ultimate resort to the Isles of the Blest: that Cadmus and his wife became leaders of a people in the west of Greece called the *Encheleis* or Eels, that they themselves turned into snakes, that Delphi was destined to be sacked by foreigners. Perhaps the snake-transformation reflected Cadmus' essential connection with the soil of Thebes (rather than with the underworld, another possible association), for the 'house-snake' was a symbol of stability and possession; the birth from the dragon's teeth of the 'Sown Men' who became ancestors of the Thebans likewise stresses their autochthonous nature. If so, this is a good example of a charter myth that is doing its best to confirm a politically desirable but historically dubious idea; for if there is anything we know about the Thebans, it is that they were subject from early times to displacement and migration. As for the foundation itself: its association with the oracle, and the use of the standard theme of founding a city where an animal performs a certain action, are presumably not earlier than the ninth or tenth century B.C., and the fight with the guardian monster, closely parallel with Apollo's fight against the Python-snake at Delphi, need be no older. The sowing of the teeth is reproduced in the story of how Jason dealt with the monster that guarded the Golden Fleece, but the Theban tale seems the earlier of the two.

What is left, then, to suggest that Cadmus goes back even so far as the Late Bronze Age? Partly that Thebes was indeed an important Mycenaean city, its inhabitants known in Homer as 'Cadmeians'; partly the association with the tale of Europa and Zeus, which is related to Bronze Age Crete; partly the mythical connections of his daughters, especially Semele and Ino. (The myth of Ino and Athamas is particularly well established, and is connected in turn with that of Phrixus and the Fleece.) There is also the cleavage between Cadmus and the later history of Thebes (from Labdacus through Laius to Oedipus and his sons), which suggests an archaic element that could not be completely integrated; and finally his Phoenician origins. These last have been doubted. Admittedly he is credited with the introduction of 'Phoenician writing' into Greece, but it is uncertain whether this connotes a Linear-B-type script or the alphabet, the latter a certainly Phoenician invention. Some scholars have thought the term 'Phoinix' to imply Cretan rather than Phoenician in this connection. Yet that seems unlikely, and we know that there were close cultural contacts between Late Bronze Age Greece and the eastern Mediterranean: for instance Ugarit (modern Ras Shamra) on the Syrian coast had a Mycenaean trading-quarter in the fourteenth century B.C.

It would be unwise to press these speculations too hard. The story of Cadmus is a particularly good example of a complex Greek myth that has attracted details from many sources and different eras: folktale motifs, miscellaneous historical details, charter-type elaborations, and so on. Modern scholarship has attacked the problem with all its power, and the result has been confusion and indecision as great as any in the ancient sources. One difficulty is that it is only with Euripides that our evidence becomes at all full for the early part of the Theban cycle. Sporadic earlier references exist, together with sixth-century artistic representations of favourite details like the marriage of Cadmus and Harmonia, but there is little else to guide us through the variants that proliferated by the time Hellanicus and Pherecydes brought their confident but crude scholarship to bear during the classical era.

The last of the selection of older heroes must undoubtedly be JASON. His myth, too, was much embroidered, but he too surely goes back into the Bronze Age. Much of the detail of the voyage of the Argo to Colchis at the eastern end of the Black Sea (the Euxine or 'Hospitable' sea as the Greeks called it to disguise or assuage its terrors) probably belongs to the age of colonization that began around 1000 B.C.; but the voyage itself is older. Iolcus, the Thessalian coastal city from which it started, was important in Mycenaean times but not later (at least, until the third century B.C.); Homer, in his single brief but apparently traditional allusion to the Argo, calls it 'well-known to all'. Hesiod, on the other hand, summarizes the union of Jason and Medea in a list of mixed marriages appended to the *Theogony*:

Aison's son [that is, Jason] led away Zeus-reared King Aietes' daughter by the will of the eternal gods, after accomplishing the many grievous tasks enjoined on him by the arrogant great king, insolent Pelias, wicked and violent. He accomplished these and came to Iolcus, after suffering much, bringing the slant-eyed maid on his swift ship . . . (*Theogony*, 992 ff.)

Unfortunately the poet is richer in epithets than in hard information. Of our fuller sources, Pindar in his fourth *Pythian* describes part of the Argo's journey quite brilliantly, but at too great length for quotation here, whereas Apollonius of Rhodes, who wrote an epic poem on the theme in the third century B.C., is both too prolix and too infected by Alexandrianism to be of great value for our purposes. Apollodorus depends heavily on Apollonius and is even more prosaic than usual. Even Pindar gives up half-way through the tale and claims that 'time constricts me, and I know a short cut' (*Pythians* 4, 247 f.); this is to give a rapid summary, and on this occasion I follow suit.

Aison has been cheated of the throne of Iolcus by Pelias, who is warned by the Delphic oracle that he will be deposed by a one-sandalled man. This turns out to be Aison's son Jason, who has been educated by the Centaur Cheiron and arrives in town wearing only one sandal. He is promptly persuaded to set off and recover the golden fleece belonging to King Aietes of Colchis – the one from the ram that had rescued Phrixus and Helle from the wrath of their stepmother Ino. Naturally the mission is meant to be fatal. Jason gathers all the young noblemen of the region for the expedition, and Phrixus' son Argos is commissioned to build a ship. As the myth grew in popularity the expedition became a Panhellenic affair; practically everyone who was anyone joined in, including Orpheus and Heracles. The Argo's distinguished crew sail north-eastward through the Dardanelles and meet various adventures, including a preliminary dalliance with the women of Lemnos who are discussed in Chapter 10. In the Propontis they kill King Cyzicus by mistake in a night landing and leave Heracles ashore searching for his beloved Hylas; then blind Phineus, in return for the routing of the greedy bird-women called Harpies, tells them how to pass between the Clashing Rocks in safety. The Argonauts seem to be in the Black Sea by now, but probably these rocks are based on a navigator's memory of the dangerous passage through the Bosporus or even the Dardanelles.

Finally they reach the river Phasis and the land of Aietes, whose father is the Sun and whose daughter is Medea skilled in magic. Athena sees to it that she falls in love with Jason, and gives him an ointment that protects him against fire or metal. This enables him to yoke the fire-breathing brazen-footed bulls that Aietes produces as a preliminary test. He then kills the dragon that guards the fleece, sows its teeth and disposes of the armed men that grow out of the ground by throwing a stone among them, exactly as Cadmus did. He rushes back to the Argo with the fleece, Medea, and her young brother

Apsyrtus; Aietes pursues, and drops behind only when Medea has the good idea of cutting up Apsyrtus and throwing the bits overboard for his father to gather. Jason is purified from the crime, and they return to Iolcus by devious routes about which the tradition was flexible: usually round the stream of Okeanos somehow, or up the Danube, into the North Sea and then through Libya. Back in Iolcus, Pelias is removed when Medea persuades him to be 'rejuvenated' by being boiled in a cauldron, a process she has just made work with an old sheep. She and Jason are expelled for the murder and find their way to Corinth, where eventually Jason acquires a proper Greek wife. Medea murders her children in revenge, at least according to Euripides' *Medea*, and finds refuge for a time with Theseus at Athens; Jason dies when a bit of the now rotting Argo falls on his head.

Plainly the tale as a whole is an amalgam of diverse elements. Folktale motifs are the most prominent: recognition by token (the sandal), disposing of an enemy by sending him on a dangerous quest (both Pelias and Aietes try this), killing a friend by mistake (Cyzicus), the barbarian enchantress, love-charms and magical gadgets, tricks to make enemies fight each other, delaying pursuit by scattering objects that have to be collected (Atalanta had done so more humanely, with golden apples), killing someone under pretence of doing him a favour. Next there is a strong geographical interest, no doubt in response to explorations in and rumours about the Black Sea and Danube. It has been suggested that Miletus on the Asia Minor coast played a part in forming the myth; it was populated by Greeks, including 'Minyans' from Orchomenus near Iolcus, after 1100 B.C., and took a prominent part in the exploration of the Euxine. Finally great care has obviously been taken to connect the myth with as many others as possible, not only through the heterogeneous crew (the Dioscuri and the sons of Boreas the North Wind, as well as Peleus, Orpheus and Heracles), but also through Pelias at

Iolcus, the relation of Jason to Cheiron, the fleece connected with Phrixus and so with the Ino–Athamas myth, and through Jason at Corinth and Medea at Athens.

Most of the details of Jason's adventures fail to mark him with any particular clarity as an 'older hero', yet such, at heart, he undoubtedly must be. His name 'Iason', 'Healer', suggests an originally rather different role. He is clearly not on a level with younger legendary heroes like Agamemnon or Achilles, yet in a sense his diversity is typical of the difficulty in distinguishing older and younger traits in the subjects of heavily elaborated myth complexes. Ultimately we have to take the tale of the Argonauts as we find it in our sources: complex in detail but straightforward, almost ordinary, as narrative. It contains few significant overtones (except for those added by specifically literary sources like Apollonius, for example, that Jason is indecisive and unheroic by comparison with Heracles), and the myth as a whole does not respond easily to special interpretations: no charter aspects, no aetiology beyond feeble explanations of place-names in the Propontis and Black Sea, no creative evocation, heavily muted fantasy. It is enthralling but bland, even superficial; and that, in the end, may be a fault in varying degrees of most of the heroic myths as they survive in the literary sources.

*The 'younger' heroes* must be treated no less selectively. As examples I take OEDIPUS, AGAMEMNON, ORESTES, ODYSSEUS and ORPHEUS; they suffice to make certain additional distinctions clear as well as to stress the difference between historicizing and non-historicizing myths.

OEDIPUS is one of the best-known and most powerful figures of Greek myths, and it may be disconcerting to see him labelled as a 'younger hero'; indeed I do not deny that in some respects his origins may go back into the Bronze Age. Yet his 'real' mythical essence is contained in Sophocles' plays: his murder and marriage, his self-discovery, his agony and blinding, his miraculous assumption in the grove of Colonus near

Athens. Most of this is likely to be comparatively recent in anything like that form. Homer knows about his killing his father and marrying his mother (although he gives her name as Epicaste not Iocaste), but differs over the aftermath. Here is Odysseus describing the figures he saw in the underworld:

And I saw the mother of Oedipus, fair Epicaste, who committed a dreadful deed in the ignorance of her mind by marrying her own son; and he married her after slaying his own father – deeds the gods immediately made notorious among men. But he in grief ruled over the Cadmeians in lovely Thebes through the destructive counsels of the gods, whereas she went to the narrow-gated strong house of Hades, tying a steep noose from the lofty hall, possessed by her own grief . . . (*Odyssey* 11, 271 ff.)

Here is no self-blinding, no immediate and self-imposed exile from Thebes. A passage in the *Iliad* (23, 679 f.) confirms that Oedipus died not in exile at Colonus but at Thebes itself, and that funeral games were given for him as a still-established monarch. Indeed the whole Theban saga (as one may rightly call it, since it obviously has a legendary and quasi-historical basis) was the subject of considerable elaboration between the time of Homer and the fifth century B.C.

Oedipus does not fit well with the early history of Thebes or the descendants of Cadmus and the Sown Men. His grandfather, who had started a fresh dynasty, is called Labdacus, a curious name which, if it is indeed related to the Phoenician letter *labda* (Greek *lamda*), is not particularly old, since the Phoenician alphabet did not reach Greece till around 900 B.C. and had been formed in Phoenicia itself not more than three centuries before that. Oedipus' father Laius incurs a family curse for abducting the beautiful boy Chrysippus – the curse theme was applied to the house of Atreus also, and was an effective device for interrelating tales about different generations. Oedipus himself has a bizarre name redolent of folktale, if indeed it means 'swollen-foot'; his exposure by his parents, his rescue by a shepherd, his winning the kingship of Thebes by solving the Sphinx's riddle – all these, too, are folktale elements. These, rather than the dramatic and deeply evocative tale developed by Sophocles (whose main point is the idea of a man relentlessly exploring his true situation at the risk of his own destruction), are the most traditional elements in Oedipus. He is a mixed figure, therefore, but one who unlike Perseus, Heracles and the rest only became an important hero of myth after the end of the Bronze Age.

There is a similar distinction of dynasties at Mycenae. Atreus is founder of the Atreid dynasty, and his famous son is AGAMEMNON. Beyond Atreus, but seemingly in a different landscape, stands Pelops, brought to southern Greece from Asia Minor by his father Tantalus, himself a shadowy figure associated with the gods; and behind Tantalus, as one of the earliest kings of Mycenae or its near neighbour Tiryns, is Perseus. Atreus quarrels with his brother Thyestes; the theme of the quarrelling brothers is a folktale one, but is similarly applied to quasi-historical dynastic problems through Proetus and Acrisius as well as Eteocles and Polyneices. Thyestes seduces Atreus' wife Aerope and gets the kingdom by a trick, then Atreus regains it after serving up Thyestes' own children for him to eat. These are the highly indirect consequences of a curse once laid on Pelops by Oenomaus' charioteer Myrtilus. Agamemnon inherits the curse, which is why he has to sacrifice his daughter Iphigeneia on the way to Troy, why he is slain by his wife Clytaemnestra on his triumphant return, and why his son Orestes has to kill his own mother Clytaemnestra and her lover Aegisthus. This all forms the material of Aeschylus' great trilogy, the *Oresteia*. The curse is finally ended after Orestes, driven mad and so punished for the crime of matricide, is set free by the Furies on the Areopagus (the Hill of Ares in Athens). This is an aetiological and validatory myth of the foundation of the Athenian High Court of historical times. It is obvious that Athens is here appropriating an Argive myth and turning it to her own greater glory, much as she did with Oedipus at Colonus in Sophocles' play, or less effectively with Medea.

Here we have fifth-century developments of the myth, powerful but undeniably recent. Yet Agamemnon himself is a considerably older figure, established as leader of the Achaean forces in Homer's *Iliad* and indeed as one of the key figures of the Trojan War. Why then should he be classified as a 'younger' hero? The answer is that the Agamemnon of the *Iliad* is predominantly a realistic character, a historical picture of a man. His actions there are legendary and not mythical in the stricter sense. His direct connection with the era of the older heroes is mainly through his brother Menelaus who married Helen, and superficially by the political inheritance stressed by Homer:

Strong Agamemnon rose, and stood holding the sceptre made by Hephaestus. Hephaestus had given it to Lord Zeus, son of Kronos, and then Zeus gave it to the Messenger [that is, Hermes] ... and Lord Hermes gave it to Pelops, whipper of horses, and Pelops again to Atreus, shepherd of the people. Atreus when he died left it for Thyestes rich in sheep, and Thyestes again left it to be carried by Agamemnon, to rule over all Argos and many islands. (*Iliad* 2, 100 ff.)

But here Homer is trying to bolster Agamemnon's position as a 'Zeus-born' king by tracing his staff of office back to Zeus, and the untraditional nature of the attempt is strongly suggested by his omitting Perseus and ignoring Thyestes' quarrel with Atreus.

With ORESTES the case becomes clearer, mainly because he is an explicitly post-Trojan-War figure. *His* relations to the distant Pelops are not stressed; he is an entirely realistic character whose one fantastic experience, being driven mad by the Furies for his pious matricide, is little more than a pathological interlude. Homer reduces the killing of Aegisthus and Clytaemnestra to a precise and pseudo-realistic chronology:

For seven years Aegisthus ruled over Mycenae rich in gold after killing the son of Atreus, and the people were subjected to him. But in the eighth year Prince Orestes came back as a bane to him from Athens, and slew the murderer of his father ... After slaying him he gave a funeral feast to the Argives for hateful Clytaemnestra and cowardly Aegisthus, and on the same day Menelaus came ... (*Odyssey* 3, 304 ff.)

Orestes draws Agamemnon with him, as it were, away from the Bronze-age past, from Pelops and Helen and the Dioscuri, into the historical period that is initiated by the Trojan War itself and develops with the emergence of Athens in the eleventh, tenth and ninth centuries B.C. Homer, around 700, knows that Orestes comes *from Athens* to take vengeance on Aegisthus; could that detail have formed part of the tradition for long?

One of the difficulties of drawing a distinction between 'older' and 'younger' heroes is that even those suggested by historical associations as belonging to the latter class tend to be involved in folktale-type actions from time to time. For Martin Nilsson that was a sign of great antiquity. I am sceptical. The use of standard motifs, some of them of the kind we associate with folktales, was so deeply rooted in the Greek mythical tradition from its earliest known phases to its latest ones that I doubt whether we can take it as a sure sign of age. Admittedly, where a myth is almost wholly composed of folktale motifs, like that of Perseus, we can suspect a highly traditional quality; but Atreus is not necessarily made an ancient figure by cooking his nephews, any more than Oedipus by accidentally killing his father. Conversely a detail about an oracle does not turn the whole of its surrounding myth into a recent creation.

With ODYSSEUS we become involved in a different and rather special situation. He obviously goes back at least as far as the first versions of the *Odyssey* – and that means, in the light of the long and cumulative oral epic tradition, close to the time of the Trojan War. Yet he is a 'younger' hero in comparison with Perseus and others, since none of his affiliations take him beyond that point by more than a generation or so. He is simply not involved in the elaborate network of mythical events outside the range of Troy. His father Laertes is otherwise devoid of myths, and so to all intents and purposes is his mother Anticleia; his maternal grandfather Autolycus is something of a trickster and lives near Mount Parnassus, but again is not integrated into the general heroic pattern. Odysseus takes full part in the events at Troy and its aftermath; his son Telemachus is incorporated into the later fictional tradition and is even married off to Circe in one unhappy version. But we cannot take Odysseus' feats at Troy as 'mythical' in the same sense as those of Cadmus at Thebes. Admittedly he is represented as being under the special protection of Athena (see p. 123 f.), and the intervention of gods is something that gives the whole Trojan *geste* a touch of mythical glamour. But it is no more than a touch, except in the specifically divine parts of the poems, and most of the actions of Odysseus and his fellow-fighters are a mixture of realism and ordinary non-mythical fiction, no doubt with a dash of genuine historical memory.

What makes Odysseus a special case is his involvement in the well-known folktale adventures that he describes to the Phaeacians in the ninth to the twelfth books of the *Odyssey*. The Lotus-eaters, Polyphemus the Cyclops, Aeolus king of the winds, the huge Laestrygonians, Circe, the journey to the underworld, Scylla and Charybdis, the cattle of the Sun, Calypso's island, the Phaeacians themselves – it would be pleasant to recount these tales once again, but they are too extensive and too familiar for that, and in any case Homer's version is best. Now this *is* genuinely mythical material. It includes many folktale themes, of disguise and ingenuity and the rest, but they have been formed into homogeneous narratives that are both fantastic and other-worldly. They have a quite different appearance from the automatic and rather tired look of many later mythical complexes, in which quests are accomplished almost as easily as proposed, heiresses are offered by the handful and the air hums with errant discuses fulfilling highly predictable oracles. Yet most critics would agree, I believe, that Odysseus' sea adventures (which begin when a storm blows up soon after he leaves Troy and end when he is set ashore in Ithaca by the semi-divine Phaeacians) are for the most part not only independent from but older than Odysseus himself, or mythical Troy, or Ithaca.

Admittedly these adventures include different strata. Scholars have demonstrated, for instance, that north-eastern details from the exploration of the Euxine have been added to events envisaged as belonging to the western seas. The Homeric poets undoubtedly carried out certain elaborations in this and other respects, and we should not be dealing with oral traditions if it were not so. But these accretions were added to a substantial nucleus that can claim to be far more ancient than the war at Troy. There are folktale elements, too, in the tale of Odysseus' return to Penelope and Ithaca: the theme of the faithful wife, or how to keep one's suitors guessing, or the husband in disguise. But in his more realistic actions, which vastly predominate, Odysseus is based on the conception of a real if provincial chieftain from north-western Greece. The association with the folktale adventures and a powerful vengeance-plot made him a mythical figure in his own right – one that developed into an object of sporadic cult, or a continuing symbol of deviousness in Sophocles' *Philoctetes* and the post-classical tradition, but one that is not in itself particularly ancient.

One of the most familiar figures of Greek myths is ORPHEUS, yet he is not even mentioned in Homer or Hesiod. The first surviving reference comes in a two-word fragment of the sixth-century B.C. lyric poet Ibycus: 'famous Orpheus'. Perhaps his omission from the poetry of the late eighth and seventh centuries is accidental, or due to his being a semi-barbarian, a Thracian from across the northern borders of Greece. When he enters literature it is mainly because of his wonderful power of drawing to him birds, beasts, fishes, even stones, by his singing and lyre-playing. Simonides, in the second surviving literary reference, of around 500 B.C., writes:

> Over his head fly innumerable birds, and the fishes leap straight up from the dark water at his fair song. (frag. 62 in D. L. Page's edition)

Aeschylus said something similar, as did Euripides, but in his lost play *The Bassarids* Aeschylus gave a quite different emphasis: that Orpheus resisted the worship of Dionysus and was torn to pieces by the god's female worshippers, the Bacchants. That he died at the hands of women, at least, is a common part of his legend. Roman poetry in particular liked recounting how his scattered limbs were thrown into the sea and his head floated to the island of Lemnos, where it was taken ashore and buried, and thereafter gave oracular responses. A curious connection, this, between the gentle singer and the victim of human prejudice and savagery, and one that seems less than startling only to those familiar with the tale of Jesus Christ.

Apart from the power of Orpheus' music, it is his love for Eurydice that is best known. Yet Eurydice is hardly mentioned in the whole of surviving Greek literature, and her story is told at length only by a Roman poet, Virgil, in his fourth *Georgic*. Admittedly it is indirectly alluded to by Euripides in *Alcestis*, produced in 438 B.C., for there the odious Admetus tells his wife, about to die on his behalf:

> If I had Orpheus' tongue and song, so that I could bring you back from Hades by charming Demeter's daughter [that is, Persephone] or her husband with my strains, I should have gone down there; and neither Pluto's dog [that is, Cerberus] nor Charon at his oar, the ferryman of souls, would keep me back, until I had set you living once more into the light of day. (*Alcestis*, 357 ff.)

The tale that becomes clear in subsequent sources is that Orpheus' wife, the nymph Eurydice, dies soon after her wedding as a result of a snake-bite, according to Virgil because Aristaeus, son of Apollo and Cyrene and protector of flocks and bees, had tried to assault her. Orpheus is heart-broken and makes his way down to the underworld, where by the power of his music he persuades King Hades and his consort Persephone to release her. One condition is set: that he shall go ahead of her, and shall not address or look back at her until they reach the world of the living. He almost succeeds, but at the last moment gives in either to love or to fear (because he can see no shadow beside him) and looks round. She departs for ever; he, inconsolable, moves towards his mortal fate at the hands of the women, who are incensed, according to late versions, either because he refuses to join their Bacchic revels, or because he spurns their love in mourning for Eurydice, or because he introduces the practice of homosexuality. We need not bother about these maundering speculations, so typical of the fervent yet arid imaginations of Hellenistic and Roman mythographers. What matters more is that the whole Eurydice tale made so little impression on Greeks of the classical age, and that Aristaeus is neither seen nor heard of in this paradoxical role (since he is usually the placid and benevolent bee-keeper and protector of flocks) until the time of Virgil. This element of the tale is unlikely to be older than the Hellenistic age.

In short, Orpheus is quite definitely a 'younger' hero in the terms I am using. The idea of a singer who could charm birds and animals might go back to the Mycenaean age; some have quixotically professed to see in a fresco from Pylos, depicting a bird *flying away from* a man with a lyre, a prototype of Orpheus himself.[2] But the silence of Homer, Hesiod and the entire epic tradition is suspicious. Other aspects of Orpheus, which do not fit well with this peaceable conception, could be Dionysiac – but then Dionysus himself came comparatively late on the scene. Eurydice appeals to the romantic imagination, but made only a passing impression on classical Greeks. A completely different kind of evidence is provided by the 'Orphics', a mystical sect that as early as the sixth century B.C. propounded a form of immortality under the auspices of the sweet singer, who was already being classed with Homer and Hesiod as the source of anonymous (and usually bad) epic verses.[3] That, once again, takes us back a little way in time; but the central fact remains that the Thracian Orpheus, with his barbarically-named father Oeagrus, has no connection with the regular framework of Greek myths, heroic or divine, at least until the time when he was signed on among the crew of the Argo. His quasi-magical powers, his extreme devotion to his wife and his pathetic ill-fortune make him, for us, a powerful and evocative symbol. The Romans felt the same, but the Greeks seem to have been less impressed.

The last category of heroic myths, *the later inventions,* is a subsidiary one, but is revealing for the way in which a myth-making tradition can persist in fully literate surroundings. Herodotus has already been cited in this respect in Chapter 5, and I now offer two further examples of how a historical personage could be turned into a mythical hero. The first of them is the great CROESUS of Lydia, the second the boxer CLEOMEDES from the insignificant Aegean island of Astypalaea.

CROESUS was the last king of the Lydian empire, in Asia Minor, that collapsed with the capture of Sardis by Cyrus of Persia in 546 B.C. He made a powerful impression on the Greeks, for after seizing their cities on the Aegean coast he had behaved quite mildly and even made rich offerings at Apollo's shrine in Delphi. Pindar refers to his 'kindly excellence', and the story of his miraculous escape from death was well known, not only to Herodotus and Ctesias but also to the poet Bacchylides:

... when Sardis was captured by the army of the Persians, Apollo of the golden sword protected Croesus, who encountered a day he never expected, and, refusing to wait for tearful slavery, built a pyre in front of his palace with its brazen walls  He mounted it together with his virtuous wife and his daughters with their beautiful hair, who wept most miserably; lifting his hands to steep heaven he cried out: 'Almighty god, where is the divine favour? Where the lord that is son of Leto? The house of Alyattes goes down in ruin ... Pactolus with its golden eddies is reddened with blood, the women are shamefully taken from their well-built halls. What was hateful before, now becomes desirable: the sweetest thing is to die!' So saying he bade a soft-stepping servant kindle his wooden abode. The girls shrieked and cast their dear arms round their mother, for the death one can see coming is the most hateful for mortals; but when the terrible fire's bright strength darted through, Zeus set overhead a black cloud and quenched the orange flame. Nothing that the care of the gods creates is beyond belief, for then Apollo, Delos-born, carried the old man with his slim-ankled daughters to the Hyperboreans, and set them to dwell there on account of Croesus' piety, because he had sent to holy Pytho the greatest gifts of all men. (3, 25 ff.)

Bacchylides wrote this in 468 B.C., only two or three generations after the event he celebrates. One might think it a mere poetical exaggeration, the assignment of a mythical fate and a typical folktale reversal as a light-hearted compliment; but Herodotus, too, tells the tale, which was taken quite seriously by many Greeks of the classical age (although Croesus may, in fact, have been killed by Cyrus). There was disagreement about whether he mounted the pyre of his own will, as Bacchylides asserts, or under compulsion from Cyrus. Herodotus also differs in saying that Cyrus decided to spare him and then, when he could not extinguish the pyre, Apollo intervened; and there were of course rationalists like Xenophon who simply made Cyrus pardon Croesus at the last moment and without divine intervention. It is the idea of Croesus going to the land of the Hyperboreans (which, as we saw on p 132 f., became conflated with the Isles of the Blest) that is most remarkable in all this. He was accorded no cult by the Greeks – that would have been going too far for a barbarian monarch, however generous – but in other respects seems to have attained a status not far removed from that of a Theseus, an Oedipus or a Menelaus.

From the remote but famous monarch to a more specific and humbler character. The boxing finals at Olympia in 492 B.C. ended with CLEOMEDES killing his opponent and being deprived of the prize. This is how Pausanias, our only source, continues the story:

> . . . he went out of his mind through grief and returned to Astypalaea. There he attacked a school of about sixty children and overturned the column that held up the roof. The roof fell on the children; he was stoned by the townsfolk and took refuge in Athena's sanctuary, climbed into a chest that lay there and pulled down the lid. The Astypalaeans toiled in vain in their efforts to open the chest; in the end they broke open its planks but found no Cleomedes there, either living or dead, so they sent men to Delphi to ask what had happened to him. This, they say, was the Pythian priestess's oracular reply: 'Cleomedes of Astypalaea is the last of the heroes; honour him with sacrifices, since he is no longer mortal.' So from that time on the Astypalaeans paid honours to him as a hero. (6. 9, 6 ff.)

Admittedly Pausanias is writing some six hundred years later, which is testimony to the myth's persistence if not to its total accuracy. Credulous villagers will believe almost anything, especially a strange event like an apparently inexplicable disappearance. What is especially interesting is that Cleomedes shares some of the characteristics of Heracles himself – his madness, his brute strength and his disappearance from a lethal situation. It is curious, too, that another boxer, who won at Olympia only twelve years later, likewise achieved heroic status. He was Euthymus from Locri, a Greek colony in southern Italy, and he rescued and married one of the maidens offered each year to an unpleasant ghost called simply 'the Hero'.[4] Euthymus escaped death, departing 'in some other way', and came to be regarded as the son not of a mortal father but of the local river. He had no cult, but these other typically heroic appurtenances emphasize his Perseus-like performance. And yet he was a real man in origin, a well-known competitor at Olympia who like Cleomedes became involved in an argument over an umpire's decision there.

These later inventions are important not so much because their heroes are strongly imaginative in conception, but because they show how history can be made mythical at almost any stage. They suggest, too, that the tendency to raise certain humans to the status of demi-gods became something of a habit with the Greeks, despite their obsession with the distinction between mortal and immortal. That tells us a little about the formation of the other heroes, too. But first Heracles, the greatest of them all, requires close consideration in the chapter that now follows.

# CHAPTER 8

# THE MYTHICAL LIFE OF
# HERACLES

HERACLES is not only the most important of the heroes, he is also the most difficult to reconstruct. In some ways he was a source of mystery to the Greeks themselves, particularly because of his ambivalent status as both hero and god: he alone started as a hero and was raised up to be a god on Olympus. His myths are quite clear about that. Despite Hera's persistent hatred of him, in the end he was taken from his funeral pyre on Mount Oeta and made immortal. What is more, he was given Hera's own daughter Hebe (whose name means Youth) as wife. He was propitiated, also, in both roles, for the offerings made to gods and heroes were distinct in kind.

In the case of sacrifices to a hero, the victim, usually goat or sheep, was held with its head down over a pit and its throat was slit in that posture; then its thigh-bones wrapped in fat were burned on a low hearth. When a victim was sacrificed to a god, on the other hand, its head was lifted towards the sky and its throat slit so that the blood flowed straight on to the altar, a high table-like structure quite different from the heroic pit or hearth. These distinctions were rather strict, and even the verb used for the act of sacrifice was different in each case. Obviously the heroes were imagined as existing under the earth, and so their sacrificial victims were pointed that way; the gods, however, were envisaged as living in the sky or on Mount Olympus, and so their altars were elevated and the smoke of offerings was given a good start on its skyward journey. Heracles, uniquely, received both types of sacrifice and worship – not everywhere. but in different parts of

Greece; this is why Pindar in a striking phrase could call him *hēros theos*, 'hero-god'.

Another unusual thing about him as a hero was that he had no grave. Most of them had all too many, since it was a great advantage for a city to be able to claim the bones of a hero-protector. Athens at a difficult period sent Cimon to recover the bones of Theseus from the island of Skyros; he managed to bring back *some* bones, at least, and they were very large ones. Many places in the Greek world must have wanted to possess the tomb of Heracles, just as they wished to divert him through their territory on his mythical travels. That was easier to arrange. A grave would have caused a scandal, because the point about him was precisely that his body was burned and subsumed into heaven; nothing except the pyre remained. Moreover nearly all other heroes (many of whom met violent ends, for example being torn to pieces) were buried, not cremated like Heracles. One or two were consumed by a lightning-blast from Zeus; that is a little different, although it is significant that they include Semele, whose offspring was the god Dionysus, and Asclepius, who as a healing-daemon gained a cult that verged on the divine.

The idea of making Heracles into a god seems not to be very old, no earlier than the seventh century B.C. That can be stated with some confidence, because the Homeric poems twice specifically assert that he was mortal, but in one case he is also said to be a god – and that in a passage there are good reasons for considering as a slightly later addition. At *Iliad* 18, 117–19 Achilles says:

Not even mighty Heracles, who was dear to lord Zeus son of Kronos, escaped death, but fate and Hera's harsh anger brought him low;

but when Odysseus descends to Hades in the eleventh book of the *Odyssey* he sees there a number of dead heroes, including Sisyphus:

And after him I saw mighty Heracles – his wraith; for among the immortal gods he rejoices in feasts and has fair-ankled Hebe to wife, child of great Zeus and Hera of the golden sandals. Around him was the clangour of corpses, as though of birds, as they fled in all directions in dismay; and he was like gloomy night, with naked bow and an arrow on the string, terribly glowering as though ever ready to shoot. (601–8)

It is the words from 'his wraith' to 'golden sandals' that the ancient critics thought interpolated, and indeed they do look like an addition. Their purpose is obvious: to reconcile the view that Heracles *died* and went down to Hades like anyone else with the contradictory idea, not elsewhere recorded in the *Iliad* or *Odyssey*, that he went to Olympus, married Hebe and lived for ever. There is an exactly similar situation in a fragmentary poem by Hesiod, the *Ehoeae* or *Catalogue of Women*. The subject is Deianeira, Heracles' wife, who

did dread deeds, since she was greatly infatuated in her heart, when she smeared the poison on his shirt and gave it to the herald Lichas to bring to him; and he gave it to Lord Heracles sacker of cities, son of Amphitryon; and the end of death stood by him as soon as he received it, and he died and came to the house of grievous Hades. But now he is a god and has escaped all evils, and lives where the others possess the halls of Olympus, deathless and unageing, and has fair-ankled Hebe to wife . . . (fr. 25, 20 ff.)

Here again the last sentence is an obvious correction or amendment, and the writer of one of the three papyri that preserve the passage marks these verses with strokes in the margin to show that they were held, in some quarters at least, to be a later addition.

The *Odyssey* was composed in its primary monumental form around 700 B.C., but additions to the eleventh and twenty-fourth books seem to have been made soon afterwards. The Hesiodic poems, too, may have suffered expansion not much later. That is why the seventh century seems the most likely period for the emergence of Heracles as a god. From the sixth century on that idea is universally attested in art and literature. The question now arises whether Heracles' burning on the pyre on Mount Oeta is equally late. The story of Deianeira and the poisoned shirt is as old as Hesiod's *Ehoeae*, as we have just seen, and the Centaur Nessus, whose blood and seed made the garment fatal (see p. 196), is depicted on Proto-Attic jars of the second half of the seventh century. Such a complex tale is unlikely to have been invented and propagated in a moment of time; it was probably fully traditional by the period of Heracles' deification. But that does not necessarily involve the idea of the pyre. Heracles obviously died through Deianeira's gift, but it is just possible that he did so as a direct result of the corrosive poison, and that the purifying pyre, like the assumption into heaven, is a later elaboration.

The problem of Heracles' divinity exercised the ancient world as well as the modern, and the historian Herodotus went to great personal trouble to solve it. Unfortunately he started from the idea that one of the twelve Egyptian gods could be identified with Heracles, who must therefore be much older than a generation or so before the Trojan War, which is where the Greek myths placed him. Herodotus made a special trip to Tyre in Phoenicia, where he had heard there was a famous temple of Heracles, to pursue the matter further. The cult there was claimed by its priests to be no less than 2,300 years old. A further visit to the island of Thasos in the north Aegean suggested that the Phoenician Heracles had been established on the very borders of the Greek world for some five generations before Heracles the Greek hero. Once again Herodotus was misled, this time by the identification (common in his day, but without foundation) of Heracles with the Phoenician god Melqart, but the importance of the quest and the unique nature of Heracles' status are confirmed by the historian's determined and arduous pursuit of every clue.[1]

The difficulties of arranging the events of Heracles' mythical *lifetime* are quite distinct. There is a mass of ancient evidence, most of it from the fifth century B.C. and later. Yet the classical writers already had variant accounts before them, and Heracles was subjected, even more than other heroes, to free elaboration and adjustment. We know that there were sub-epic poems about him that no longer survive. One was called *The Capture of Oechalia* and was sometimes attributed (incorrectly) to Homer; another was a *Heracleia* by one Peisandros of Rhodes, who lived probably in the early sixth century B.C., and a different *Heracleia* was composed in the fifth century by Herodotus' uncle, Panyassis. Then the fifth-century antiquarians and local historians, and especially Pherecydes of Athens, summarized and rationalized and syncretized; their work exists only in fragments, but Apollodorus the author of the *Library* (that valuable compilation of Roman times) evidently followed Pherecydes' account of Heracles rather closely. From all the evidence it seems that most of the exploits to be described shortly were already associated with the hero by the beginning of the sixth century B.C., and many of them, as we can tell from references in Homer and Hesiod, went back at least several generations before that.

That is as much as can be said with reasonable certainty, simply because other evidence is lacking, but once again it is likely that the Heracles myth was established in its basic form for long before Homer and Hesiod – that it was at least Mycenaean and in parts much older. Unfortunately the scholarly study of the classical evidence does not help much with the pre-Homeric stage, and for present purposes that evidence can be presented in a very simple form. So too can the iconographical evidence, that is, the scenes from Heracles' life that appear copiously in vase paintings from the sixth century B.C. onwards, and in smaller numbers in other works of art, notably temple sculptures. The study of these scenes is still sporadic.[2] When brought nearer completion it will be valuable, for they often give earlier evidence for the appearance of a fresh detail than does any surviving literary source.

Even so it will have little to reveal about the pre-Homeric Heracles, and that is what we mainly want to know. I except, of course, representations that were actually made before 700 B.C. It is possible that identifiable Mycenaean pictures of Heracles, or indeed other heroes, will turn up, but it seems unlikely. Even post-Mycenaean versions in the 'Geometric' style are sparse. A few indeterminate Centaurs from the ninth and eighth centuries B.C. and a probable picture of Heracles and the Stymphalian birds of shortly before 700 are the meagre harvest so far. And yet, if a good deal about Heracles remains obscure, there is also much that we do know. In presenting it one is handicapped, as usual, by the sheer allusiveness of classical writers, as well as, in Hesiod and tragedy, the brevity and repetitiveness of their references and the arid formular descriptions of gods and heroes. But a fascinating biography still remains.

The ancient mythographers divided the hero's activities into the following three kinds: the twelve Labours, the 'incidental deeds' that were performed in the course of the Labours, and the 'expeditions' in which he was leader of an army. It is convenient roughly to follow that arrangement, prefacing it with his birth and early life and ending with his death and transfiguration. Some of the relative chronology is arbitrary and was under dispute even by the fifth century; for instance it is not clear whether he killed his children by Megara before the Labours or, as Euripides said in his *Heracles*, just afterwards. Nor does it matter much. We shall not find in the actions of Heracles any consistent development of character or moral attitude. He is a mixture of paradoxical qualities, and these are the main reasons for the random arrangement of his life. One thing is certain, and that is that the Labours always stood as his central achievement, even if some of them may not seem so significant now as other and lesser of his deeds.

Heracles has a human name, not a divine one; it means

'glory of Hera' or the like, and implies a pious dedication to the goddess by his mortal parents. Ironically, Hera was his lifelong enemy and hated him for being one of her husband's bastards. For Zeus desired Alcmena, who had just married Amphitryon, a prince of Tiryns forced to flee to Thebes for the usual kind of reason (that is, accidentally killing his uncle). Amphitryon had vowed to defeat the Teleboans in western Greece before ever sleeping with his wife, and as a consequence Zeus anticipated him in the marital bed. Amphitryon returned in triumph on the self-same night, and Alcmena duly bore twins: first Heracles the son of the divine father, then Iphicles the son of mortal Amphitryon. The proceedings are described in Hesiod's *Ehoeae*, a fragment of which has become attached to a rather poor pseudo-Hesiodic poem called the *Shield of Heracles*:

> All night long Amphitryon lay with his respectful wife, rejoicing in the gifts of golden Aphrodite. Alcmena, mastered by a god and by the noblest of men, bore twin sons in seven-gated Thebes. They had different temperaments, but yet were brothers: one inferior, the other much better, mighty Heracles, terrible and strong. She bore him to the dark-clouded son of Kronos, and the other, Iphicles, to spear-brandishing Amphitryon. (frag. 195; *Shield of Heracles* 46 ff.)

The circumstances of Heracles' birth caused him much trouble, because they led to his being made subject to King Eurystheus of Mycenae, the man who imposed the Labours on him. Zeus in a rash moment had made the following boast:

> 'Hear me, all you gods and goddesses, that I may speak as my heart in my breast bids me. Today Eileithyia, the goddess of painful birthpangs, will show forth into the light of day a man descended from my blood who shall rule over all his neighbours.' (*Iliad* 19, 101 ff.)

Zeus knew that Alcmena was on the point of birth, and he was really referring to their son Heracles; but Hera, after persuading him to confirm the statement by an oath, hastened on the birth of Eurystheus (who was also descended from Zeus by way of Perseus) and delayed that of Heracles to the next day. She then told Zeus what had happened, and he was so angry that he threw the Lady Infatuation out of Olympus and told her to dwell henceforth among men. But Heracles was irretrievably destined to be Eurystheus' vassal. This may reflect a historical memory of the relationship of Tiryns, the fortress-town of which Heracles became king, to the capital city Mycenae. For Heracles was an Argive, not a Theban, in spite of being born in Thebes. There must be some motive for the Theban detail that we do not understand; he was connected there with a figure called Alcaeus, 'the strong one', but the Thebans made no special attempt to incorporate him in their other local myths, or to relate him to the descendants of the Sown Men. His worship, admittedly, was firmly established there, both as hero and later as god, but in the words of L. R. Farnell, 'The Theban devotion to Herakles seems to have been purely personal, unconnected with any history of tribal settlement. Nor does it appear that they worshipped him as ancestor . . .'[3]

Heracles showed from the beginning that extraordinary precocity that is a mark of divine children, and Pindar recounts an 'ancient story' whereby

the son of Zeus, with his twin brother, escaped the pangs of his mother's womb into the wonderful daylight. But he was seen by golden-throned Hera as he was wrapped in the saffron swaddling-bands, and the queen of the gods, pricked on with rage, despatched serpents without delay. When the doors were opened they entered the broad inner part of the chamber, eager to coil their swift jaws round the children; but Heracles lifted his head upright and made his first trial of battle, as with both irresistible hands he seized the two snakes by their necks; he strangled them, and in time they breathed out the life from their unspeakable limbs. (*Nemeans* 1, 35 ff.)

The hero quickly grows up, and his first feat is to kill a huge lion that roamed Mount Cithaeron near Thebes; he is the guest of King Thespius and sleeps with his fifty daughters on successive nights, or in some versions on the same night. Next he defeats King Erginus of Orchomenus and delivers Thebes from tribute. This reminds us of Theseus, but there is already a touch of typically Heraclean brutality, for he cuts off the noses and ears of Erginus' envoys, ties them round their necks and so sends them back to their king. Orchomenus and Thebes were often at loggerheads, and doubtless there is a historical reference in the tale, even if only a superficial one. Heracles is rewarded with the Theban king's daughter Megara; he has children by her but suddenly kills them in a fit of madness sent by Hera. According to some accounts this was why the hero was forced to subject himself to Eurystheus in Mycenae as some kind of expiation.

Eurystheus sends him on a sequence of quests, the Labours, that lasts for several years. Their order and number reflect a degree of logical arrangement by mythographers of the classical period. First come six tasks in the Peloponnese, mostly the disposal or capture of remarkable beasts. The second group of six lies outside the Peloponnese and indeed covers the known world; the first three take him south, north and east respectively, whereas he goes west in two of the last triad, which is strongly concerned with the underworld.

His first task was disposing of the lion of Nemea, a monstrous beast that did much damage close to Mycenae itself. It was literally invulnerable, so Heracles had to trap it in its cave and squeeze it to death. He managed to skin it by using its own claws (a folktale-type ingenuity motif, for nothing else could pierce it), and henceforth wore the skin, with its jaws over his head, in place of armour. It was on this occasion, too, that he cut and shaped the famous club, although club and skin do not seem to have become his regular equipment until the mid-sixth century B.C. Before that, both in vase paintings and in references in Hesiod and Homer (like the passage quoted on p. 178), he wears ordinary armour, if at all, and wields a bow.

The next Labour is to destroy the Hydra, a many-headed

water-snake that made life difficult around Lerna, an ancient settlement on the coast to the south of Mycenae. Hesiod's *Theogony* describes the Hydra as offspring of monstrous and snakeish parents, Typhon and Echidna (who also engender two other of Heracles' opponents, Geryon and Cerberus):

As her third offspring Echidna bore the evil-minded Hydra of Lerna, whom white-elbowed goddess Hera nurtured in her unceasing wrath against strong Heracles; and he, Zeus' and Amphitryon's son, slew it with cruel bronze in company with Iolaus beloved of Ares, through the counsels of Athena ... (313 ff.)

No club is used here; the 'cruel bronze' is the knife with which Heracles cut off the monster's heads – but they grew again twice as fast, and in the end he had to sear them with torches fetched from the forest by his nephew and helper Iolaus. That is not specified by Hesiod, nor is another detail that became traditional and was certainly known in Hesiod's time, for an engraved plate-fibula (a kind of decorative safety-pin) of the early seventh century B.C. clearly shows a large crab biting his foot – an interesting refinement, rather like Sciron's turtle, that takes us beyond the usual stereotypes and presupposes an individual and slightly bizarre invention.[4] Perhaps the crab is meant to emphasize Lerna's position in the marshy land near the sea. There are underground springs there, and this is one case where a rationalizing explanation suggested in antiquity might have some merit: that the Hydra's heads represented the springs that welled up all over the plain. Yet it is difficult to imagine them as especially menacing.

The next task is the routine capture of a huge boar on Mount Erymanthus in Arcadia; the quest, that is, now moves away from the immediate neighbourhood of Mycenae. Heracles drives the beast into a snowdrift and so catches it, then carries it on his shoulders and shows it to the terrified Eurystheus, who cowers in a great jar half-buried in the earth – a favourite scene with vase-painters, and perhaps another instance of the underground-chamber idea. The fourth task is another capture (rather than killing, as Euripides has it), this time of the Ceryneian hind, a marvellous beast with golden antlers. Heracles had to pursue it for a whole year, and according to Pindar went as far afield as the Hyperboreans in the mythical north to do so. In the end he tired it out back in Arcadia, and after some trouble with Artemis (to whom it was dedicated) was able to display it to Eurystheus and so proceed to his next task, the slaughter of the Stymphalian birds. They lived in a forest near lake Stymphalus, between Arcadia and Mycenae, and were a pest either because of their great number or through their possession of terrible metallic feathers and claws. Heracles drove them out of the woods with clappers and then shot them, according to most versions (that is, he is once again the archer rather than the club-wielder); but in one of the very earliest of probably mythical pictures, on a late-Geometric jug now in Copenhagen that was made and painted shortly before 700 B.C., a man is shown gripping one of a line of birds round the neck, and probably therefore strangling it.[5]

Finally in these Peloponnesian Labours, the hero has to clean out the vast cowsheds of King Augeias of Elis, which had become completely choked with dung. He did so, after being promised some of the cattle as reward, by diverting two neighbouring rivers through the buildings – a folktale ingenuity motif, but also a realistic reference to drainage-dykes, which in other parts of the Peloponnese were traditionally credited to him on account of his unusual strength. Augeias refused payment (just like King Laomedon of Troy on a subsequent occasion; it is another well-worn narrative motif), and Heracles returned later with an army and killed him for it. This particular Labour has some odd features, particularly that Heracles performs it for payment and not simply on command from Eurystheus. Apollodorus, probably following the fifth-century Pherecydes, accordingly removed it from the canon.

The next triad of Labours ranges from Crete through Thrace to the Black Sea, and is not on the face of it particularly ancient. Heracles was sent to capture the Cretan Bull; he duly did so, and brought it back to Eurystheus. Bulls were important creatures in Bronze Age Crete, but this one is too derivative in appearance to be plausibly Minoan. The Greek poets, even Euripides, ignored it (although his prose contemporary Acusilaus evidently mentioned it), but numerous vase paintings carry it back into the sixth century. Presumably someone like Peisandros of Rhodes had described the task in an epic poem; later the bull was identified as the one loved by Pasiphäe, or alternatively as the one that carried Europa to Crete in a version in which this bull was not Zeus himself. The hero's next opponents were more formidable, for they were the horses of the Thracian King Diomedes (not the Homeric hero of that name), and they lived on human flesh. Euripides duly mentions the episode, but without the picturesque detail, which may be a later invention, that Heracles fed their own master (or a groom, according to Pindar) to the horses, after which they became tamer and could be driven to Mycenae.[6] The tale was much embellished; in another version Heracles took a small army with him, and in a battle with the Thracians his favourite, Abderus, was killed and gave his name to Abdera, later the birthplace of Democritus the Atomist.[7] Pictorial representations are rare, but again they take the incident in its basic form back to the sixth century.

Last in this group comes the task known from literature as the Girdle of Hippolyte, the Amazon queen. Eurystheus' daughter had expressed a desire for it, but there is some doubt whether it was an article of clothing or a piece of armour (that is, a bronze waist-band). Euripides described it as 'preserved in Mycenae', and evidently an ancient piece of bronze armour was shown as this 'girdle' in the famous sanctuary of Hera (the Argive Heraion) not far away. At all events Heracles obtains the girdle. Literary accounts differ over whether or

not he kills the queen in doing so, but the archaic vase paintings, which are relatively numerous and carry the episode back
to the end of the seventh century at least, never show a girdle
of any kind and represent an all-out battle between male and
female warriors. They also tend to identify the queen as
Andromeda or Andromache, not Hippolyte. One picture of
a warrior fighting an Amazon, on a clay votive shield from
Tiryns, was painted as early as 700 B.C., but we cannot tell
whether it depicts Heracles and his Amazon queen or Achilles
and Penthesileia in a separate episode known to the Homeric
tradition.[8] Such specific encounters may not have been envisaged much earlier than that; but the idea of the Amazons
themselves – of a race of barbaric female warriors – fascinated
the Greeks and could be older, whether or not it embodies
an observation of matriarchal constitutions overseas.

Here the evidence of figure-representations becomes really
important, for they not only establish these three Labours as
older than the classical period, they also suggest that the tasks
were simple and unembellished: no girdle, no feeding of
Diomedes to his horses. That draws attention once again to
the high degree of mythical elaboration in the classical age; it
also renders these particular Labours relatively uninteresting as
evidence for Heracles as an older hero – or even, some might
say, in themselves.

The last three Labours are very different, for they take
Heracles to the western borders of the earth and down into the
underworld itself. First comes his task of bringing back the
cattle of the triple-bodied giant Geryon, also called Geryones
and Geryoneus. Geryon lived in the island named Erytheia,
'Red', beyond the river Okeanos; it was imagined as early as
the sixth century B.C. as lying off the Atlantic coast near
Cadiz. Hesiod briefly tells the tale:

Chrysaor sired three-headed Geryoneus by mingling with Calli-
rhoe daughter of famous Okeanos. Strong Heracles slew him close by
the shambling cattle, in sea-girt Erytheia, on the day when he drove

the broad-foreheaded cattle to holy Tiryns, after crossing the strait of Okeanos and killing Orthus and herdsman Eurytion in the windy stalls beyond famous Okeanos. (*Theogony*, 287 ff.)

Not great poetry, admittedly; Hesiod simply fills in the bare outlines without even mentioning that Orthus is Eurytion's dog. His audience must have known this already, and therefore the tale was traditional in the early seventh century. It was illustrated in the art of the latter part of that century, and copiously in the following two hundred years; fifth-century literature has many references to Geryon, and already in the late seventh century Stesichorus had devoted a long poem to the episode. It is the most fully attested of all the Labours.

Geryon's father was the giant Chrysaor who had sprung, with Pegasus, from the severed neck of the Gorgon Medusa. One would expect the son to be formidable, but Heracles disposes of him quite easily (whether with bow or with club), and also of his helpers, the hound and the herdsman. Late-archaic and classical versions concentrated rather on the difficulties of crossing Okeanos, and in particular of getting the cattle back, and on the journeys to and from the far west (Hesiod's apparent assumption that he returned in a single day being, perhaps, an accident of his formulaic language). Stesichorus told how Heracles used as his ferry-boat the floating cup in which the Sun returned each night from west to east round the stream of Okeanos; he was promised the loan of it when he threatened Helios with his arrows as he crossed the parched African desert. On the way he also destroyed sundry Libyan monsters and set up his Pillars at Gibraltar and Ceuta. Returning by a different route through Liguria (which is southern France), he killed brigands and then defeated the natives, after summoning from Zeus a shower of stones when he ran out of other missiles – apparently an aetiological tale connected with the rock-strewn *Plaine de la Crau*. From there he passed through Italy and Sicily, where he eliminated King Eryx, across to Greece, up to Thrace and back through Asia

Minor before presenting his diminished herd to Eurystheus at Mycenae. It was this adventure, more than any other, that enabled the western colonists to bring Heracles to their far-flung territories and so create their own local versions of his original monster-slaying feats in the Peloponnese.

Even more significant is the probability that Geryon was really a 'Herdsman of the Dead'. A clear indication is given in our ancient sources, for this is how Apollodorus (who seems to follow the fifth-century Pherecydes particularly closely for this Labour) describes Heracles' arrival:

> He reaches Erytheia and camps on Mount Abas; the dog sees him and rushes at him, but he smites him with the club, and also kills the herdsman Eurytion as he comes to the aid of his dog. Menoites, who was grazing Hades' cattle there, told Geryones what had happened; Geryones caught Heracles driving off the cattle by the river Anthemus, joined battle and was shot to death. Heracles put the cattle in the cup, sailed across to Tartessus and returned the cup to Helios. (II, 5, 10)

The significant detail is that *Hades'* cattle are kept nearby. Menoites seems to be a double of Geryon, or vice versa, and encourages us to draw the obvious comparison between the dog Orthus (or Orthrus as he is sometimes spelt) and Cerberus, the many-headed hound of Hades that Heracles brings up from the underworld in the next Labour. In fact Hesiod makes Orthus and Cerberus brothers, offspring, together with the Lernaean Hydra, of the ghastly snakeish couple Echidna and Typhon.[9] If so, Geryon belongs to the underworld in some form, and this adventure, like the Cerberus one, involves penetrating and in some sense conquering the world of the dead. The Dutch scholar J. H. Croon has shown Heracles to be especially associated with hot springs, which are found in various parts of the Mediterranean world and were connected not only with healing but also, because of their sulphurous vapours, with the underworld: they were entrances to the realm of the dead. Geryon, too, seems to have belonged originally to mainland Greece, quite probably to the hot-spring region of Thermopylae, and to have been progressively shifted westward with colonization.[10]

Here one of Heracles' other deeds is relevant, for in a list of his outrages against the gods Homer mentions that

Huge Hades, too, endured a swift arrow, when this same man, son of aegis-bearing Zeus, shot him in Pylos, among the corpses, and caused him great agony . . . (*Iliad* 5, 395 ff.)

'Pylos' must refer to one of the entrances to the underworld, literally its 'gate', rather than to Nestor's Mycenaean city of that name. The episode is further confirmation of an ancient tradition that one of Heracles' chief functions was to come into conflict with death; so is the incidental deed whereby he went down to Hades to rescue Alcestis (subject of Euripides' play of that title), who had reluctantly offered to die in place of her husband Admetus, a Thessalian king whose name, 'Unsubdued', has been rather improbably taken as a reference to Hades himself.

The eleventh Labour involves bringing up the monstrous dog Cerberus who guards the underworld against intruders and escapers. Once again the tale is definitely old. It is the subject of numerous vase paintings and several references in tragedy, as well as being alluded to in Hesiod (as we saw) and in the *Iliad*, where Athena complains that Zeus

does not remember that I often rescued his son when he was worn down by Eurystheus' tasks. He was always crying toward heaven, and Zeus sent me speeding down to help him. Had I known what I now know in my cunning heart, then Heracles would not have escaped from the steep streams of the waters of Styx, when Eurystheus despatched him to the house of gate-guarding Hades, to bring from Erebus the hound of hateful Hades. (8, 362 ff.)

With the help of Athena and Hermes, the god whose task it was to escort dead souls to the underworld, Heracles succeeded in his quest; he carried off the dangerous beast and showed it to Eurystheus, who cowered in his bronze jar and begged the hero to return the hound to its owner. While Heracles was below he incidentally released Theseus, trapped there with Peirithous in their foolish attempt on Persephone; he also encountered the shade of Meleagros and promised to marry his sister Deianeira, who was to be the unwitting instrument of his own death and apotheosis.

Finally comes the voyage to the Garden of the Hesperides, the nymphs whose name means 'western' (or 'of the evening star') and whose task was to look after the garden of the gods and the golden apples given by Gaia as a wedding present to Zeus and Hera. No literary reference to this Labour survives from before the classical period, and vase paintings take it back no earlier than the late sixth century B.C. It was represented, however, according to the traveller Pausanias, on two slightly earlier works of Peloponnesian art, the Amyclae throne and the chest of Cypselus (see p. 156). Moreover the fifth-century versions include the detail that Heracles sought the help of Atlas, whose task it was to support the sky on his shoulders, and this conception of Atlas goes back at least to Hesiod's *Theogony*. Yet we must reserve judgement on whether or not the Apples of the Hesperides are a very old element in the mythical history of Heracles. The classical versions differ (either he plucked the apples himself after killing the conventional dragon that guarded them, or he persuaded Atlas to do so while he himself supported the sky), and this could be used as evidence for either point of view. Whatever the date, there is a clear implication that this adventure, too, lies in the far west (one of the Hesperid nymphs is actually called Erytheia, the same name as Geryon's island, which probably refers to the colour of the sinking sun) and is connected with the idea of an afterlife. The golden apples may recall the golden blossoms that according to Pindar grew in the Isles of the Blest (see p. 133). Moreover, according to a fragment of Stesichorus' Geryon poem there was an island in the Atlantic, and therefore near Erytheia, called Sarpedon's Island, and we know from the *Iliad* that Sarpedon was a son of Zeus and was divinely carried after his death to Lycia. There he was embalmed, but it is a not implausible conjecture that in some versions he ended up in the Isles of the Blest.

The golden apples must once have had a significance more pointed than the one they retain in our slightly etiolated myth, where Eurystheus does not know what to do with them and simply hands them back to Heracles, who offers them to Athena. They may well have been envisaged as a 'food of life', or symbol of immortality or the renewal of youth (which is why they were so closely guarded by the gods); magical apples of this kind are known from the folklore of other nations. At the same time Heracles' acquiring them may be a comparatively recent development, like his connection with Atlas, and we should not count the tale as more than a slight reinforcement of his ancient role as Harrower of Hell.

Thus Heracles came at last to the end of his Labours and was free of his servitude to Eurystheus. The mythical tradition is far from clear about what he did next, for the 'incidental deeds' are performed in the course of the Labours themselves, and so are some of the Expeditions, for example that against Augeias of Elis for his refusal to pay the wage for clearing his cowsheds. According to Apollodorus, at least, the hero proceeded to marry off Megara (the wife whose children he had murdered in a fit of madness) to his nephew Iolaus; then he tried to win a new bride, Iole the daughter of King Eurytus of Oechalia. Eurytus liked arranging archery contests as a means of choosing a bridegroom, but took care to win them himself – much as Oenomaus had behaved, in order to keep his daughter Hippodameia. But Heracles, like Pelops, defeated the father; Eurytus none the less refused to hand over his daughter. Her brother Iphitus, by some accounts, had favoured Heracles, but when he visited Heracles in Tiryns the hero treacherously murdered him by throwing him from the walls.

Apollodorus says that this was in another fit of madness, but Homer in the *Odyssey* had done no such whitewashing and stated quite bluntly:

Heracles murdered him when Iphitus was a guest in his house – the act of a wicked man who had no regard for the disapproval of the gods or the hospitality he himself had set before him; but he slew him and kept the strong-hooved mares [which Iphitus had come to recover] in his own halls. (21, 27 ff.)

This is one of several indications that Homer drew on a source for Heracles that was thoroughly hostile to the hero, or at least did not try to disguise his destructive and anti-social side. At all events the killing of Iphitus made Heracles both ritually polluted and physically ill; he came to Delphi for advice from the oracle, which refused to give it, so the hero snatched up the oracular tripod and wrestled for it with the god Apollo himself. Zeus had to separate them, for they were both his sons, and the oracle consented to announce that the hero would have to sell himself as a slave for a year, or possibly three, to purge himself. He was bought by Queen Omphale, about whom more later; afterwards he returned to Oechalia, captured it and Princess Iole as well, and was on his way back with her to Trachis (where he was now living with his second wife, Deianeira, whom he had acquired in the interval) when Deianeira's fatal gift of the poisoned tunic reached him. The chronology and the wives have become a bit confused, but at least it is the knowledge that Heracles has a new woman, Iole, that causes Deianeira to send him the tunic and so bring an end to his career on earth.

That is the outline of Heracles' biography after the Labours: now to return to some of the more fascinating incidental deeds before elaborating the problems raised by his death. He deals with a whole assortment of monsters and malefactors apart from those already mentioned: for example, Cycnus, a son of Ares and brother of another victim, King Diomedes of Thrace; Busiris, an evil king of Egypt who sacrificed strangers (his name is historicizing and contains a reference to the god Osiris, although according to Herodotus the Egyptians had never engaged in human sacrifice); Antaeus, a giant who lived in Libya and was son of Earth, and could only be killed when Heracles lifted him clear of his parent and squeezed him to death, much as he had the Nemean lion; and Alcyoneus, another giant, who lived near the Isthmus of Corinth. In some accounts he helped the gods dispose of the whole race of giants in the so-called Gigantomachy, a favourite subject of monumental sculpture in the classical period. Indeed the tale is familiar as early as Hesiod, and so is the embellishment of the Prometheus story whereby it was Heracles who released him from the Caucasian rock (see p. 136 f.).

These encounters have their interest, but are not exactly novel in appearance. The contacts between Heracles and the Centaurs are in complete contrast, and form one of the oldest, most original and most important parts of the whole narrative complex. The Centaurs are firmly established in the mythical tradition by the time of Homer and Hesiod, our earliest literary sources, and they appear in Geometric art from 900 B.C. onwards. Homer refers more than once to the wise Centaur Cheiron (see p. 208), but describes the tribe as a whole as 'mountain-roaming beasts'.[11] We shall see later that this contrast between 'good' and 'bad', savage and civilized Centaurs is strongly emphasized in their contacts with Heracles.

First came his meeting with the Centaur named Pholus, who derived his name from Mount Pholoe on the western borders of Arcadia. Heracles stayed with him on his way to capture the Erymanthian Boar; Pholus, who was kind and hospitable, cooked a meal for him (although his own food is carefully specified by Apollodorus as raw), and was then persuaded to open a special jar of wine. Apparently it was the common property of all the Centaurs who lived on the mountain; anyway, they immediately scented it and came galloping up in fury. In the fight that followed Heracles routed them with burning embers and shot down some of them with arrows; the rest fled to Cape Malea in the far south of the Peloponnese. It was there that Cheiron now dwelt, because he had been driven from Mount Pelion in northern Greece after the disgraceful affair at Peirithous' wedding (see p. 154). It seems to be the rule that 'good' Centaurs suffer for the greed and lust of the rest. Heracles pursued them to Malea and there shot Cheiron by mistake; Pholus, too, died in an accident with one of the hero's (poisoned?) arrows back on Mount Pholoe. The others scattered once again, and some of them were mysteriously hidden under a mountain at Eleusis. There is an acropolis there, almost quarried out of existence in recent years, but it is hardly a mountain.

Eurytion, a Centaur who had already behaved abominably at the Lapith wedding, now managed to insinuate himself into the affections of a daughter of King Dexamenus ('Receiver' or 'Hospitable') back in Arcadia; Heracles disposed of him, and in some versions the girl is Deianeira herself. She at any rate is the innocent cause of the next incident, for the Centaur Nessus offered to ferry her across a river and tried to rape her in midstream; Heracles shot him, and the dying Nessus surreptitiously advised the girl to collect his blood and seed in a phial and use it if necessary as a love-philtre. This was the poison she later smeared on the fatal tunic.

That, in briefest outline, is the extent of the Centaur myths, together with the clash at the Lapith wedding and the whole conception of Cheiron as a wise and kindly healer and an educator of heroes in his cave on Mount Pelion. The closeness of their involvement with Heracles is very striking. Many of his actions are related to other mythical scenes, actions or characters, but the links are mostly superficial and could be due to the progressive organization of the whole tradition.

That is not so with the Centaurs, to whom I shall return later. There seems to be an early and integral connection to which even classical authors responded, so that it seemed natural for Euripides in *Heracles*, for example, to make his chorus refer extensively to the Centaurs in the course of a list of the hero's greatest deeds:

First he rid Zeus' glade of the lion, and skinning it he covered his blond head with the beast's terrible tawny jaws. At another time he brought down with his lethal bow the mountain-roaming race of wild Centaurs, and slew them with winged arrows. The fair-streamed river Peneius knows his presence . . . and so do the habitations of Pelion . . . (*Heracles* 359 ff.) [After further description of the Centaurs' haunts the chorus revert to the Labours proper.]

Two other of Heracles' actions are especially remarkable. The first is his foundation of the Olympic games from the spoils gained from King Augeias, described as follows by Pindar:

In Pisa the strong son of Zeus assembled his whole army and all the spoils, and measured out a holy precinct for his almighty father; he fenced round the Altis [that is, the sacred precinct at Olympia] . . . and after dividing out the fruits of victory, the gift of war, he made sacrifice, and established the four-yearly festival with the first Olympiad and its contests for victors. (*Olympians* 10, 43–6 and 55–9)

Elsewhere the poet tells how Heracles noticed that the site lacked shade, and brought back trees from the Hyperboreans to plant there. In all this he is seen in one of his regular if slightly paradoxical roles, as a culture-hero, the founder of rituals and cities and establisher of warm springs and shrines of healing.

The second notable episode is his servitude to Omphale, which results from the darker side of his character and his treacherous killing of Iphitus. Omphale seems to have been first envisaged as a queen of Epirus on the north-western borders of Greece, where there was a town of a similar name.

Later she was located in Thessaly, further east, and later still, but already by the time of Sophocles, in Lydia in Asia Minor. Perhaps she was carried across the Aegean by Greek colonists after the end of the Bronze Age; yet she remains rather a mysterious figure, one who makes no appearance in surviving art or literature before the fifth century B.C. The Hellenistic tradition, including Apollonius of Rhodes in his *Argonautica*, made her fall in love with her dashing servant (although Pindar tells us, rather surprisingly, that Heracles was quite a short man).[12] That is certainly a late embellishment; another detail known only from Hellenistic and Roman sources, that he exchanged roles with the queen, so that he wore her dresses and she dressed in the lion-skin and wielded the club, could well be earlier. It might be a learned deduction from the matriarchal and therefore in some ways mannish institutions with which the Lycians rather than the Lydians were credited, but it could also be a further development of the whole theme of servitude, an intentional and firmly established reversal of his primary role. Much the same motif underlies the whole plan of the Labours and his service to Eurystheus, and it seems to be characteristic of this man that from time to time he is placed in situations of inferiority and weakness, whereas on other occasions his strength gets the better of him and he goes berserk. At the same time transvestism is a familiar feature of 'rites of passage', in which the transition from one social status to a quite new one, for example from virgin to wife, is stressed by deliberate interruptions of the normal flow of events. Heracles' priest in Cos (with which the hero was associated as early as Homer) wore female garments for certain religious occasions; it would not be surprising if the transvestism with Omphale had a ritual reference also, and was not simply a scholarly elaboration. Achilles' disguise as a girl in Skyros and Pentheus dressing as a female bacchant to spy on the effeminate Dionysus may have similar implications.

While he was with Omphale Heracles came across two

arrogant characters called Syleus and Lityerses, in some respects variants of each other. Syleus seems to be of Thracian origin and has a famous vineyard; he intercepts passers-by and makes them labour there, and in the end, as often as not, he kills them. Heracles is put to work and responds by tearing up the vines and doing all kinds of damage. Lityerses is a famous harvester, and he too presses strangers into his service and ends by cutting off their heads and fixing them in the sheaves. Heracles turns the tables in a way that reminds us of Theseus with *his* brigands and bullies. But Lityerses has one special distinction, that he seems originally to have been not a man but a song: a harvest-song, in fact, of a kind known in Phrygia.

Later, Heracles encountered two originally Thessalian brothers known as the Cercopes, which means something like 'the long-tailed ones' and gave rise to the idea that they were turned into monkeys. Their habit was to attack travellers, steal their clothes and then kill them. They pounced on Heracles while he was sleeping, but he had the better of them and carried them off by slinging them head downward from a pole across his shoulders. From there they had a good view of his hairy rump, and remembered their mother's prediction that they would come to grief when they encountered Melampygos, 'Black-bottom'. But they made so many lewd jokes on the subject that Heracles burst out laughing and let them go. Obscenity, of course, was common ritual practice, useful for keeping away evil spirits or for promoting fertility. Iambe, one remembers, had made Demeter laugh when the goddess was mourning for Persephone, and she did so by telling jokes; that was part of the Eleusinian mysteries, and behind Iambe there probably lies Baubo who pulled up her skirts (see p. 267). So the Cercopes may not always have been figures of fun, nor Heracles' hairy bottom an unimportant detail, although he was of course sometimes treated, in the classical age and perhaps earlier, as a burlesque figure – as in Euripides' *Alcestis*, where he gets roaring drunk, and indeed in the same poet's lost satyr-play *Syleus*, based on the tale just described.

The servitude to Omphale resulted from his treacherous killing of Iphitus, and that was connected with his love for Iole which in turn led to his death. We should like to know more about this. Sophocles' *Trachiniae* gives a full version of the preceding events (also summarized by Bacchylides), but ends with Heracles being carried still living to his funeral pyre. There is no extended description of his assumption to heaven, even of the kind given for the miraculous disappearance and presumed transfiguration of Oedipus (but into a daemon and not a god) at the end of Sophocles' *Oedipus at Colonus*. This, in any event, is how Apollodorus summarizes his fate:

He came to Mount Oeta, which is in Trachis, and there made a pyre, mounted it, and told them to light it. No one was willing to do so until Poeas, who was passing by in search of his flocks, kindled it, and Heracles gave him his bow. It is said that while the pyre was burning a cloud enveloped him and with a clap of thunder conveyed him up to the sky. Then he won immortality, and being reconciled with Hera married her daughter Hebe . . . (II, 7, 7)

Poeas was father of Philoctetes, the Achaean prince abandoned in Lemnos on the way to Troy because of his festering snake-bite; according to other versions it was Philoctetes himself that lit the pyre and was rewarded with Heracles' famous bow, destined to be the instrument of Paris' death and Troy's downfall.

That the pyre was lit, whoever the precise agent, is an agreed part of the tradition. This may merely have been to make the scene more dramatic – one thinks of the drama of Croesus on his funeral pyre (see p. 173). But Heracles' un-bearable suffering is an important part of an even earlier tradition, for his flesh was burnt away by the corrosive con-coction derived from the Centaur Nessus, and that detail goes back at least into the seventh century and probably a good deal earlier. Burning is a traditional means of purification, one with which the Greeks had long been familiar, and it is a reasonable as well as a common conclusion that the mortal parts of Heracles' nature were consumed by fire so that the immortal part might be free to ascend to heaven.

It would be easy to construct a complicated and superficially attractive theory about Heracles' death, drawing out the possible significance of the Centaur's blood and semen, and opposing the purgation by fire to the hero's earlier involvement with water (Hydra, hot springs, Nessus and the river). That would be very much in the current fashion. It is not hard to build apparent systems out of the diverse materials and manifold variants of classical Greek myths, and Heracles provides more opportunities for this sort of thing than any other mythical figure. Yet one must resist such temptations, while at the same time trying to give proper emphasis to strands of meaning that do really seem to run through his mythical biography down to and including his death. In any event the first impression is of incoherence. The Labours form a roughly homogeneous group (although, as we saw, even they include distinct kinds of action), but how do they accord with the expeditions against Pylos or Sparta, the foundation of games and cults and the origin of curative springs? And why should Heracles so unpredictably kill his children, or his music-teacher Linus in a fit of uncontrollable rage? How does the long-suffering servant of Eurystheus accord with the impatient devourer of whole oxen, or the Prometheus-like benefactor of mankind with the lustful and treacherous enemy of Eurytus of Oechalia?

Part of the answer to these questions undoubtedly lies in the cumulative manner in which the Heracles cycle, and Greek heroic myths in general, must have been assembled, and in the scholarly and literate processes of organization to which they were progressively subjected. Yet some of the contradictory characteristics appear to go back as early in the tradition as we can trace it, even if others are due to the proliferation of local versions and the centripetal attraction of the greatest of the heroes for otherwise unattributed motifs and actions. The Italian scholar Angelo Brelich has noted that something of the same contradictory quality is to be found in most Greek heroes, who by their nature tread dangerously close to the border between human and divine.[13] Even a paradigm of wisdom and justice like King Aeacus of Aegina is found indulging in unseemly attacks on the ladies, in his case the sea-nymph Psamathe. Brelich also argues that all the major heroes have a wide range of activities extending from combat and monster-slaying to the foundation of oracles, cities, games and healing shrines, as well as to initiation rituals and the organization of life in city and state. Further common qualities are an association with mystery cults and with death and the propitiation of the dead. Yet it is doubtful whether all these properties belonged to each of the heroes as of right. *Of course* the heroes became associated with tribal institutions and the ritual life of the people. They were, after all, relics of a glamorous past, and in addition they had strong regional associations and heavily localized cults. As for mysteries and death, Heracles is said to have been initiated into the lesser Eleusinian mysteries before descending to Hades to bring back Cerberus, but that is probably an Eleusinian claim of no great age. Most of the heroes rather expectedly die remarkable deaths, usually violent ones, and continue to operate from beneath the earth as protective spirits or daemons. That provides a special association with death and the tomb, but it does not mean that many beyond Heracles were concerned with death as such or with trying to overcome it. As for the foundation of cities and games, the Greeks were determined that every institution should have its proper originator, a deeply mythical attitude in itself, and the heroes were again the obvious choice for the more universal institutions, at least those beneath the notice of the gods. Cults of healing tended to gain heroic connections for the same sort of reason, and also because the heroes turned into chthonic powers with the gift of life as well as death.

Perhaps this last statement reveals one of the more significant aspects of the contradictoriness of heroes; perhaps their duality depends as much on that of the earth itself, as both life-giver and death-receiver, as on the natural tendency to resort to the mighty as founders and initiators. For their cult after their demise is connected with the earth. With that in mind we can return to Heracles in particular. Curiously enough his varied life did not provide the plots of many tragedies (as distinct from satyr plays). Sophocles' *Women of Trachis* and Euripides' *Heracles* are those that survive, and significantly they deal respectively with his impending death and his madness. The Labours were perhaps too lacking in obviously profound content to be intensely dramatic, and Heracles won greater fame in the theatre as a burlesque figure, as lecher, drunkard and picaresque performer of great feats of strength, than as an august character deserving ultimate divinity. That is partly a question of fifth-century religious attitudes. Few people, in any case, at least in the larger cities, would be likely to regard him as anything like the equal of Apollo or even Dionysus. Making a man into a god was a difficult business, as the Romans found when they tried to deify their emperors. Finding an underlying harmony in Heracles is something the ancients did not succeed in doing, and perhaps were not much interested in; his cults, after all, depended on special local aspects and functions, rather like those of a Roman Catholic saint. Yet it may be worth looking for such a unity from our remoter position, which for all its disadvantages still affords a certain objectivity.

These are the striking aspects of his mythical doings: his killing and capture of monsters and malefactors; his wanderings far and wide; his interludes of madness and slavery; his bestial aspects on the one hand, his cultured ones on the other; and his encounters with death and the underworld. The first of them, disposal of monsters and so on, is a typically heroic activity that has its roots as much in folktale as in the faint memory of legendary kings and warriors. It seems that any hero associated with a really remarkable feat, like Theseus and the elimination of the Minotaur, or Bellerophon and the impious flight on Pegasus, had also to be equipped with a set, three at least, of suitably horrible and anti-social routine victims. Heracles demonstrated his pre-eminence by having an unusual number of them, centred upon the Labours. Some, as we saw, probably reflect memories of political dispositions in the Peloponnese, others overlap the association with death. Yet it seems doubtful whether tests and quests as such reveal Heracles' individual essence. He is usually interpreted as a culture hero who makes the earth habitable by men, a type familiar from African and Amerindian myths. Yet no specific evidence for this survives, and the choice of Labours does not really support the interpretation. Some of the Peloponnesian monsters (the Lion, the Hydra and the Birds) are envisaged as causing destruction in their immediate region, and that is a typical function for such creatures; the Calydonian Boar hunted down by Meleagros in Aetolia and the Chimaera that was Bellerophon's monstrous victim had the same local and anti-social properties. Other Labours, however, such as cleansing the cowsheds, fetching the Amazon's girdle, or all three western adventures, are not of this type. They do not involve purging the earth of its primitive dangers and making it fit to live in. The classical age envisaged Heracles as giant-slayer *par excellence*, and it was he who helped the gods dispose of the whole race of giants in the Gigantomachy, but this conception of him as a bulwark against barbarism does not seem particularly old. Other aspects of the Labours and incidental deeds are similarly uninformative on this point. Moreover their far-flung quality reflects two specific practical preoccupations – with exotic geography for its own sake and with the need to establish cultural and ritual links between distant colonies and the motherland – rather than anything unique in the hero himself. To discover his underlying essence we shall have to look at other of his special qualities.

The slavery motif has already been discussed, and is uncommon among the heroic myths at large, although Apollo himself once had to do a year of service to Admetus. It reinforces the paradoxical side of Heracles and is no mere incidental detail, for it underlies the whole scheme of the Labours. It is connected, as I believe, with his fits of madness. Again, this is not a unique motif (for instance Athamas kills one of his children in a fit of madness, also heaven-sent, and the general murder-of-children motif recurs with Atreus and others), yet its reduplication in Heracles' case (Linus, as well as his children by Megara) suggests it as an essential part of his character. I am still assuming that his kind of madness is an extension of sheer rage and brute strength; the attack on Linus is certainly that, rather than pure insanity. The alternative is that the madness does not arise out of his character as a whole, but is completely extraneous. In the case of the attack on his children it is, after all, sent by his enemy Hera, and might be regarded simply as a more drastic form of the Infatuation that according to the *Iliad* is so frequently sent by gods upon men. Yet the borderline between the martial inspiration the Greeks called *menos* ('might', in its conventional translation) and going beserk is not a sharp one, and Heracles' madness could be the occasional and extreme result of a supernatural strength and vitality that were always potentially dangerous. Ajax and Achilles exemplify the same trait. If so – and I myself think this a quite probable explanation – then here is a further connection with the bestial side of Heracles, of which brute strength is one obvious component. Admittedly we should be cautious about treating him as a real person whose character is an amalgam of psychologically compatible trends. He is, of course, a largely fictitious creation, and certain parts of him, like the inclination to found cults and games, quite certainly reflect the institutional needs of widely scattered communities rather than the plausible nuances of an individual psyche. Yet the arbitrary quality cannot be absolute, and there must be a specific and significant nucleus to which the more random properties can attach themselves.

This nucleus may exist in a general polarity between Nature and Culture. The hero's civilized actions, which from now on I consider under the heading of 'Culture', have been summarized already and include the founding of the Olympic games and presiding over initiation-rituals. His bestial or barbaric actions will be considered under the heading 'Nature', implying the untrammelled working of 'the world of nature' as opposed to human law and convention. Animals live according to Nature, and it is startling to observe how many animal aspects there are to Heracles: his hairiness, which so much amused the Cercopes, his clothing of lion-skin, the head of which covered his own head and made him resemble a rampant lion, his club hacked out of a tree instead of being artificially made like a spear or arrows. Admittedly club and skin are not shown in the earliest representations, but that may be a question of artistic habit rather than a sign of late invention. A possible parallel is provided by the Akkadian Epic of Gilgamesh, where Gilgamesh himself seems to represent Culture in contrast with Nature in the form of his friend Enkidu (who was not only brought up among the animals but is covered with hair until weakened by luxury and the decadence of city life); although Enkidu soon moves across to Culture, and suffers a lingering death for it. Gilgamesh in desperate fear rushes into the desert and abandons his clothes for skins; he seems to be trying to defeat death by rejecting Culture and returning to Nature, but that of course is an idle hope.

Another part of Heracles' 'natural' behaviour is his freedom over love, food and wine: the normal social restraints are not for him. His prodigious strength marks him as superhuman, lion rather than man, and the fits of rage and madness are bestial rather than human. Incidentally they recall Cleomedes of Astypalaea, the 'last of the heroes' (see p. 174), who went mad through frustration and pulled down a whole building like Samson – but on a group of children. There are occasional signs, too, that Heracles may once have possessed trickster-like qualities; for instance he deceives Atlas by a trick into taking back the burden of the sky. Many of his folktale-type feats inevitably contain elements of ingenuity, but the question is whether he goes beyond that and in the direction of the cunning Odysseus; for Odysseus, too, has some of Heracles' contradictory quality and also, incidentally, becomes involved with the Cyclopes, another kind of creature halfway between Nature and Culture. It is difficult, perhaps, to separate the picaresque hero, the good-hearted but rather violent simpleton who gratifies the peasant's taste for rustic success and humour, from the more subtle figure that might emerge from a preoccupation with contradictions between Nature and Culture. Heracles probably has something of both. But the chief reason for not considering his character as the product of chance or naïveté is that remarkable affinity of his to the Centaurs, whose friend and enemy he is in the myths that so often bring them together.

The polarity of Nature and Culture formulated by the Greek Sophists under the heading of *physis* and *nomos*, nature and law or custom, and given modern currency by Rousseau and more recently by Lévi-Strauss, was embodied in a concrete fashion by the Centaurs. Their human torsos and equine quarters symbolize their ambivalence and emphasize a possible association between cerebral and human, animal and sexual. Most of them fall firmly on the animal side of the fence, and the mythical imagination evidently preferred to express their ambiguity by separating Cheiron, and to an extent Pholus, as particularly humane in contrast with the rest rather than by exploring tensions within a single character.

The opposition between the restrained and civilized Cheiron and the brutish behaviour of the Centaurs as a whole has struck many students of myths, and various ingenious and unconvincing attempts have been made to explain it. In the background, no doubt, lies a general feeling about Nature itself that we all share: that it can be either hostile and repellent, or sympathetic, uncomplicated and desirable. The combination of horse with man to represent that feeling is no less understandable. The horse was a relatively recent arrival in Greece, being introduced from Asia Minor to draw chariots around 1700 B.C., and could still be regarded as in some way strange and monstrous as late as the seventh century, when a Theban vase-painter drew the Gorgon Medusa with a horse's body. At the same time horses could appear wise, tame and friendly. But that does not altogether explain the role that Cheiron achieved as the greatest educator of his day, the teacher of all the arts both liberal and military, to whom heroes like Jason, Asclepius, Aristaeus, Achilles and even, in some sources, Heracles himself were sent for instruction.

There was a story that Cheiron saved Achilles' father Peleus from being murdered by the other Centaurs when stranded on Mount Pelion by a lethal plot of King Acastus. That typifies the tension between Cheiron and the rest; yet it was still to him, now a refugee at Malea, that the survivors from Mount Pholoe fled. Pholoe was the scene of another paradigmatic confrontation between Nature and Culture, with Pholus representing hospitality and Culture (although Apollodorus, as we saw, carefully specifies that he ate his meat raw, something incidentally that horses would find especially repellent), and the other Centaurs as superficially civilized wine-drinkers sent berserk by the mere smell of wine and the thought of their liquor being illegally expended on a stranger. This was a repudiation of the laws of hospitality on which civilized Greeks prided themselves, and their running wild was similar to what happened as a result of too much champagne at the Lapith wedding. There it was Theseus, in so many respects a pale imitation of Heracles, who chastised them. On Mount Pholoe, fortunately, there were no women, but once again the Centaurs were slaughtered by a hero, this time Heracles himself. He has, as we have seen, more than a few of their own qualities, lechery and hairiness and love of drink – even the possession of a club, since great tree-branches were the Centaurs' traditional weapon. It was with those that they beat the Lapith hero Caeneus into the ground, Caeneus who had been made invulnerable by Poseidon and therefore had to be eliminated in that unusual manner. Incidentally he was a complex figure with possibly phallic connotations – he set up his spear as an object of worship – and a sex-change history that might conceivably bear some relation to Heracles in his transvestite role.

The Centaurs, then, serve to reinforce the feeling that Heracles' apparently contradictory attitudes to Nature and Culture are no mere accident, but rather reflect a continuing preoccupation among those that developed the myths in their formative stages. Lévi-Strauss's studies of the Amerindian myths of Paraguay and Brazil have proved (and this, I think, is indisputable) that the apparent contradiction between the laws of the jungle and those of the village, between the complex regularities of the natural world and the artificial rules imposed by men, between the freedom of animals and the constraints of society can form a major concern of myth-forming societies in their pre-literate phases. The preoccupation is revived in our own 'environmental' myths and has never completely disappeared. There is nothing preposterous, then, in the idea that this was an underlying concern in certain Greek myths also.

It might be pressing the polar analysis too far to claim that Heracles' special connections with death are the antithesis to his exceptional vitality, the force that sometimes boils over into madness. The death aspect is the last of the special qualities in which we hoped to find the key to his evident mythical power, but we should be careful not to be carried away at this point. What, after all, do the western adventures amount to? Do they necessarily make him an enemy of death? And if so, does he fight death on behalf of mankind? The answer to the last two questions is probably no. Admittedly he killed Geryon who seems to be a servant of Hades, but Cerberus was simply displayed at Mycenae and then returned to the underworld, and there is no implication in the versions of this Labour that King Hades himself was particularly incommoded. Indeed Heracles had struck a kind of bargain with him, just as he did with both Hades and Persephone over the release of Theseus. Moreover the quest for the Apples, even if they were properly speaking the food of immortality and corresponded with the Mesopotamian Food of Life, does not necessarily imply the conquest of death on behalf of men. At most it may be a relic of a tale about a particular semi-divine creature who, like Gilgamesh, sought immortality for himself and then as second-best turned aside to seek an elixir of youth. Heracles did, after all, marry Hebe whose name means 'Youth'. There is no implication in these themes that he was acting on behalf of men in general, like Prometheus, nor does this emerge from the rescue of Alcestis, who should never have gone below in the first place. The possibility must be borne in mind that the adventures in or near the underworld owe part of their development to the fact that this was the most terrible kind of test a hero could undergo. At the same time most other heroes, even great ones, are not subjected to it. It seems that there is something special about Heracles that makes such experiences appropriate to him in particular.

He does, after all, bring death in manifold forms to others. In that he is not unique, but the killing of his own children through inexplicable madness shows that his quality of excess spills over into lethal forms as well as into vitality and life.

He is superhuman, but still, until the gods decide otherwise, all too mortal. And then his own death by burning, followed by resurrection and glory, must have some bearing on the situation. His pyre was built on the summit of Mount Oeta, and there was understandable excitement some fifty years ago when the remains of a heap of ashes were excavated there, to reveal that small human figurines had regularly been cast into bonfires from as early as the seventh century B.C.[14] It was easy to explain this as a kind of new-fire rite, a widely diffused European folk ritual whereby bonfires are lit at crucial times of the seasonal year to renew the forces of Nature and in particular of the sun. If that were so, then the myth of Heracles' death in that particular spot might be an aetiological tale designed to explain the practice of casting effigies into the flames. Martin Nilsson and others accepted this explanation, which could indeed be relevant to the association of Heracles with Oeta, but I doubt whether the whole idea of his self-cremation can be so easily accounted for.

There is so much more to mark his death as a culmination of power and violence, quite apart from its implications of purification and sacrifice. It results directly from one of his many adulterous adventures and the capture of Iole by force; indirectly it is the result of his conflict with the Centaurs (so close to him in many ways) and Nessus' attempted rape of Deianeira. Classical sources saw a connection of an almost proto-Christian kind between Heracles' life of labour and his eventual divinization, and when he appears as a god at the end of Sophocles' *Philoctetes* he himself is made to refer to

> my own fortunes,
> all those labours that I toiled over and won through
> to gain glory and immortality, as you can see.
>
> (1418–20)

That is a sophisticated nuance, but nevertheless an implied connection does exist between his remarkable and often violent life, his unusual and violent death, and his ultimate condition of divine bliss.

There is, no doubt, much of the folktale hero in Heracles, and much too that is fortuitous and derivative. Yet the central themes of contradiction – of madness and slavery, Nature and Culture, and the testing of the boundaries between life and death – single him out as a truly mythical being in the profounder sense, as one whose actions both express and determine men's attitudes to the central parts of their experience. The short chapter that follows relates these conclusions to the problem of heroic myths in general, and in particular to their probable modes of origin.

# CHAPTER 9

# THE DEVELOPMENT OF THE HERO-MYTH

THE Heracles myths have vastly extended our idea of the heroic tale. Some of them, naturally, are derivative and were accreted to the cycle relatively late. Others were attracted to Heracles from lesser figures. Yet the whole collection amounts to a significant whole, in which the hero's characteristics, even if sometimes contradictory, seem to reflect a persisting intention. In this respect he is a true counterpart of the Akkadian Gilgamesh, for in the Epic of Gilgamesh originally independent tales, some of them Sumerian, came together to form an essentially new myth in which the valuation of life and death emerges as the dominant theme through the interplay between Enkidu and Gilgamesh.[1]

These instances indicate, even more clearly than before, that heroic myths can achieve a structural unity by means of very disparate materials. *Folktale motifs* are always important, and some of the main heroic actions, tests and quests most conspicuously, are of strongly folktale character. *History* provides a separate constituent, even in myths that are not so obviously historicizing as to deserve the special title of legends. It is reflected either in implied relationships (of Mycenae and Tiryns, Athens and Crete, the southern and northern axes of Mycenaean Greece) or in more obvious charter functions, for example Theseus killing the Marathonian Bull and unifying Attica. *Cults and rituals*, too, play their part, and the next chapter will consider them in more general terms. For the moment it is enough to concede that the tomb of Ariadne in Naxos or the supposed pyre of Heracles on Oeta were factors in shaping their particular myths, just as a desire to reproduce mainland hero cults ensured the extension of heroic adventures to colonial lands. Other components are *speculative* in kind and intention: infringements of heaven and hell, explorations of Nature and Culture, mediations of recurrent human dilemmas. Along with these under the too-general heading of *aetiology* come more concrete and sometimes trivial explanations of place-names and specific customs. *Deliberate organizing* plays a special role, since it results in the introduction of subsidiary motifs from different myths, in the rationalizing as well as the extension of personal and regional relationships and in the suppression of odd and possibly important details. Such influences and tendencies are particularly marked in the literate era, but I feel relatively sure that they began in a smaller way long before the diffusion of the alphabet in Greece from the ninth to the seventh century B.C. Finally *wish-fulfilment* and other emotional factors affect the formation of a complex myth, not only by the imposition of simple folktale patterns but also in less obvious ways.

The heroic myths are manifold in their constituents and enormously rich in range and variety – on one level, at least. They are wide-ranging and various in their attachment to different cities and regions of the Greek world, in their complex cast of characters and the care with which it is deployed, in their incidental use of gods and goddesses. Yet they are surprisingly narrow, when one comes to think about it, in range of narrative theme. Similar ideas are employed over and over again in relation to different *personae* and in different regional contexts. The use of tricks to surmount difficulties; transformations of physical shape; fulfilment of a task or quest, often involving a giant or monster; accidentally killing a friend or relative; attempting to dispose of an enemy by setting him an apparently impossible task; winning a contest for a bride; being punished in various dramatic ways for impiety; killing one's own child for various reasons; displacing a parent or an old king; taking revenge by seducing a wife or killing children; defending one's mother against an oppressor; circumventing the wiles of a lecherous or an ambitious woman; founding a city or an institution; making use of special weapons to overcome seemingly impossible odds; journeying to the underworld or trying to overcome death; falling in love with a god or goddess – these and a very few others, together with the basic narrative motifs of prophecy and cursing, cover most of the action of most known heroic myths. It is true that variant mixtures of these elements can produce narratives surprisingly distinct in feeling and effect, and that *all* kinds of narrative can be reduced to a relatively small number of basic situations. Yet Greek heroic myths remain exceptionally repetitive in thematic terms, and the divine myths little less so.

The ultimate standard of comparison must be other sets of myths from other periods and places. Mesopotamian myths, for example, mainly concern the gods, so mortal themes like killing a relative by mistake do not appear; they also have their own special *schemata* and repetitions. Nevertheless, considering the small number that survive, they display a relatively wider variety of theme and incident and a freer range of fantasy and imagination. The point can hardly be emphasized too often: Greek myths are limited in fantasy (apart from a few conspicuous exceptions like the Labyrinth tale), and that is the probable result of progressive organization and rationalizing both within the literate era and before it. Heroic myths are less fantastic, for obvious reasons, than divine ones, again with a few conspicuous exceptions. Greece is almost unique in its proliferation of heroic myths as distinct from divine or heavily supernatural ones. No other ancient culture is similar, and the best parallel is the heroic world of Nordic myths and sagas. That Greece went through a 'Heroic Age' in the Mycenaean period – an age of military and baronial values, of the elevation of honour in its most material form to be the ideal of manhood – is the most obvious explanation, and establishes an immediate parallel with the Viking age. Yet there were other reasons too. It is probable, for example, that certain charter-type activities were progressively detached from high gods and given to daemons and heroes; and that folktale-type actions, also, were often found more suitable to the latter. At all events the results were scarcely conducive to the more inspired forms of imagination.

That still leaves the question of why heroes became established in the first place. Some tales, at least, were likely to attach themselves to historical persons, either great kings and generals or men involved in exceptional adventures. The Egyptian tales of Sinuhe or Wen-Amon are instances, and so are some of the Sumerian short tales about Gilgamesh. Yet it is difficult to pick out any particular Greek hero as being of this kind – except, probably, for 'younger' heroes of legendary myth such as Agamemnon of Mycenae. Even Theseus, despite his sometimes historicizing actions, may be a fiction; his name means something like 'Establisher' and is almost too functionally good to be true. One presumes nevertheless that many of the Greek heroes must once have been men, or at least composed out of reminiscences of actual individuals. It used to be believed, on the contrary, that they were 'faded gods', and that this is why they are so close to the Olympians, often their blood relatives, in surviving myths. A few heroes or heroines (Helen and Semele, for instance) might be of this kind, but the details of individual hero cults preclude it as a general rule. What these cults – the acts of worship and sacrifice carried out at their supposed tombs right down to classical times – emphasize is that the heroes continue their existence under the earth, not down in Hades, like ordinary mortals, but just beneath the life-giving soil itself. Are they, then, kinds of 'chthonic' daemon or minor god, in contradistinction to the Olympian gods who dwell in the sky? A few of them may be, like Trophonius who after his death operated an underground oracle in Boeotia, but most, like Perseus, Pelops, Jason,

Oedipus, or Heracles himself, are surely not, and abstract ancestor figures like Aeolus and Danaus even less so. They may have become chthonic powers, as Hesiod implies in some cases; if so, that was the result of the worship at tombs rather than their original nature.

Martin Nilsson was inclined to believe that tomb-cults were the crucial factor, and that it was specifically Mycenaean tombs that were important.[2] The Greeks of the Late Bronze Age tended to build conspicuous repositories for their dead kings and noblemen. The huge bee-hive tomb known as the 'Treasury of Atreus' at Mycenae is the most imposing example of all, but apart from these large *tholos* tombs there are scores of well-built chamber-tombs scattered round the Mycenaean world and especially the Peloponnese.[3] One of their most significant characteristics is that they were mainly but not completely underground. A revealing mound often surmounted the roof, and a passage-way, filled in after each burial and cleared for the next, ran down to the door of the chamber. They were conspicuous antiquities, therefore, known to be the tombs of great men and their descendants. Offerings were made at them during the Bronze Age itself, and pottery excavated in and around the passage-ways reveals that occasionally the practice continued into the early Iron Age. Yet by this time the cult can hardly have been a family affair, in most cases at least. Presumably the great dead were now regarded as something other than mere ancestors. They had become heroes, powerful spirits remembered to be associated with the glorious age that vanished in the cataclysms of 1200 to 1000 B.C. That age had seen the wars against Thebes and Troy and the first large-scale exploration of the Black Sea. Some of its deeds would still be familiar through informal story-telling – even, perhaps, through poems that were ancestors of the *Iliad* and *Odyssey*. The protagonists of such tales would almost inevitably be connected with these revered but largely unknown occupants of the tombs – would be credited with almost superhuman powers and sometimes even related to the Olympian gods themselves. And yet they had, after all, died, and so in a way were still men. They were heroes; they had elements of both human and divine.

This Nilssonian approach has much to be said for it. Yet I also suspect that many of the themes of myths, if not the exact divine or human status of their participants, had developed long before the early Iron Age or indeed the Mycenaean Age itself. If that suspicion turns out to be well-founded, it represents a crucial qualification, for it allows the possibility of a period almost totally unknown to us during which myths were substantially different from their later forms, and in which their social and speculative functions could have shown up far more plainly than they do now. That would have the advantage of bringing Greek myths, or at least their proto-types, more closely into line with the myths of most other societies that have not passed through a long period of literacy. Nothing is known, or at present can be, that proves this to be so, but on the other hand nothing disproves the possibility.

It is generally believed that Nilsson, in *The Mycenaean Origin of Greek Mythology* of 1932, demonstrated this very fact of 'Mycenaean origin'. Actually he did not do quite that. What he proved, by one of those simple but compelling observations that are so tantalizingly rare in scholarship, is that most Greek myths go back *at least* to the Mycenaean Age, because they are essentially related to cities and power groupings that were important in the Late Bronze Age but at no later period. But supposing some of the myths were actually *pre*-Mycenaean: they would still, surely, have been adjusted to the social and political conditions of the highly organized Mycenaean epoch. Nilsson was well aware of the folktale-motifs so liberally strewn around the heroic myths; these of course are plausibly pre-Mycenaean, but the significant point is that the process of combining them with other elements to make the myths as we know them had probably begun, and advanced some way, long before the acme of Achaean civilization in the fourteenth and thirteenth centuries B.C., or even before the sixteenth century when Mycenae itself first became an imperial power. There were, naturally, specifically Mycenaean elements too: the Labyrinth theme, if it was really a memory of Athenian subservience to Knossos; Theseus' unification of Attica; the tale of the Danaïds pursued by their Egyptian cousins, or of Io and Belos, if those tales reflect (as they seem to) contacts between Greece and Egypt towards the end of the Bronze Age. The historicizing components can be dimly and erratically discerned; others, for example speculative or cultic elements, usually cannot. Even so, the *pre*-Mycenaean origin of much Greek mythology remains highly probable, in my eyes at least.

The Greek hero myths add further support to some general conclusions that are plainly emerging: that myths are extremely complex entities; that they do not necessarily originate in one specific period; that their development is gradual and to a large extent unpredictable; and that their central figures are woven out of several different strands, narrative, historical, social and religious, among others. The last of these, the religious aspect of myths, brings us back to the relationship between myths and rituals.

# PART III

\*

# INFLUENCES AND TRANSFORMATIONS

# CHAPTER 10

# MYTHS AND RITUALS

THE persistence of cults of the dead at originally Bronze-age tombs is one important element in the development of the idea of heroes; so much was concluded in the last chapter. How far does that strengthen the case of those who assert that there must always be a close connection between rites and myths? It is time to return to this topic, now that the different types of Greek myths have been surveyed; and the immediate answer must be that simple tomb rituals may generate *heroes*, but they do not thereby generate heroic (or any other) *myths* – or they do so only in an indirect and unimportant way. Closer examination of the myths has confirmed that they grow out of all sorts of interest and situation, religion and ritual included; but to make those the primary or unique source seems no more attractive than before. Once it is firmly established that many of the heroic tales are real myths that cannot be shoved aside as 'saga' or 'oral literature', then it becomes plainer than ever that the universal myth-and-ritual theory is false.

The heroic myths, in particular, offer hundreds of instances for which no ritual precedent is known or plausible. It may be permissible to argue that heroic myths are in some restricted sense 'sacred', either because in an earlier form they were part of the solemn structure of communal life or because they include secondary references to divine beings. Yet it remains quite difficult to identify or even conceive of *rituals*, sacred or otherwise, that might give rise to myths like that of Cadmus and the Sown Men, Oedipus and Iocaste, Bellerophon and Pegasus, Perseus and Andromeda, Heracles in countless of his activities, or the Lapiths and Centaurs. Admittedly one has to be careful in making such lists of counter-instances, since there are certain heroic themes (including Theseus in the Labyrinth, Perseus and Medusa, Heracles' killing of his children, Ino's parching of the seed-corn) that might just conceivably have had a ritual origin, even though no sign of ritual survives. Escaping from a maze *might* be an initiation-test, decapitating an ugly creature in effigy *might* be ritual magic to end winter or drive off pest and disease. I have also avoided predominantly folktale-type myths, as well as 'younger' and more legendary tales that lack the profounder qualities of many acknowledged myths. Yet the final result is unaffected: several Greek heroic myths have some kind of ritual association, but many more do not. Therefore the universal theory is wrong.

The divine myths, as opposed to those about heroes, could not alter this conclusion even if they all appeared to be based on rituals; in fact, of course, that is not the case. Out of the relatively small range of separate narrative acts attributed to gods only a few are plausibly ritual in origin or colouring. Neither the means by which Zeus came to power, nor the transformations he undergoes to win mortal mistresses, nor his other acts of revenge or governance, are concerned with rituals either actual or potential. Apollo's birth in Delos is a little different. It is presumably related to some kind of early cult there, but which came first, the cult or the assumption of Apollo's birth, is uncertain. His defeat of the dragon Python at Delphi might reflect the imposition of a new kind of worship on an older and cruder cult, but that is a historical rather than a ritual precedent, and in any case the details of the encounter do not appear to be determined by ritual features. His vengeance, with Artemis, on Niobe (who boasted that she had surpassed Leto as a mother) or Tityus (who tried to rape Leto) is obviously independent of ritual; so are his affairs with Cyrene and Coronis, or his punishment of the Cyclopes for supplying the thunderbolt that destroyed Asclepius, his son by Coronis. Poseidon's part in building the walls of Troy, or his sending of a sea-monster to punish Laomedon, are neither based on nor celebrated in ritual; neither is his marriage to Amphitrite or, apparently, his contest with Athena for the possession of Athens. On the other hand he is also father of Arion, the marvellous horse that rescued king Adrastus from Thebes after the attack by the Seven; this recalls his earlier association with horses, perhaps even an equine shape of his own. That idea is preserved in cult, for Arion is offspring of Poseidon and Demeter together, and at Thelpousa in Arcadia they were worshipped as Hippios and Hippia ('Horsey') and had horses' heads.[1] The local tale was that Demeter turned into a mare to avoid Poseidon's attentions, and he into a stallion to further them: a common motif, familiar from Zeus' amatory disguises, but given a special slant by the local cult and the ancient religion.

Some divine myths, then, are rooted in cult and ritual, but many others are not. One might, of course, claim that all such myths depend on the very concept of gods, and that this was associated from the beginning with acts of worship presumably ritualistic in some sense. But that is not what the proponents of the myth-and-ritual theory mean. They mean that the detailed elements of mythical narratives about the gods are developed primarily as explanations of obscure ritual actions, or at the very least that myths and rituals are parallel phenomena, products of the same psychic forces and always interrelated.

The truth is, of course, that religious acts and beliefs, and the traditional tales we call myths, *are* quite often related and do to an extent overlap, but that they quite often do not. We need not therefore accept theories like that of the anthropologist Clyde Kluckhohn that myth and ritual are 'symbolic processes for dealing with the same type of situation in the same affective mode', in which the one is a 'system of word symbols', the other 'a system of object and act symbols'; although that is a moderate view when compared with functionalist statements like that of E. R. Leach that 'myth implies ritual, ritual implies myth, they are one and the same.'[2] We do not even have to follow Joseph Fontenrose (who has himself done much to destroy the extreme position adopted from Robertson Smith by Frazer and his followers) when he argues that the name 'myth' should be applied only to 'traditional tales of the deeds of daimones'.[3] Traditional tales, yes; but *daimones*? Admittedly Hesiod, in his Myth of the Five Races (pp. 132, 273), held that the men of the golden and silver races turned into daemons after their death; admittedly the worship at the tombs of heroes tended to treat them as daemons – that is, as spirits that could hurt or help the living. Yet in the myths themselves we see that heroes, and sometimes even gods, are viewed for the most part as ordinary beings. It is the situations in which they become involved, rather than the fact that they themselves can be called in some sense daemonic or supernatural, that give their actions a mysterious power and meaning.

In short the myths, both divine and heroic, are indeed supernatural in places, and that is important; yet many of their details and functions are unaffected by this, and that is important too. For alongside the stream of religious imagination there runs a stream of purely narrative invention that can sometimes be identified with folktale but is really much broader. I remind the reader of the discussion of 'traditional tales' in the first chapter, where it was shown that they often reflect the interests and preoccupations of the people quite independently of polytheism and the practice of religion.

The matter should not be left there. One needs to survey the rituals, too, in order to be persuaded that many of them did not give rise to myths, or at least to early and important ones. It is a difficult undertaking, since the scope of Greek rituals is so extensive. Only a highly selective and summary treatment can be attempted; yet it is worth doing, if only because there is an important area in which myths and rituals do overlap, and because rituals, like myths, were a vital and revealing part of Greek life.

Walter Burkert, professor of Greek at Zürich, has recently published a fascinating book called *Homo Necans* ('slaughtering man' as opposed to *homo sapiens* or 'thinking man') in which he relates the Greek obsession with animal sacrifice – *that* kind of ritual – to biological urges in the direction of aggression (of the sort studied in animals by Konrad Lorenz) and to the relentless but sometimes almost apologetic attitudes of primitive hunters to their prey.[4] It is true that we cannot begin to understand the culture and literature of ancient Greece if we overlook the ubiquitous altars reeking with fresh blood, the constant throat-slitting of bulls, cows, sheep, goats, pigs, and occasionally dogs. Greek cities had no abattoirs; the slaughtering was done mainly in front of the temples. The priests were butchers, hacking up animal corpses, tearing out thigh-bones and wrapping them in fat to be burned for the god, dabbling in entrails, jointing the rest of the carcase and selling parts of it to the worshippers, keeping back specified portions for themselves. Zeus' most hallowed place at Olympia was a great heap of ashes, the ashes of burnt offerings, and in the precincts of Apollo at Delphi and Delos there towered piles of horns, a concrete record of piety by slaughter. In the Panathenaic festival at Athens no less than 41 minas' worth of cattle, about fifty head, were slaughtered at the great altar of Athena on the Acropolis in 335 B.C.; after the usual pickings by priests and officials the rest of the edible meat was carried down, presumably in steaming cart-loads, through the market-place and to the Cerameicus quarter for distribution to the people.[5] All this was the public side of sacrifice. Within the home smaller but similar rituals were *de rigueur*, much of it no doubt little different from the farmer's wife going into the farmyard and wringing a hen's neck for dinner; or perhaps Kosher butchery, with its ancient obsession about correct blood-letting, would be a more telling parallel.

That is only one kind of ritual, although a striking one. It is strange that the theme occurs so little in myths, and so few of them are strongly concerned with the nature of offerings and so on; Prometheus' deceit of Zeus at Mecone (see p. 137) is the one prominent exception, apart from the special case of human sacrifice. Other rituals (or rather other parts of complex sequences of ritual action in which sacrifice would form a climax) were often concerned with fertility. Again, one must distinguish the elaborate city festivals, for which Athens provides the fullest evidence, from the little rural cults and rituals that were often, and especially in remote areas like Arcadia in the central Peloponnese, both ancient and curious. I propose first to survey some of the main Athenian festivals to see how far they are reflected in myths, and then to make a selection of local rites from those observed by Pausanias (our chief source for this sort of thing) in his travels through Greece in the second century A.D.[6] No ritual will be omitted that seems to have generated an important myth.

Of the festivals to the city goddess Athena the most important was the *Panathenaea*; its foundation was credited to Erichthonius, a mythical king, then to Theseus. A sheep was slaughtered for Pandrosus, a daughter of King Cecrops (another early king), but that is all in the way of mythical association. Pandrosus and her two sisters are connected with a more promising ritual called the *Arrhephoria* that was preliminary to the Panathenaea. Two (or four) little girls spent several months in the year in the priestess's house on the Acropolis, helping to weave the new robe for the goddess. On a certain night they carried on their heads bundles, whose contents were unknown, down to a precinct of Aphrodite below the Acropolis. They handed them over to the priestess and received other bundles in return, which they carried up to the priestess of Athena. Then they were discharged.

That is the ritual, and there is a myth that corresponds with it in important respects. King Cecrops had three daughters,

Pandrosus among them; they were given a box to guard by the goddess Athena and told not to look inside it. Curiosity overcame two of them, but not Pandrosus; inside they saw a snake (which later grew into Erichthonius), product of seed spilled on the ground by Hephaestus when he tried to rape Athena. They went mad at the sight and cast themselves from the Acropolis to their deaths. There is nothing here about carrying bundles down the hill, or different ones up again, and the girls are three in number, not two or four. But there *is* a secret object in a box (not bundle), and it is associated with Athena, and less directly with Aphrodite. Presumably the ritual was connected with fertility, and the myth suggests the same in a way, for the daughters of Cecrops (also known as the Cecropides) have names that mean All-dewy (Pandrosus), Dew, and Shining, and look like references to life-giving moisture. But several details of the myth – Hephaestus' attempt on Athena, Erichthonius as serpentine, King Cecrops himself – existed independently, and so of course did the motif of objects in boxes. Yet the myth is, after all, clearly associated with the ritual. This looks like a good start for those who believe that rituals always create myths, but unfortunately the Cecropides instance is almost unique, as we shall see.

Athena was also concerned in a rather mysterious festival called *Skira*, although it belonged primarily to Demeter. There was a procession from the Acropolis to a place called Skiron on the ancient borders with Eleusis; an Eleusinian priest walked under a baldachino; a sacred act of ploughing took place. A fertility-rite, then, but also probably a symbolic union with the town of Eleusis; there was almost no mythical reference, except fleetingly to King Erechtheus of Athens. A more famous festival to Demeter and Kore was the *Thesmophoria*; again it was a fertility rite, for these were fertility goddesses. On its second day pigs were placed in underground chambers by selected matrons and left to rot, to be mixed eventually with the seed-corn. On the last day came purification before childbirth, with ritual obscenity and the handling of model female sex-organs, these last two being a probable feature of the Eleusinian mysteries also. But there is no proper reference to the myth of Kore's disappearance and Demeter's search for her, only a feeble *aition* for the pig-ritual: that the pigs of a swineherd called Eubouleus (that is, Hades) were swallowed up in the chasm through which Persephone was carried below. Another Demeter festival that specialized in sexual reference was the *Haloa* (from a word connoting 'fertile land'), attended by prostitutes as well as by other women. Clay phalluses were set in the ground and watered like plants, and there was the usual obscene joking and display of model female organs. No special myth is mentioned as *aition*, except by the palpable confusion of a much later scholiast.[7] The greatest of all festivals to Demeter and Persephone was, of course, the secret one at Eleusis, on which more later. The chief thing to notice is that, although there is an obvious connection between myth and ritual, the myth seems in many respects to have come first, or at least to be an independent phenomenon. It was not 'created' by the ritual.

Next, Dionysus: his rituals are at least as varied and unusual as Demeter's, for he too represents fertility (although of ivy, vines and trees rather than of crops), and this is aided by all sorts of dramatized actions that draw freely on the supposedly parallel powers of human reproduction. Greatest of Dionysiac feasts was the *Anthesteria*, held in the month of Anthesterion or January-February; it united Dionysus and the dead and expressed the dual function of the earth. It also celebrated the opening of the new wine, for on the first day the huge jars were unsealed and on the second the participants gathered to try it, each with his own pitcher (from which the day was known as *Choes*, 'Pitchers'). On the third day they cooked a *panspermia*, a mixture of seeds and fruits of the earth, in pots that gave the day its special name of *Chytroi*. On *Choes* there was a drinking-contest as well as a ritual marriage of the god with his priestess (perhaps her husband acted the divine part), while the old women carried out their own secret rites. The souls of the dead ascended on this day, too, and were dispatched below again on *Chytroi*.

Here, surely, are ritual actions that were striking and varied enough to have generated special and original narratives – if that is really how myths are made. Indeed, certain mythical explanations *were* attached, but they are typically feeble affairs. Why did everyone drink out of his own pitcher at *Choes*? Because Orestes came to Athens on this day of the year when he was seeking purification from his matricide, and the Athenians prudently gave him his own drinking-vessel because he was polluted; they also politely used separate ones themselves, and that is how the custom began. As for eating the *panspermia* on the following day, it is said by the Hellenistic historian Theopompus (who presumably took the idea from earlier sources) to have celebrated the first cooked meal made by the survivors of Deucalion's flood. In other words, *pre-existing* myths, or faintly plausible details from them, are dragged in as *aitia*, which is a very different process from solid mythical invention.

Another Dionysiac festival called *Aiora* ('Swinging') does slightly better. Girls swung on swings suspended from trees; it was said to commemorate the suicide of Erigone, an Attic girl who hanged herself from a tree because of the death of her father Ikarios, killed by his own villagers for introducing them to wine (they thought he had poisoned them!). Swinging, for reasons that are not certainly understood, is a fertility charm that can be paralleled elsewhere. It must have seemed to call for some sort of explanation, and the Erigone story at least makes a connection with Dionysus, from whom her father must have received the vines. Again, however, the story seems to have existed independently of the ritual, which is applicable only to a small part of it. Another rustic festival was the *Lenaia*, named after ecstatic female worshippers who made offerings of wine before a statue of the god formed as a draped pillar topped by a mask. The mask probably pre-dates the theatre and its masks, of which the god was patron, and curiously enough it generated no mythical *aition*. Finally the *Oschophoria*, the 'Branch-carrying': a procession set out from one of Dionysus' sanctuaries in Athens and made its way to a shrine of Athena by the sea; it was led by two boys dressed as girls and carrying vine-branches and grapes; there was a race between teams representing the ten Athenian tribes, and the winner drank out of a special five-fold cup. Who were these boys and why were they dressed in female clothes? One might expect a myth to tell us, if that is the purpose for which myths are made. As usual, however, there is merely a more or less inappropriate and tangential connection with a myth already formed: the procession was said to recall one that went to meet Theseus when he returned with the freed captives from Crete after killing the Minotaur.

Apollo had two particularly important festivals: the *Thargelia* in late April and the *Pyanopsia* in late September. On the first day of the former, two 'scapegoats' (the Greek word is *pharmakoi*, 'cures') were driven out of the city; one wore a necklace of black, the other of white figs, and they represented the two sexes. In non-Attic versions of the festival they were struck seven times on the penis with fig-branches and squill. All this is routine, if fascinating, fertility ritual, and it evidently gave rise to a variety of mythical 'explanations': either one Pharmakos had stolen some cups from Apollo and was stoned to death by followers of Achilles (for heaven's sake!), or the death in Attica of Minos' son, Androgeos, led to a plague that was purged by driving out scapegoats. The central acts of the *Pyanopsia* were likewise connected with fertility, and included the cooking of a kind of *panspermia* soup and the carrying of harvest-wreaths in procession; they too were connected, no more convincingly, with the myth and legend of Theseus.

Apollo's sister Artemis had her own festivals, of which the *Brauronia* and *Tauropolia* are among the more notable. The former features her 'bears', the name given to little girls in saffron dresses who spent a year in her temple at Brauron. There is some connection here with the myth of Artemis and Callisto, a nymph loved by Zeus and turned into a bear by the jealous Hera – but only in so far as both myth and ritual are independent expressions of the association of the goddess with bears. The *Tauropolia* included nocturnal revels and the ritual scratching of a man's neck with a sword. Euripides made this a reminiscence of the tale of Orestes narrowly escaping death by being sacrificed to Artemis by the barbaric Taurians; but again the ritual, if it was at all ancient, probably had some quite different purpose, although in this case the myth would seem less ineffective than usual as an *aition* for it.

The *Kronia*, a kind of harvest-festival in honour of Kronos, involved masters and workers in the fields feasting together: a natural kind of thing to happen once a year, whether or not intended as a *rite de passage* role-reversal. Equally naturally, if unconvincingly, it was assumed to be a reminiscence of the 'Age of Kronos' or Golden Age. Kronos' son Zeus had a more impressive range of festivals. Greatest of all was the *Diasia*; the first day was grim, with sacrificial animals burnt whole and other gifts flung into the flames. Afterwards came relief and feasting, but no sign of a myth. Perhaps the proceedings were too indefinite, but that was not so with the *Dipolieia*, the festival of Zeus Guardian of the City, which included the charade known as *Buphonia* or 'Ox-slaughter'. Corn or barley was laid on the god's altar, an ox was led up and left to commit the 'sacrilege' of eating it; he was then killed for his sacrilege by a priest, who took flight but left his axe behind. The axe was tried and found guilty, and the priest was allowed to return; meanwhile the ox's skin was stuffed and then displayed yoked to a plough. Aristophanes, the fifth-century comic playwright, thought these proceedings very old-fashioned.[8] Their original point is not fully understood, although it has been often suspected that the ritual was intended to appease man's feeling of guilt at slaughtering tame animals who are also his friends and helpers. Indeed Pausanias relates that the ox ate the grain by accident in the time of King Erechtheus, and explains the ritual as being 'in memory' of that event; the priest in question was one Thaulon, and his family still served in the priesthood.[9] Other authors gave different explanations, but again the degree of myth involved was minimal and the generation of real narrative extremely slight.

Finally some rituals connected with less august figures. The *Prometheia* included a torch-race in which it was essential that the winner's torch did not go out. That gives the clue: it was originally a new-fire ritual, in which a fresh flame had to be brought directly and without replacement from the altar of the fire-god into the city. The purpose was to keep the power of fire undiminished, for ritual and technological purposes, much as in the ritual carried out annually on the island of Lemnos (see p. 244 f.). The present application might imply a reference to the tale of Prometheus' theft of fire, but the details of the race do not stress that idea. Once again, myth and rite seem to evolve independently out of the nature of the god himself. Next is the *Adonia*, a festival introduced into Greece from Syria and points east: the women mourn for effigies of a dead man and carry crocks sown with fast-growing seeds on to their roofs. A fertility cult, then, at heart, but one connected with the Mesopotamian myth of the disappearing god known to the Sumerians as Dumuzi and to the Akkadians and Babylonians as Tammuz. In its Greek form the myth explains that Adonis (from Syrian *adon*, 'lord') was loved by Aphrodite; he was a prince of Assyria or of Cyprus, through which the ritual seems to have passed to Greece; he was killed by a jealous god and sent down for part of each year to solace Persephone in the underworld. The general theme is similar to the tale of Persephone herself, but the ritual, with its 'gardens of Adonis' that bloom and decay so quickly, is more specific and is only cursorily accounted for in the myth.

Lastly, the *Apatouria*, a three-day festival celebrated by all Ionian cities, including Athens, was quite specifically concerned with initiation. The first day was for feasting, the second for the solemn throat-slitting of animals, the third for the ritual hair-cutting of young men about to enter adult status. Nothing much to generate a myth, perhaps; various gods and goddesses were involved, Zeus and Athena above all; the young men drank a toast to Heracles before their hair was shorn, but that is the only detail to connect this hero – who was adopted as a mascot by the *ephebes*, or young warriors, in other contexts (see p. 238) – with the ritual, or with the process of initiation itself.

There were other festivals at Athens, but I have mentioned the most important and striking ones. The result is that from this point of view, once again, the rituals do not seem to generate myths except in rare and exceptional cases. What they more frequently do is to encourage half-baked *aitia* in the form of loosely applied or ill-chosen details from other and obviously independent tales. The same will be found to be the case outside Athens, also. We happen to know a good deal about festivals at Delphi, mainly from the essayist Plutarch, and they exactly accord with this conclusion. At the *Stepterion*, celebrated every eighth year, a straw hut was burned and a group of boys fled to Tempe, purified themselves and made a triumphal return. It was a fertility and scapegoat ritual of some kind, and the best the Delphians could say was that it represented Apollo's victory over the serpent Python, original possessor of the sanctuary. The action of the myth bears no resemblance to that of the ritual: an extreme case, but not altogether untypical. At the festival called *Charila*, barley was ritually handed out to the people but ignominiously refused to a doll named Charila, which was taken away and buried with a rope round its neck. The grave of a girl of the same name stood nearby, and the myth related that she was an orphan who was once refused food during a famine and hanged herself in chagrin. That exemplifies a different aetiological technique whereby a special but somewhat pointless and improbable tale is manufactured to match the manifest details of the rite. Again, the doll presumably had some scapegoat function; rituals involving puppets and unusual actions were especially prone to generate narrative *aitia*. The most important case, as we saw, is the tale of Heracles cremated on Mount Oeta, where there was indeed some kind of new-fire ritual that involved throwing figurines on to a blazing pyre. That is one of the rare examples of an important mythical detail (as distinct from a whole myth) apparently being shaped by a ritual.

The large, organized festivals, particularly those from Athens that are best known, suggest strongly that rituals only rarely generate anything like an important myth. Are small rural cults and rites any different? They are less likely to have been elaborated or altered during the passage of centuries: do they then exemplify the allegedly universal rule that strange ritual behaviour gives rise to myths, that this is the way myths are developed?

Pausanias started the account of his travels through Greece at Athens, where one of his lesser observations concerns a yard-wide cleft in the floor of an ancient sanctuary of Earth near the later temple of Olympian Zeus:

And they say that after the deluge in Deucalion's time the water flowed away by this route; and every year they throw into the hole wheat-grain mixed with honey. (I. 18, 7)

This, then, is an example of the facile connection of ritual circumstances with well-known myths. Proceeding to Megara, Pausanias saw among other things a rock near the town hall:

They call it *Anaclethris* ('Recall'), because Demeter (if one can believe these things), in her wanderings in search of her child, called
her back at this place also. The women of Megara still, down to our
own times, perform actions imitating the story. (I. 43, 2)

This represents a trivial aetiological explanation of an odd
place-name and draws on an obvious mythical paradigm; its
special interest is that Pausanias notes it as a case where a
ritual, the pageant by the Megarian matrons, is generated by
a myth – the precise reverse of the myth-and-ritual theory.
Some time later he visited the sanctuary of Athena at Titane
near Corinth; it contained an old lightning-blasted statue of
the goddess, and below it at the foot of the hill he found
that

there is an altar of the winds, on which the priest sacrifices to the
winds on one night in every year. He also performs other actions,
which may not be spoken of, into four pits, to tame the winds'
fierceness; and they say in addition that he chants spells derived from
Medea. (II. 12, 1)

These actions were so unusual that they might be expected to
have generated a mythical *aition*, but they did not do so,
perhaps in this case because the rituals were in some sense
secret. Even so, it was hard to resist connecting the priestly
incarnations with Medea, the mythical archetype of a sorce-
ress, who had lived in Corinth close by.

At Sparta our traveller described a remarkable ritual,
obviously part of the elaborate training and initiation of
young Spartan warriors, that was performed at a place called
Platanistas. There was a kind of island there ringed by plane-
trees and a moat; access to it was by two bridges. Two
companies of youths went on to the island, each by their own
bridge. They had previously sacrificed puppies and organized
a fight between boars, now they fought each other with no
holds barred and pushed their opponents into the water. The
only myth that is faintly similar is a tale told by Pherecydes of

Syros in the sixth century B.C. concerning a fight between Kronos and his followers on the one side, and Ophioneus (a serpentine, Typhoeus-like figure) and his followers on the other; the winners, who would gain possession of the sky, were to be the party that succeeded in pushing the others into the waters of Okeanos.[10] I doubt whether (as has been held) the Spartan ritual generated the myth, which incidentally is so far unknown outside the context of Pherecydes. There is not so very much in common, only a fight between two groups that try to push each other into water. It's an unusual idea, on the face of it, although not if the fight happens to take place, for other reasons, close to water. Perhaps what is really surprising is that such a well-marked contest ritual was not related to any more familiar myth. Heracles was involved in the proceedings (since his statue stood by one of the bridges), no doubt as a hero connected with the initiation of young warriors; yet none of his many contests was drawn on for a mythical precedent, nor so far as we can see was any of them invented with the ritual as model.

Pausanias now passed through Achaia in the northern Peloponnese, where he witnessed, among much else, an Artemis-festival called the *Laphria*, in which the participants relentlessly hurled birds and beasts of every kind, as well as fruit, into a blazing pyre. No mythical explanation is offered. He then proceeded southward to Arcadia, a backward and mountainous region that proved richest of all in curious rites. The strangest of them, perhaps, was the sacrifice to Zeus that took place annually in his sanctuary on top of Mount Lykaion. The precinct, incidentally, included an area forbidden to men; whoever entered it found that he had lost his shadow and died within the year. Furthermore,

they say that since the time of Lykaon [an early king, on whom more below] someone has always turned from man into wolf at the sacrifice for Lykaian Zeus – not for his whole life, for if while a wolf he witholds from human flesh, then they say that in the tenth year after that he turns back into a man from being a wolf. But if he has tasted it, he remains as a wild beast for ever. (VIII. 2, 6)

Pausanias was even told of an Arcadian boxer called Damarchus who had won an Olympic victory around 400 B.C. after having changed into a wolf and then back again nine years later (VI. 8, 2). He refused to believe all this, but surprisingly accepted the story that according to him gave rise to the ritual: that Lykaon, son of Pelasgus and second king of Arcadia, had sacrificed a baby to Zeus and was instantly changed into a wolf for his crime (VIII. 2, 3). Apollodorus gives a slightly different version: that Lykaon's fifty sons were to blame, and Zeus visited them in disguise to see if they were as vicious as he had heard; they slew a boy and mixed his innards with the sacrificial meats offered to the stranger; Zeus overturned the table in disgust (at the spot known as Trapezos, 'Table') and blasted Lykaon and his impious sons with a thunderbolt – all except one, of course, the common folktale motif; and the great flood followed shortly thereafter (III. 8, 1). Still another version was recorded by Pliny after Varro, who got it from a Hellenistic writer called Euanthes. It restricts the werewolf theme to members of a certain family; they regularly led one of their young men to the edge of a lake; he took off his clothes and hung them on an oak-tree, then swam across the lake and disappeared; he became a wolf and changed back again eight years later, provided he had tasted no human flesh.

Is this a case of a relatively substantial myth created to explain a ritual? I answer the question with some reserve, for the ritual, whatever it was, was obviously an old one, and something unpleasant to do with human flesh seems to have continued right down to Pausanias' time. Yet the myth that was based on it is not as substantial as at first appears, or rather, there is a doubt about its primacy in Arcadia. A closely similar story was told of Tantalus and Pelops (see p. 134 f.). Tantalus, like Lykaon, lived in the age (reign of Kronos, Golden Age) when men feasted with gods; he too offered the gods the flesh of a child (his own son Pelops). They instantly recognized it (except for sorrowing Demeter, who absent-mindedly ate a bit); Tantalus was drastically punished, the Golden Age, presumably, came to an end, and of course the flood followed shortly thereafter. There are some additional details here, but which came first, Tantalus or Lykaon? It's a difficult question, admittedly; my own feeling is that the Tantalus story, being more widely known and more fully integrated into the pattern of other heroic myths, is likely to be the earlier. It was then drawn in as the obvious mythical precedent for the sacrificial practices on Mount Lykaion, but in this case the names were changed and the offering of child-flesh to the gods was performed by the eponymous King Lykaon himself, or by his sons.

One particular element of the Arcadian myth and ritual is not reproduced in, and cannot be derived from, the myth of Tantalus and Pelops, and that is the idea of turning into a wolf. It is, of course, a not unsuitable punishment for eating human flesh; that is a thing wolves notoriously do, therefore the man who tastes human flesh is behaving like a wolf, and it is poetically and mythically appropriate that he should actually become one. Yet the matter is not quite so simple: how had the cannibalistic practice become regularized, and what about the Euanthes version whereby turning into a wolf did not (it seems) depend on the sacrifice? There is the further point that the names of Mount Lykaion and King Lykaon might be connected (as they certainly were by the Greeks themselves) with the word for 'wolf', *lykos*. There may, too, as Walter Burkert thinks, be an initiation practice behind all this, whereby young men joined for a period a 'wolf-pack' that lived in the wilds, rather like young Spartans at one stage of their long military training.[11] That must remain conjectural, but in any case the *myth* of Lykaon and his sons seems to owe much to Tantalus and Pelops, and that means that the ritual only supplied certain details. This is, in short, an interesting case where a ritual does seem to have contributed to a myth; but the myth is not an important one, or rather it only became so because of themes taken from another myth rather than from the ritual itself.

Not far from Megalopolis in Arcadia was a shrine of the Furies, and near it a tomb surmounted by a stone finger; here, went the popular tale according to Pausanias (VIII. 34, 2), Orestes bit off his finger after being driven mad by the Furies for killing his mother. That kind of superficial aetiology went on continuously; the question is whether something analogous can have created myths in the first place. The people of the city of Pheneos, also in Arcadia, were evidently much given to mythical precedents, but even so they did not create a myth to explain a truly remarkable ritual that took place there near the sanctuary of Demeter:

> Beside the sanctuary of Eleusinian Demeter there is made what is called Petrōma ['place of the rock'], two large rocks fitted against each other. Every other year they celebrate what they call the Greater Ritual, when they open these stones; they extract from them writings that pertain to the ritual, read them out so that the initiates can hear them, and replace them again on the same night. I know that most of the men of Pheneos swear at Petroma in the most solemn matters. Furthermore there is a round appendage on top of Petroma, containing a mask of Demeter Cidaria; the priest wears this mask in the Greater Ritual and beats with rods, for some reason or other, those who dwell beneath the earth. (VIII. 15, 2–3)

Admittedly this is to some extent a secret ritual, since there are initiates. It seems to bear a loose relation to the Mysteries at Eleusis; but Pausanias was able to learn much of what went on, and it is surprising that none of it was related to a special myth. After all, the Eleusinian rites were openly connected with the myth of Demeter and Kore.

My last Pausanian example comes from the Arcadian city of Tegea and concerns the festival of Apollo Guardian of Streets:

'They perform actions in honour of Scephrus, and the priestess of Artemis chases someone as though it were Artemis pursuing Leimon.' (VIII. 53, 3) This ritual action, which looks most like a scapegoat ceremony, must have been for long related to a tale about two early kings or princes of Tegea, Scephrus and Leimon, who were brothers; their father was Tegeates the founder of the city, and he was a son of Lykaon himself (and had not, it seems, been thunderbolt-blasted or turned into a wolf). Apollo and Artemis were travelling through the land, seeking out and punishing those who had refused to help their mother Leto when she was looking for a place in which to give birth. Scephrus drew the god on one side and had a private conversation with him; Leimon thought Scephrus must be informing against him, and so killed him; Artemis forthwith shot him down. Again this is an example of a simple ritual being superficially connected with a well-known myth (that about Apollo, Artemis and Leto); but here local prehistory is an additional ingredient, since the man pursued by the priestess becomes an early king or prince remembered to have quarrelled with his brother. The result is a 'new' myth of a singularly feeble kind, a compound of antiquarianism, aetiology and charter in their lowest forms.

The country rites, then, like the great urban festivals, speak clearly against the theory that myths are invariably created on the basis of existing rituals. There are a few other myth-associated rites not covered by these headings. Some, like fireless offerings and ritual cursings at Lindos, have been already briefly described as attracting trivial aetiological inventions. Tenes, the mythical founder of Tenedos near Troy, presents a similar case, for the mention of Achilles or the presence of a flute-player was forbidden near his tomb. Then there is the tale told by Euripides of Medea killing her children and burying them in the sanctuary of Hera Akraia, across the water from Corinth. The actual rite involved seven boys and girls being kept there for a year, at the end of which a black she-goat was sacrificed; it may have been an ancient initiation ritual which then promoted the idea of Medea slaying her children, rather than an expiation rite that followed the murder. Here the probabilities are hard to determine; but that is not so with two exceptionally important cases, the Hyperboreans and the Lemnian women, which deserve fuller consideration.

Herodotus is sceptical about the Hyperboreans (on whom see also p. 132 f.), but provides the following intriguing account:

It is the Delians that are by far the most informative about them. They say that sacred objects packed in wheat-straw are conveyed from the Hyperboreans and reach the Scythians; from the Scythians they are received and passed on from country to neighbouring country, until they reach their westward limit at the Adriatic. From there they are forwarded southward, and the men of Dodona are the first Greeks to receive them; from them they descend to the Malian gulf and cross over to Euboea, where city sends them to city as far as Carystus. From there Andros is omitted, for it is the Carystians that bring them to Tenos, and the Tenians to Delos. This then is how they say these sacred objects reach Delos, but originally the Hyperboreans despatched two girls to bring them – their names according to the Delians were Hyperoche and Laodice. For safety's sake the Hyperboreans sent with them as escorts five of their citizens, those that are now called 'Perpherees' and have great honours in Delos. But since those who had been despatched failed to return home, the Hyperboreans, resenting the prospect of continually losing their envoys, brought the sacred objects wrapped in wheat-straw to their borders and enjoined their neighbours to forward them to another country. (IV. 33, 1–4)

Herodotus goes on to say that Thracian women likewise wrap their sacred offerings to Artemis in straw, and that the two Hyperborean girls were buried in the precinct of Artemis in Delos. Girls before marriage, as well as children, laid locks of hair on their tomb. Moreover there was another and earlier pair of Hyperborean girls, and a hymn was addressed to them by the mysterious Olen of Lycia. Pausanias, too, refers briefly to the passage of the straw-wrapped offerings, but places the route further east and makes its last stage Athens; significantly he describes the offerings as 'first-fruits' (I. 31, 2).

The realities of the situation seem to be, first, that secret straw-enclosed offerings, probably of fertile implication, arrived each year in Delos by way of northern Greece, Euboea and Tenos (the last being an island just north of Delos); Athens succeeded in inserting herself into the route in later historical times. Secondly, there was an ancient tomb of two girls associated with the sacred objects and with the northern regions from which they came. The offering of hair at the tomb, as well as the second pair of girls and Olen's hymn, look like secondary developments. The passage of the offerings was highly unusual and intensely dramatic. It surely cried out for a striking mythical explanation, yet all it received was the dull rationalistic tale of how the two Hyperborean girls and their escorts stayed on, somehow, in Delos, so that the Hyperboreans were obliged to invent a kind of postal service. Who, precisely, originated the offerings, which actually arrived each year? That remains a mystery – probably some priest of Apollo and Artemis. As Greek contacts expanded northwards, so the place of origin might be pushed further away until it reached the mythical people 'beyond the north wind'. Other fascinating possibilities, such as that the route takes in part of the 'amber route' from northern Europe into Greece, do not affect the implication of the performance as a whole, namely that a remarkable and widely known ritual signally failed to generate a decent and substantial myth.

The second important ritual was carried out annually in the island of Lemnos in the north-eastern Aegean and leads to a different conclusion. We know from Philostratus, a member of a Lemnian literary family active in the second and third centuries A.D., that each year all fires were extinguished in the island for nine days, during which invocations were made to chthonic deities. New fire was brought by ship from Delos, and the ship had to lie offshore until the nine-day period, during which cooking and crafts like pottery and metal-working ceased, was complete. Then life started up again, the power of fire (and of fertility, perhaps, with which fire is often associated) was renewed. Philostratus explicitly connects the ritual with an ancient crime committed by the women of Lemnos. They had been afflicted by Aphrodite with a bad smell, punishment for some kind of impiety or neglect; their husbands found them intolerable and took Thracian slave-girls to their beds instead; the wives slew their menfolk in revenge (except, of course, for the folktale exception, since Hypsipyle spared her father, King Thoas). They then lived without men, with the consequence that, when the Argo-nauts called in on their way to or from Colchis, there was a protracted love-in.

This story is related, among others, by Apollonius of Rhodes in his *Argonautica*, but a more significant piece of in-formation for our purposes is preserved by a far lesser author. An ancient commentator on the Apollonius passage reported that according to one Myrsilus of Lesbos it was Medea and not Aphrodite who sent the foul smell upon the women, and that there is still a day in each year when the women keep their menfolk at bay by means of a smell.[12] The variant about Medea is unimportant, a mere piece of learned variation; but the ritual abstention from sex with the aid of an artificially induced odour is highly significant. Exactly the same thing happened in the Athenian festivals of Thesmophoria and Skira: the women chewed garlic to help them achieve tem-porary chastity. The purpose of the practice is almost certainly to increase the sympathetic power of human fertility after a period of abstention, much as the strength of the new fire was all the greater by contrast with the total absence of fire in the nine days preceding. In short, both fire ritual and smell ritual can be explained as typical fertility acts quite independent of the myth. Yet the myth is explicitly connected with the rituals by our admittedly late sources, and it looks very much as though it was developed as a means of accounting for them. Most of this was discerned by Georges Dumézil in 1924; in 1970 Walter Burkert added the subtle observation that the structure of myth and rite is remarkably similar: in each case a period of barrenness followed by a renewal of life and energy after the arrival of a ship. Coincidence? Perhaps so, but the general similarity between myth and ritual can hardly be denied, any more than the probable antiquity of the ritual in this case. It is justly conceivable that the fire and smell were connected with some kind of marsh-gas for which the island was famous, and that Philoctetes' stranding there with his malodorous wound (see p. 200) was also related. Even so, the probability remains that in this case ritual gave rise to an explanatory myth.

Moreover the myth of the Lemnian women is a substantial one. It admittedly includes folktale motifs like the lone survivor, but then what myth does not? On the whole it is fresh, interesting and inventive, no mere embroidery (as the Lykaon tale appeared to be) of an older and neighbouring myth. It stands out, then, as the one clear case in the whole range of Greek heroic myths – with the Cecropides tale (see p. 228 f.) as a weaker ally – in which the myth-and-ritual theory is vindicated. Or rather, *slightly* vindicated, for the theory, it will be recalled, claims that all myths are based on rituals, whereas what we have discovered is that one or two substantial Greek myths appear to be so based. Still, that is a consoling result, even for those who reject the monolithic theory. It would be strange if no clear and important case could be found in which the aetiological analysis of rituals, so clearly exemplified in the period of literature and learning, was successfully applied at an earlier date. Myths, as has now been abundantly demonstrated, are a diverse phenomenon with disparate causes and lines of development. When ritual was so prominent an aspect of Greek social behaviour, it would be extraordinary if its inevitable overlap with myth did not occasionally take this particular form. What is important is to distinguish between different grades of interaction; to see quite plainly that, if Achilles' son Neoptolemus was killed with a sacrificial knife in a brawl at Delphi, that was a minor invention that drew on the ritual use of knives there in an unimportant way, and not a major instance of creative interplay between the two forms of cultural expression.

The myth-and-ritual theory was developed with special reference to the myths of western Asia and Biblical lands, although it also drew support from classical instances adduced by Frazer, Cornford and others. It is true that religious rituals were even more marked a part of communal life in Mesopotamia, for instance, than in ancient Greece. All the same, nearly all known Sumerian and Akkadian myths are independent of ritual. They contain no reference to ritual acts, or only slight and unimportant ones, and the events they describe do not look as though they ever referred to, or were determined by, the kinds of rituals that are locally attested. Take the Epic of Gilgamesh: little or nothing in this fascinating product of the mythical imagination bears any relation to rituals, known or probable. The Epic of Creation, so-called, is different, but that is a cosmogonical text that was adapted as a charter for the titles and prerogatives of Marduk, the great city-god of Babylon; no wonder it was recited as part of the diverse activities of the New Year festival![13] One other instance among many, far from Mesopotamia and the ancient world, is worth citing. I referred earlier to the myths of the Tsimshian Indians of the north-west Pacific coast, so scrupulously studied by Franz Boas (see p. 30 f.). Their rituals, too, were of great interest, and the central characteristic of these was the potlatch, that extraordinary custom whereby neighbouring chieftains vied with each other in the destruction of precious objects (mostly blankets and ingots of copper) in order to gain 'face' and prove their superiority.[14] One would expect, if the myth-and-ritual theory were anything like correct, that Tsimshian myths would be full of potlatch situations. The reality, as the reader will not be surprised to learn, is that they are virtually innocent of potlatch. Instances from tribal societies could be widely extended, but the point has now perhaps been adequately made.

Apart from invalidating the universal theory in its crude form, our analysis of Greek myths and rituals suggests strongly that careful discrimination needs to be made between different kinds of ritual. The term itself is almost as misleading as 'Myth' or 'mythology'. There are several different types of 'ritual' behaviour, and it is only their formal aspect – as socially accepted repetitive acts believed in some way to be effective – that is common to all. Their underlying motives differ, and so do their origins and assumed effects. That being so, it is highly probable that their relations with myths will vary also. There is indeed an area in which myths and rituals overlap, but the degree and kind of interaction are controlled by, among other factors, the particular type of ritual.

There is, to begin with, the difference between ceremonial behaviour and specific rituals. The former, whether in private or in communal relations, has its own rules and intentions; it does not usually generate fresh tales, although it may be associated with charter-type recitals as at tribal jamborees (or school speech-days). Stricter rituals, on the other hand, must be subdivided into non-cultic and cultic ones. The non-cultic include those designed to promote fertility in the broadest terms and those connected with social and biological status. There is some overlap, naturally, but the former tend to become associated with myths, partly because they often involve sympathetic magic and therefore make use of puppets or scapegoats, whereas the latter are usually rites of passage; the ritual behaviour required of a new mother, an initiate or a dying man and his relatives cannot be so easily paralleled by a narrative, unless by a simple charter-type paradigm. As for cultic rituals, they may be subdivided into ritual actions on behalf of the gods (offering them food or gifts, cleaning their temples and statues), and ritualized rehearsals of their deeds accompanied by requests for aid (in other words, hymns and prayers). Clearly the first sub-division tends not to be allied with myths, whereas the second makes use of pre-existing myths rather than generating new ones. Future research would do well to recognize and define these differences and the varying relations to myths they imply, rather than hammering away at crude and unworkable universalistic theories.

To end this chapter I revert to the warmer realities of a particular myth, perhaps the most pervasive of all Greek divine tales – the tale of Demeter and her daughter Kore ('the girl'), otherwise known as Persephone. It has been outlined already and can now be assessed in a wider context, for it is, of course, closely integrated with the most famous of all Greek rituals, the whole proceedings undergone by initiates in the Mysteries at Eleusis near Athens. The details are not entirely clear, precisely because they were secret and there were heavy penalties for divulging them. It was not until late antiquity that some of the Church Fathers, undeterred by pagan threats, were prepared in the interests of Christ and the suppression of heresy to blow the gaff. But even Clement of Alexandria and Hippolytus of Rome were not well-informed. They were working on the basis of rumours, and naturally selected the most sensational and equivocal ones. The Mysteries contained 'things said, things shown, things done', and the initiates undoubtedly had to handle sacred objects, taking them from a box, doing something unknown with them, placing them in a basket and then back into the box. According to the Christian sources these objects were of a sexual nature, models of male and female organs. That is not improbable in itself, for this was in essence a fertility ritual; among the less secret actions was the drinking of a drink made from barley-meal, mint and water. The Mysteries gradually developed a wider symbolic meaning, and the renewal of crops became a pledge of renewal for the initiates themselves, of life after death. Yet in an earlier form the Eleusinian rites were probably designed to persuade the goddesses not to withdraw their power of fertility from the earth. Most of the ritual actions demanded of the worshippers were standard for this kind of fertility magic. The eating or drinking of representative fruits of the earth is paralleled by the *panspermia* of Apollo's festival of *Pyanopsia* (see p. 232) or Dionysus' *Anthesteria* (see p. 230 f.), and the handling of sexual objects at Demeter's other festivals of *Thesmophoria* and *Haloa* (see p. 229 f.). The joking that made Demeter laugh in the myth was probably reproduced in the secret rites and is paralleled at the *Haloa* and elsewhere.

That is the ritual: now for the myth, which is given in full in the *Hymn to Demeter* composed, probably, in the seventh century B.C. Hades snatches Persephone while she is gathering flowers and carries her off to his underworld kingdom. Demeter goes wild with grief, searches everywhere for the girl, refuses to eat and avoids the company of the gods; she learns that Hades is responsible and that Zeus has connived; she settles in Eleusis and 'conceals' the crops for a whole year. Mankind is in danger of destruction; Zeus and the other gods fail to win her over, and eventually Zeus insists on Persephone's release. Hades persuades her to eat a single pomegranate-seed before leaving, which binds her to return to him for a third of each year. But Demeter is overjoyed at her release, restores fertility to the fields, reveals the finer points of agriculture to Triptolemus prince of Eleusis, and so returns to Olympus.

Much of the hymn is concerned with the goddess's stay at Eleusis and the foundation of her worship there. It is, in that respect, a local charter myth. Yet her year's isolation in her new temple is also the cause of world-wide famine, and both aspects are made plain in the following passage:

Keleos called his numerous people into the market-place and bade them make for lovely-haired Demeter a rich temple and altar on a jutting hill; and they swiftly obeyed and listened to his words and did as he commanded, and the temple grew according to the goddess's decree. When they had finished it and rested from their labour they each went home; and brown-haired Demeter sat there far apart from all the blessed gods and stayed wasting away through longing for her deep-girdled daughter. That was the most dreadful, the worst of all years that she made over the fertile earth for all mankind. The soil sent forth no seed, for Demeter of the fair chaplet concealed it. Many were the curved ploughs the oxen drew in vain across the fields, much was the white barley that fell to no purpose into the ground. And the whole race of articulate men would have been destroyed by grievous hunger, and would have deprived those who possessed the Olympian halls of the glorious honour of gifts and sacrifices, had not Zeus noticed and observed it in his heart. (296–313)

The word translated as 'year' can mean 'season', but even so it is clear that what Demeter effected was a rare and total famine, not just the infertility of winter. Yet that lesser and regular infertility is implied by Persephone's subsequent need to spend four months of each year in the underworld. Demeter tells her:

But if you *have* partaken of food there, then you shall fly back down under the hiding-places of the earth and dwell there for a third part of the season, year by year, and the other two parts with me and the rest of the immortals. And whenever the earth burgeons with fragrant spring flowers of every kind, then you shall rise again from the misty darkness, a great wonder for gods and mortal men. (398–403)

Is the myth really trying to say that seasonal infertility is the result of some major famine in the past? Is it trying to explain why a 'dead' period is necessary for the growth of the crops? I doubt it; there seems to be a deeper ambiguity in the relationship of different parts of the account. A more plausible solution is that the myth contains a version of a widely diffused Asiatic prototype. The theme of the disappearing fertility deity takes several different forms in Near-Eastern myths: the visit of Inanna-Ishtar to the underworld, or the death and temporary reappearance of Dumuzi-Tammuz, or, closest to the Greek version, the rage and disappearance of the Hurrian fertility god Telepinu, who is eventually persuaded to return to the other gods and so end the famine that is threatening to destroy mankind. Now this mythical archetype relates to the fear of total famine, of a long period, from one to seven years, without rain. That was a continual threat in parts of western Asia, but it simply did not apply to Greece with its regular winter rainfall. Hence some of the ambiguity of the myth in its Greek form. What we are faced with (I suggest) in the developed Demeter myth is a conversion of a Mesopotamian famine myth into a crude *aition* for seasonal agriculture; moreover the adapted form is then applied to a particular fertility cult that had been known in Eleusis at least from the Mycenaean period. The new amalgam then becomes the basis for a wider initiation ritual in early historical times, in which the rebirth of corn becomes the token of human renewal.

It is a complicated pattern, and the results of converting Mesopotamian themes to Greek uses will be further explored in the next chapter. What most concerns us here is the relation between the myth and the ritual, and that is not a simple matter of cause and effect in either direction. Some parts of the ritual of historical times were certainly engendered by the myth; for example it appears that Demeter's search for Kore was imitated by the initiates, or at least Clement of Alexandria could write: 'Deo [that is, Demeter] and Kore have turned into a drama for initiates, and Eleusis celebrates with torches their wandering and rape and mourning.'[15] Moreover a part of what was revealed to the highest initiates by the Hierophant, the 'revealer of sacred things', was probably concerned with the reunion of mother and daughter and the consequent re-establishment of fertility. Other ritual actions – drinking the potion, obscene jokes – had presumably long been established in the fertility cult and helped to determine minor details of the Near-Eastern myth in its new, Eleusinian guise; the potion is what Demeter drank to end her fast at Eleusis, and she was heartened to do so by the jokes made by Baubo or Iambe (see p. 199).

Myth affects ritual, ritual affects myth. Originally, perhaps, each was independent: the prehistoric Eleusinian fertility cult before the imposition on it of the Mesopotamian myth pattern, the Mesopotamian myth as a self-contained means of averting or assimilating periodic droughts. The potentially complex relations between the two overlapping forms of social behaviour (the telling of significant tales, the performing of significant acts) could hardly be better expressed than by this mysterious, manifold and in every way salutary affair of Demeter and her lost daughter. Yet the fact also remains that *on all the evidence the great majority of Greek myths were developed without any special attention to ritual.*

# CHAPTER II

# THE INFLUENCE OF WESTERN ASIA ON GREEK MYTHS

THE exceptional disappearance of a Mesopotamian deity, representing one of the occasional disastrous droughts that afflicted the region, seems to have been converted at Eleusis into a myth concerning the regular withdrawal of a Greek goddess representing seasonal fertility. Indeed we now have two deities instead of one. Strictly speaking, Demeter stands in the place of the drought-causing deities, Inanna or Dumuzi or Telepinu, whereas Persephone is closer to the Asiatic Adonis, whose birth and death were celebrated each year and who more nearly represents the seasonal crops and vegetation. Nevertheless the Eleusinian myth and ritual present a mixture of the two ideas, and Demeter's withdrawal, in particular, seems to depend unmistakably on the Mesopotamian mythical background. In the developing Greek context she is ostensibly motivated by the psychology of a sorrowing mother who blames the gods for an arbitrary act of violence. Even so the famine that afflicts the whole earth and the unexpected terror and submission of the gods come as a surprise, and not just of the kind that emerges from mythical inconsequence. They are, indeed, directly derived from the Mesopotamian archetype. In Mesopotamia, however, they present no problem, indeed constitute a typical motif, for the simple reason that occasional great droughts and famines, like periodical floods, were part of ordinary experience.

This instance raises two interesting possibilities: that there are other such Asiatic themes lurking in Greek myths, and, if so, that their original context has had peculiar effects on the Greek product.

First, a word of caution: tracing the Near-Eastern origins of recurrent motifs in Greek myths is a fascinating but perilous occupation. The chief danger lies in one's necessarily subjective assessment of the degree of specific resemblance needed to demonstrate a dependent relationship between the myths of separate peoples. The Near East and western Asia in the third and second millennia B.C. (and that is roughly the period under discussion) were a cauldron of customs and ideas that passed from Mesopotamia to Egypt and occasionally back again, to Syria and Asia Minor and into the Aegean, to Cyprus and Crete and the Greek mainland. Semitic tribes absorbed concepts from Indo-Iranian ones and vice versa. Indo-European-speaking Hittites derived their theology from the non-Indo-European Hurrians, the Semitic Akkadians from the non-Semitic Sumerians. The Aegean peoples were in contact during the second millennium with Trojans and Hittites in Asia Minor, with Egypt through casual trade and mercenaries, with the Levant through Cyprus and trading posts in Syria and Palestine. The main fountain-head of culture and beliefs was certainly Mesopotamia. Even Egypt was affected, especially in the third millennium B.C., although she rapidly developed her own highly idiosyncratic civilization.

The existence of this great continental culture area, maintained by military, commercial and political diffusion and spreading into the eastern Mediterranean itself, means that the appearance in different places of vaguely similar or very general ideas (like those of a mother goddess, a storm god or the moulding of mankind out of clay) does not necessarily indicate the direct influence of one particular region on another, for example of Egypt or Mesopotamia on Greece. It is only when a rather complex and specific motif occurs in two distinct places and not elsewhere that a probability of direct influence arises, and even then the occurrences may stem from an unknown archetype and not be directly interdependent. That still leaves the problem of deciding on the degree of complexity at which all this becomes plausible. Of theological themes known from Greece, only the violent displacement of older by younger gods, and possibly the consequent disposal of a final monstrous opponent by the storm god before he establishes his supremacy, are complex and specific enough to prove significant links between Asiatic and Greek myth-makers. Greece is unlikely to be the initiator here, since many details of the common account are unmistakably Asiatic. This suggests a definite borrowing from some west-Asiatic source, perhaps in Asia Minor or the Levant, since the theme of violent displacement is more fully developed in the Hurrian–Hittite Kumarbi fragment than in the Babylonian Creation Epic, where it occurs in skeleton form in the displacement of Apsu by Ea and of Tiamat by Marduk.[1] The time of borrowing is in doubt, except that it can hardly be close to the date of Hesiod himself, who first records the Greek version of the theme in his *Theogony*. The probable spread of broader mythical concepts like that of the geography of the underworld, although it cannot be proved, nevertheless argues for a date in the second millennium for the passage of the specific Kumarbi/Kronos theme.

The same difficulty confronts us if we try to trace narrative motifs in the heroic myths. It will always be a question (at least until new evidence turns up, or is deciphered) whether the Homeric tradition owes anything to the Mesopotamian Gilgamesh tradition, which became widely diffused over western Asia as early as the second millennium and was still being recorded in Assyria at the time of the composition of our *Iliad* and *Odyssey*. Achilles' affection for Patroclus is not an exact parallel to the spiritual companionship of Gilgamesh and Enkidu, yet it does have something in common with it. Achilles, like Gilgamesh, has a goddess for mother, and in each case the goddess supports her son, not unnaturally, at a time of trial. The most specific resemblance, and one that encourages speculation about definite contact, lies in the brief reappearance of the companion's ghost from the underworld and his account of the grim state of affairs there; this happens with Enkidu in the twelfth tablet of the Epic of Gilgamesh and with Patroclus in the twenty-third book of the *Iliad*. Other possible echoes of Gilgamesh occur in Heracles (the wearing of skins, the attack on giants and monsters, the concern with death) and Odysseus in his travels through magic lands. Yet in the end such resemblances may be accidental, or simply part of a vague common language of folktale motifs that had developed over millennia and ranged all the way from India to the western Mediterranean. That might account, also, for ideas like that of a great bow used by a hero to kill suitors (by Greek Odysseus and Hurrian Gurparanzakh) or that can only be drawn by its owner (Odysseus and Hindu Rama). Such typically folktale ideas travel more widely, perhaps, and as a result of more ephemeral contacts, than more abstract ideas about cosmogony and the development of gods. Yet the general point remains: specific influence can only be demonstrated by complex and specific similarity, and that is still restricted to the theme of violent displacement.

At a level below that of proof the most suggestive cases are not occasional narrative similarities, which become no more compelling when one doubtful instance is added to another, but rather certain broader similarities of personnel and worldview. Several constituents of the Greek mythical cosmos point towards Mesopotamia, one or two towards Egypt. First, the gods themselves.[2] Some important members of the Greek pantheon are clearly non-Greek in derivation. Despite Herodotus, who thought that everything ancient in Greece came out of Egypt, they are not Egyptian but rather western Asiatic. Apollo comes probably from Asia Minor; his epithet *Lykeios*, despite an intrusive 'e', points to Lycia rather than to any connection with wolves (see p. 240); he had widespread cults in Asia Minor, and his name, apparently not Greek, has a close analogue in a functionally similar Hittite god called

Apulunas. If his connection with the Hyperboreans and the curious ritual passage of offerings to Delos (see p. 243 f.) point northward, then it is quite probably to north-eastern Asia Minor and the Caucasus rather than to the Balkans. His sister Artemis is again strongly rooted in Asia Minor, as a multimammary fertility goddess at Ephesus and also as 'mother of animals'. She is akin to the Cretan goddesses Britomartis and Dictynna, but that does not reduce the probability of Asiatic origin, especially since her mother (and Apollo's) is Leto, who has been plausibly connected with 'Lada', a Lycian goddess and also the Lycian word for woman – Lycia being the south-western part of Asia Minor and presumed home of Apollo Lykeios.

Aphrodite presents an even clearer case. She is the Greek version of Sumerian Inanna, Akkadian Ishtar, Canaanite Anath, the 'queen of heaven', the love goddess, and her famous cult at Paphos in Cyprus, where in Greek myth she was supposed to have been born, marks one stage in her passage from Asia to Greece. Hephaestus belongs to the island of Lemnos not far from the Asia Minor coast; he is the Lemnian version of an Asiatic craftsman god. Dionysus, a relatively late import from the uplands of Lydia and Phrygia, develops special Greek forms but retains something of the role of a fertility consort to the Asiatic Great Mother known to the Greeks as Cybele and sometimes confused with Rhea, the wife of Kronos and mother of Zeus. Demeter's Asiatic origin is more speculative. In her Eleusinian connection she behaves like an Asiatic disappearing deity of fertility, but may also retain elements of some indigenous pre-Greek vegetation goddess. I do not count the Indo-Iranian weather-and-bright-sky god who left his mark in western Asia but was introduced into Greece as Zeus by the first Greek-speakers; nor Ares who is some kind of Thracian interloper. That leaves, of the main Olympian pantheon, only Hera, Athena, Hermes and Poseidon as predominantly local. There are enormous areas of doubt in all this, and I am prepared to concentrate solely on the three most assured cases: Aphrodite, Apollo, Artemis. How crucial they are to Greek divine myths as a whole, and how central to Greek religion! If *they* came from western Asia at some relatively early date – surely, in the case of the two goddesses at least, well before the Mycenaean age in the latter half of the second millennium B.C. – then we have absolutely no right to reject the possibility that other important elements of myth came too. In fact that becomes an *a priori* probability.

The early history of the gods provides some confirmation of this probability, even apart from the theme of violent displacement that is apparently Mesopotamian in origin and finds no analogue, incidentally, in Egypt. The mere succession of gods, displacement or not, takes a similar and fairly specific form in Mesopotamia, Egypt and Greece. The general idea is that the first nature gods, representing cosmic divisions like Ouranos and Anu (Sky), or Apsu-Tiamat and Egyptian Nun (Water), give way to more specific functional and regional gods that are also more fully anthropomorphic: deities like Enki, who loses much of his watery aspect and becomes the city god of Eridu and the embodiment of ingenious wisdom, or Atum of Karnak, or Hera and Athena, the guardians respectively of Argos and Athens. Some of the many Egyptian theogonies resemble Mesopotamian ones: Nun as primeval water generates Shu and Tefnut as air and moisture, and they separate Geb and Nut as earth and sky, who generate the fertility god Osiris.[3] The production of related but opposed pairs who then mate with each other is typical both of the early stages of the Greek theogony according to Hesiod and of the Babylonian succession described in the opening verses of the Creation Epic. Here it is a thought-pattern rather than a specific motif that is held in common.

If there is influence on Greece from either Egypt or Mesopotamia, then once again the latter seems the more plausible, for the Greek conception always seems to fall closer to the

Mesopotamian, and less abstract, end of the spectrum. For example, Re is the sun god who becomes supreme in parts of second-millennium Egypt, whereas Mesopotamian Shamash is a more restricted figure closely matched by Greek Helios, who like Shamash is guardian of oaths. Egyptian Hathor or Isis is the mother goddess, who can be destructive and takes the form of a cow; the Mesopotamian mother goddess known as Ninhursag, Ninmah or Mammi lacks this destructive side and is (unusually) less specific, rather like Greek Demeter and Hera. Among water deities, Poseidon is closer to Enki/Ea than to Nun, who has no strongly particularized descendants.

The idea of an underworld where men live some kind of grim half-life after death is common to Mesopotamia and Greece. Ancient Egyptians also thought at certain periods that the dead lived in an underworld, but their whole eschatology was radically more optimistic in tone. The Mesopotamian House of Dust or Land of No Return has marked resemblances to, as well as certain differences from, the Greek Hades.[4] Both are the domain of a ruler and his or her consort: Hades with Persephone in the kingdom to which he gave his name, Ereshkigal and her husband Nergal in the House of Dust. There are underworld judges in both places, and the condition of dead souls differs according to their life on earth, their burial and their behaviour after death. The Mesopotamian realm, unlike the Greek, is equipped with subsidiary gods and demons, but that matches the more complex organization of the theocratic state to which living Mesopotamians belonged. The way to the Mesopotamian underworld passes through seven gates that have no precise Greek parallel, but the very exact idea of a river over which the dead must be carried by an infernal ferryman is common both to Greece and to Mesopotamia. (Admittedly it also occurs, not very conspicuously, in Egyptian eschatology at one period.) In each case a terrifying monster guards the boundaries of the underworld: Cerberus with his two, or three, heads in the Greek conception, the ferocious bird Zu or the like in the Mesopotamian. Yet neither Mesopotamian nor Greek underworld contains anything like the famous Egyptian dragon Apophis, who tries to waylay the sun on its nightly passage. Perhaps the largest concrete difference is in the idea of the Mesopotamian dead as covered with feathers like birds, and of their normal diet as clay and dust. Greek myths also lack the idea of deities who go down to the underworld for a short period, like Inanna or Enlil himself, to be released only when a substitute is provided. Visits by heroes such as Heracles, Theseus and Orpheus provide no real parallel, but then the immortality of the Greek gods is much more emphatic than that of the Mesopotamian, and consequently their association with the underworld far slighter.

The possibility remains that the Mesopotamian and the Greek underworlds are independent conceptions, and that the latter is in no way affected by the former. It is not in my opinion a very strong possibility, but it exists. Let us therefore turn for contrast to a theme with which every Greek was familiar and which quite certainly comes from Mesopotamia: that of a great flood in the mythical past, one that destroyed all mankind except for a favoured individual and his wife and family. That man was Deucalion, a son of Prometheus himself according to Hesiod in the *Ehoeae*; his wife was Pyrrha, and they recreated mankind after the waters receded by throwing stones over their shoulders in an etymological act of reproduction (see p. 135 f.). And yet Deucalion was not quite so firmly attached to the flood as one might expect; in rare later versions it is associated rather with Ogygus or with the sons of Lykaon (see p. 239). The cause is in most cases roughly the same: the flood was sent by Zeus as a punishment on men for impiety, bloodshed, cannibalism or mere meat-eating. There are many loose ends, but the important central fact is the deluge tself, an overwhelming cataclysm that destroyed virtually the whole of mankind and covered the face of the entire earth. Why and how did such an idea ever occur to the Greeks? Surely not because flooding was a danger that they either experienced or particularly feared in their mountainous land with its moderate rainfall and relatively well-disciplined torrents and drainage-beds? There are a few myths of localized flooding in the Peloponnese (at Lerna, or in the Tegean plain, or in the realm of King Augeias of Elis), but Heracles was fully capable of dealing with these, and they are in any case an agricultural and pastoral nuisance rather than a threat to life and limb for all mankind.

If the Greeks were primarily responsible for dreaming up such an idea for themselves without outside influence, it was a remarkable act of the imagination, unaided by anything much in the way of practical experience or specific fear. One would like to credit them with such a feat, but it would be quixotic to do so in the light of certain other pertinent facts: notably that a myth of a great flood destroying all mankind, save for one pious survivor and his wife and family, was firmly established in Mesopotamia as early as the third millennium B.C. and spread from there all over western Asia during the next two millennia. Furthermore the Mesopotamians, unlike the Greeks (or indeed the Hebrews) had every reason to fear great floods and to regard them as an important factor of life and death. For the river Euphrates, fed by snows in the mountains of eastern Anatolia, periodically overwhelmed the settlements built along its banks, at least until an elaborate system of drainage and irrigation canals had been completed by the end of the second millennium B.C. Whole cities as well as villages could be destroyed by floods: that is the almost irresistible conclusion from the layers of mud that separate habitation-levels in the stratified mounds marking the ancient cities of Ur and Kish, Shuruppak and Uruk – Uruk being the city of which Gilgamesh himself was king early in the third millennium. One particularly deep band of mud three to four metres deep, found in the strata of Ur, is dateable to around

3500 B.C., and it was Sir Leonard Woolley's guess that this is a relic of a truly prodigious deluge, the very one that gave rise to the myth. Yet the occurrence of lesser but still highly destructive floods, at long intervals but still within the range of human tradition, would be enough by itself to distinguish destruction by cataclysm as one of the chief ways in which jealous or resentful gods might punish mankind.[5]

A few of the details of the Asiatic myth are lacking in Greece. Deucalion is prompted to take avoiding action by his father Prometheus rather than by the king of the gods himself. His wisdom is not stressed as was that of the figure variously known in Sumerian and Akkadian as Ziusudra, Atra-hasis, Utnapishtim – the 'Exceeding Wise'. The charming folktale-motif of the release of birds to see if the waters had receded, meticulously reproduced in the tale of Noah, has slipped out of the Greek versions if it was ever in them. But the great flood itself is there, the sole survivor is there, the ark is there, and it grounds on top of Mount Parnassus itself. The Greek flood myth is unquestionably derived from the Mesopotamian exemplar by one means or another. Obviously, when that exemplar was so widely imitated through the length and breadth of western Asia, we cannot say that the Greeks derived their version directly from Mesopotamia. That would in any case be unlikely. Perhaps they got it from Asia Minor (although as it happens no Hurrian version survives), or perhaps from Syria or Palestine. That is not the most important factor, for what is indubitably true is that in this case an established Greek myth is known to be closely modelled on a widely diffused Mesopotamian one.

We can be quite certain, in any event, that the flood theme was not borrowed by the Greeks from Egypt, for the simple reason that flooding there was a necessary phenomenon on which the economy of the whole country depended. It might occasionally cause inconvenience, especially in the Delta, but it was never a national disaster. There is no trace in Egypt of anything like the myth of the great flood, and the totally different conditions of the Nile valley would effectively preclude it. It is one thing for the myth to be accepted in a region like Greece from which large-scale floods are absent; it is another for it to intrude on a second riverine culture for which the concept of flooding has a totally contrary and benign value.

The Greeks were uncertain about the date of the flood. Sometimes it seems to come at the end of Hesiod's Bronze Age, a period of harsh and evil men, but it is also envisaged as terminating the Golden Age. It is to this concept of a Golden Age that I now turn, for it, too, seems not to be native in origin. Unlike the themes of flood and disappearing fertility god, it cannot be clearly related to Mesopotamian circumstances or specifically dissociated from Greek ones. The contrast between the desert and the fertile is admittedly strong in Egypt and Mesopotamia, and might have sharpened the concept of an ideal oasis life for men; yet imagining a time when everything is peace and abundance is an almost universal occupation. There are indications, nevertheless, that the idea came into Greek myths from abroad. Chapter 6 showed that there is much in common between the Greek idea of a Golden Age for all men, at some time in the past, and a blessed afterlife for favoured souls after death. The last idea is associated either with Elysium, also known as the Elysian Plain, or with the Isles of the Blest, and it is on this point that there is some evidence, not copious but probably significant, of Egyptian influence.

This is what Proteus, the old man of the sea, tells Menelaus in the *Odyssey* about his ultimate destiny:

For you, Menelaus, Zeus-nurtured, it is not fated to meet the doom of death in horse-rearing Argos, but the immortals will convey you to the Elysian Plain and the ends of the earth, where golden-haired Rhadamanthys lives and livelihood is easiest for men. There is never snow or harsh storm or rain, but Okeanos continually sends forth the shrill-blowing Zephyr's breezes to bring men coolness. This is because you have Helen as wife and are son-in-law of Zeus. (4, 561-9)

Now the Elysian Plain bears some resemblance to the paradisal lands known in the Egyptian Coffin Texts of the second millennium B.C. as the Field of Offering and the Field of Reeds, where the blessed dead till the earth and reap marvellous crops. This degree of labour is not specifically excluded by the brief references to the Elysian Plain in Homer, Hesiod and Pindar, although in the Isles of the Blest, according to Pindar's second Olympian ode, the earth brings forth its fruits of its own accord and without the need for labour, and so too for the men of the Golden Age in Hesiod's myth of the Five Races (see p. 132 f.). Mesopotamian myths, also, refer to a land where sickness, suffering and toil are absent, but that is most commonly the land of Dilmun where the gods lived in a blessed earlier age before the creation of mankind.[6] Rare Mesopotamian references to a privileged life for men are hard to integrate with the Mesopotamian world picture and its associated eschatology, and it seems possible that the influence was from Egypt to Mesopotamia rather than vice versa.

There is further evidence for Egyptian influence on the Aegean in this respect. The mention of Rhadamanthys in the passage just cited from the *Odyssey* directs our view to Crete, where Rhadamanthys had been brother to Minos and son of Zeus and Europa. Minos and Rhadamanthys are sometimes cast as judges in Hades, but the latter is specially associated with Elysium and the Isles of the Blest. Crete in the Minoan period, and particularly during the second millennium, was in undoubted communication with Egypt, as is clearly demonstrated in both Cretan and Egyptian art. One of the most famous and mysterious testimonies to the funerary beliefs of the ancient world is the Haghia Triadha sarcophagus, excavated in the rich Minoan residence at Haghia Triadha near Phaistos, and made and painted soon after the middle of the second millennium B.C.[7] On each of the longer sides are scenes of offerings. There seem to be two separate processions, one to a shrine containing a double-axe and a tree, the other to a shrine whose most prominent feature is a less-than-life-size statue of a man, presumably the dead man whose remains were contained in the sarcophagus. Three priests or worshippers bear offerings to this second shrine and its statue; they are wearing a kind of skirt made out of animal-skins, the first of them carrying a model boat, the other two, animals that may also be models. What matter here are the hair skirts and the boat, for the skirts are closely similar to a regular ritual garment worn by Egyptian priests and illustrated in tomb paintings, and Egyptian model boats can be seen in practically every museum in the world, since for long periods any respectable Egyptian tomb had to have one in order to convey the dead man across the waters of the underworld to the place of blessed souls.

Egyptian ideas of the afterlife may well have entered Greece through Crete, although that raises a whole set of fresh problems about the conceptual (as distinct from material) connections between Mycenaeans and Minoans in the Late Bronze Age. Certainly the Elysian Plain idea, with its associations and overlaps with the Isles of the Blest and the Golden Age, looks Egyptian in inspiration. It can hardly in any case be Mesopotamian, because it implies an interaction between human and divine (for example in those famous shared banquets in the time of Tantalus and Peleus) that was absolutely excluded by the universal and persistent Mesopotamian conception of men as slaves and manual workers of the gods.

There is little else that looks Egyptian in Greek myths, except perhaps at the folktale level. The Potiphar's wife motif, which was a favourite in Greece, is exploited in the Egyptian Tale of Two Brothers known from a papyrus of the thirteenth century B.C., but is too widespread to be very significant. A more striking resemblance occurs in the 'Contest of Horus and Seth' that survives from roughly the same period, although it is probably older in origin.[8] The god Re is sorrowing because Seth seems likely to win, and can only be roused from his gloom by the goddess Hathor who displays her privates to him and makes him laugh. In the *Hymn to Demeter* Iambe makes the sorrowing Demeter laugh by telling her jokes (they were probably dirty ones once, but the poet has bowdlerized the whole episode), and Clement of Alexandria has a version in which it is Baubo that cheers up the goddess by, precisely, lifting her skirts and displaying her private parts.[9]

That Greek myths were infected by Near-Eastern themes is of exceptional importance in itself. That is so not only because it casts a faint glimmer of light on the development of Greek culture and ideas in their formative stage, but also because it makes it easier to isolate the specifically Hellenic contribution, the particular intellectual and imaginative ingredients that made Greek civilization such a very different phenomenon from those of western Asia and Egypt. We are, of course, dealing here with possibilities that are little understood, and in addition present serious problems of ethnic and cultural definition. The very term 'Greek' is full of ambiguity. 'Greek', like 'Akkadian', denotes a language rather than a people. The Greek-speaking people began to enter the Greek peninsula shortly before 2000 B.C., but they found there an indigenous population that already had cultural and perhaps linguistic connections with Asia Minor. The names of prominent geographical features like Mount *Olympos*, or the sea itself, *thalassa*, of settlement-sites like *Korinthos*, *Lindos* or *Mukenai* (Mycenae), of vegetation like *kuparessos* (cypress) and *huakinthos* (hyacinth), have close west-Asiatic parallels, and are definitely not Greek in type and origin. They were taken over by the Greek-speaking immigrants, together with heaven knows what else in the shape of myths, deities, cults and rituals. The somewhat separate culture of Early Bronze Age Crete complicates the issue, and so do the Greek-speakers themselves – where did they come from, proximately and ultimately? Presumably, by the *thalassa* criterion, not from near the sea, otherwise they would not have needed to borrow a word for it. At present it looks more probable than not that they came from somewhere far to the north-east of Greece, and moved down into the peninsula partly through Asia Minor and across the Aegean and partly through the eastern Balkan area. If so, they may have brought with them further west-Asiatic ideas, as well as older Indo-Iranian ones such as that of the sky god Zeus.

The western-Asiatic influences, in short, may have acted in different ways and at different periods: on the indigenous inhabitants of Greece, perhaps from the Palaeolithic age onwards; on Crete, both from south-western Asia Minor and from Egypt, which was itself affected by Mesopotamia; through Crete on the Mycenaean cities of Greece; and directly on the Greek-speakers before their entry into Greece. Finally, cultural contacts must have continued sporadically through the second and the early part of the first millennium B.C., culminating in the transmission of the alphabet. These contacts were no doubt concentrated in places like Troy, Miletus, Rhodes and Cyprus, and Ugarit and Poseideion in Syria. Trying to pick out one cardinal route for the passage of ideas is a waste of time, and in any event vastly over-simplifies the probable situation. There is insufficient evidence for saying more than that influence was possible through any or all of a number of different routes.

The presence of western-Asiatic elements in Greek myths and religious ideas has another important implication that I have not seen mentioned elsewhere. Greek myths, as we observed, were reduced to a system. Even the divine myths appear to form some kind of coherent whole, at least on the biographical level. One result of systematizing was the disappearance of nearly all problematic overtones. Nevertheless some curious gaps appear in the semantic rather than the narrative structure, and several vital problems are touched on and then left, as it were, in mid-air. What this implies is that some of these omissions are due not so much to the distortions and suppressions of the organizing process itself, but rather to the incorporation of foreign material that in certain aspects was unsuited to the developed Greek context, and therefore generated anomalies and lacunas. In short, the conceptual framework may have become distorted in places through the difficulty of accommodating some essentially alien themes. That would not, of course, be anything inherently unusual. Many cultures can show a similarly complicated cultural history and comparable anomalies of myth and belief. The fusion in British culture of Saxon, English, Norman and Celtic, and of pagan and Christian, is just one instance. Here literacy becomes a factor: in one way it makes the domestication of alien elements more efficient, since suppression of the irrelevant and the inconsistent becomes more thorough. By contrast, societies that have never been exposed to literacy are often, though not always, culturally isolated, and as a consequence their myths express social and speculative concerns more purely and with fewer diversions.

One of the most assured instances of the borrowed myth was found to be the Flood. As we saw, it is incompletely integrated into Greek mythical pre-history. It is variously associated with Deucalion, Ogygus or Lykaon's sons. It is sent by Zeus to punish a specific sin – but also as part of a plan to relieve the teeming earth, as in the post-Homeric *Cypria*. Moreover it is integrally connected with two other borrowed themes, each with its own special area of vagueness. The first is that of the Golden Age, or more generally a succession of mythical ages including, in Hesiod's formulation, that of Bronze. Why did the Golden Age, in particular, come to an end? How far was it related to the behaviour of Kronos? Obviously those are critical questions for the whole problem of the relation of men to gods and the existence of unfairness and evil. Admittedly myths have to remain somewhat mysterious over these particular issues, but the Greek myths are not so much mysterious as lacunose and confused. Hesiod's myth of the Five Races simply avoids the problem by stating that the earth 'concealed' each of the first three races, including the golden one. That is ambivalent in a different way: were they just buried, or perhaps swallowed up? Rather I suspect that the imprecise phrase was found useful for evading those other issues about Kronos and the rest. For, like the Flood, the Golden Age seems to have arrived in Greece from abroad. The concept of a time in the past when all men shared the conditions of divine bliss was, for the Greeks at least, an uneasy one. Mortality was for them an essential part of the human condition. Admittedly they strained at the question whether grim old age and disease, at least, were really necessary, and the concept of a swift death as in sleep was a reflection on that particular problem. It was a component of Hesiod's description of the golden race, but fails to appear as a regular element of the Golden Age situation, which was almost too divine in its proper application to be easily assimilated as a detailed narrative relating explicitly to humans.

The second theme concerned with the flood is that of the gods trying periodically to destroy mankind. Mesopotamian myths are replete with gods and goddesses with an itch to wipe out men. Irra is the Akkadian god of plague and is constantly on the *qui vive* for a chance to annihilate them; he would have done so, too, had it not been for the restraint exercised by his more kindly vizier, Ishum. In the Akkadian poem about Atra-hasis the gods are disturbed by men's quarrelsome and riotous behaviour and send pestilence and famine against them.[10] The virtuous Atra-hasis pleads for his fellow-men, and Ea reprieves them. But they break out once again, and this time the gods send the Flood to destroy them. Atra-hasis, who is the equivalent of Sumerian Ziusudra and Utnapishtim in the Gilgamesh Epic, survives with his wife and family in a kind of ark. The eleventh tablet of the Gilgamesh Epic itself gives a somewhat different version of the flood story. There are signs of the conflation of certain details, no doubt because the theme of destruction was so widespread. At one point Ishtar seems to be the prime mover in attacking men, but at another it is Enlil himself, the chief of the gods, who is accused by Ea of bringing on the deluge. For even in Mesopotamia there is an underlying ambiguity in the whole concept of divine hostility to men, so that the gods who most give way to it are in due course restrained and rebuked by the others, who tend to show remorse for their previous anger or indifference. Much the same is the case in Egypt, where the theme seems once again to be borrowed from Mesopotamia. Hathor, mother goddess and goddess of fertility, who is also Sekhmet and Isis, runs amok among men and fills the land with blood. At last Re manages to deter her by a trick, for he dyes beer red to look like blood, she drinks it greedily and gets so drunk that she forgets her anger. The rest of the gods are then relieved.[11]

This theme of divine destruction only makes sense, even in mythical terms, in Mesopotamia, where men were assumed to have been created for one purpose only: to be the servants of the gods and save them the trouble of preparing food and drink for themselves and looking after their own temples. This is what Marduk says to Ea when he has destroyed Tiamat and established the heavens: 'Blood will I mass and cause bones to be. I will establish a savage, 'man' shall be his name. Verily, savage-man I will create. He shall be charged with the service of the gods that they might be at ease!' (translated by E. A. Speiser). Later these men come to be known as the black-headed ones': 'May food-offerings be borne for their gods and goddesses. Without fail let them support their gods! Their lands let them improve, build their shrines, let the black-headed wait on their gods.'[12] Against an assumption like this the idea of the gods trying to destroy what they have created, once men no longer seem to be performing as planned, is acceptable and indeed logical. Without such an assumption the idea is senseless, or presupposes divine malice for its own sake.

The Greeks, and to a large extent the Egyptians too, were innocent of concepts like these. Men and gods live together in the same world, are part of the same order of things. Pindar regarded them as in a sense offspring of the same mother, the earth itself; moreover men were also descended from the heroes, and the greatest of the heroes were children of a god or goddess. Provided they were properly treated, the gods of the Greeks were normally benign or at worst aloof. Neglected or offended, as Odysseus offended Poseidon by blinding his son Polyphemus, they were dangerous – but discriminating. Men as a whole had made serious mistakes in the course of their history, but they paid for it by disadvantages like having to toil for their livelihood, not by having to withstand repeated attacks by the gods aimed at their total destruction. The Flood is the one well-known occasion on which such an attempt was made. It must always have seemed slightly alien to the common conception of the Olympian gods, and that is an important reason why the myths are imprecise at this point.

Mesopotamian men were created by the gods to be their slaves, and there were varying descriptions of precisely how this took place. Either a god was slain – in the Creation Epic it was Kingu, who was found responsible for the monstrous behaviour of Tiamat and was killed at Marduk's orders – and his blood was mixed with clay to form mankind, or clay was moulded by itself. Sometimes this was done by a craftsman god acting as though he were making figurines in a mould, sometimes by the mother goddess in a womb, or series of wombs, that themselves came close to being potters' matrices. Such ideas were conflated with each other, and there were other more abstract accounts. In any case there were plenty of myths of this kind for would-be borrowers to choose from. Yet the

Greeks, who borrowed so much, seem to have turned their backs on this particular idea of the creation of man. Indeed, their myths are almost silent on the topic, or leave a vacuum to be filled by folk etymologies like Deucalion's creation from stones (p. 135 f.). Hesiod's *Theogony* and *Works and Days*, where something on the subject is only to be expected, devote enormous attention to the creation of *woman*, but men were simply assumed to exist, and how and why they were created remains something of a mystery. The myth of the Five Races goes so far as to admit that the golden and silver races were made by the Olympian gods and the bronze and heroic ones by Zeus, the bronze out of ash-trees. But compare that vague and evasive information with the specific nature of the Mesopotamian myths, or indeed with Greek accounts of the creation of the first woman! Admittedly *Genesis* gives special attention to the making of Eve out of Adam's rib in its second chapter, but it at least allowed them to be created equally in the first: 'male and female created he them'.

The creation of woman was a special concern, partly because of folktale jokes about women being greedy and expensive, but partly because of their crucial physiology. But it becomes all the more important to devote some care to putting men on the scene already. Apollodorus has a story that men were moulded by Prometheus out of clay, and that accords with the view of him as benefactor of man and patron of potters. There might be a residue here of one of the Mesopotamian conceptions, and Pausanias saw the signs of Prometheus' handiwork at Panopeus in Boeotia (see p. 140). Unfortunately these versions do not seem particularly early, and the gaps in Hesiod and to a lesser extent Homer are still significant. Again, the common Greek idea that men in certain places were 'autochthonous' was designed to express their claim to those particular places rather than to imply anything about their creation from the earth in itself. They were charter and not creation myths. In short, the Greeks evidently did not wish to include in their myths any detailed account of the creation of men, even though the various Mesopotamian motifs must have been available, and even though allied themes, in particular the periodical destruction of men, were themselves alluded to. Why?

The existence of the problem has been clearly recognized by Hugh Lloyd-Jones in *The Justice of Zeus* and Peter Walcot in *Hesiod and the Near East*.[13] The latter feels that Hesiod's emphasis on the creation of the first woman fills the gap left by omitting the creation of men in general, but I am sure that is not so. The kind of answer I propose will already be plain to the reader: *it was because the idea of men as slaves of the gods was repugnant to the Greeks that they rejected Mesopotamian stories of their creation and passed over this whole topic*, or adopted details of such stories only erratically and in minority or sectarian versions. They pursued their neglect even at the cost of contradictions implied by the tale of the first woman, a tale they felt free to elaborate since it concerned woman's relation to man and not mankind's to the gods.

We have uncovered a complex of four interlocking themes – the creation of men, the Golden Age, their attempted destruction, the Flood – that are crucial for men's place in the world, and yet are glossed over or defectively treated in Greek myths because their foreign models had irrelevant or unacceptable associations. The range of this kind of approach could no doubt be extended. Not only the disappearing-god motif from which the inquiry started, but also certain aspects of the underworld, of the status of heroes, of the role of prophecy and divination, and of the concept of *moira*, fate, and its relation to the *me's* or Ordinances of Mesopotamian myths, could be freshly examined from this point of view. I leave that for others, or for another place. The general point has been made, if in the nature of things not completely demonstrated, and is intensely relevant to the evaluation of Greek myths as a whole, and in particular their speculative roles. These are not the exclusive roles of myths, or necessarily the most important ones. Yet the problematic aspects – or their absence – are more than ordinarily absorbing for the modern reader, because it was against the background of the myths that there evolved a kind of imaginative reasonableness that became the foundation of western philosophy and science. Babylonia made its most obvious contribution to Greece through mathematics and astronomy in the historical period, but it begins to look as though Mesopotamian culture had already made an earlier and even profounder impact through the medium of myths.

# CHAPTER 12

# FROM MYTHS TO PHILOSOPHY?

IT would be easy to write, in a final chapter, about the later development of Greek myths, whether by Stoic and Neo-platonic allegorical interpreters, by Hellenistic and Roman poets, by scholarly mythographers, or in Medieval and Renaissance literature. Some of these are fascinating subjects in their own right. Yet the nature of Greek myths themselves, except in decadent forms, is not strongly illuminated by such studies. Rather I want to conclude by examining the complicated stages by which a myth-dominated culture gradually turned into one in which *philosophy* was an important element. For this is what happened in Greece between the time of Homer, or before, and that of Plato and Aristotle. It is obviously an important question, and illuminating for the nature of myths themselves, whether they were the ancestors of philosophy in some real sense – whether the chronological priority of one to the other implies some kind of causal relationship.

Before the First World War a famous historian of early Greek thought, John Burnet, stated that 'with Thales and his successors a new thing came into the world'.[1] Thales of Miletus was the first Greek 'physicist' according to Aristotle, and he worked in Ionia in the early part of the sixth century B.C. Burnet was prepared to concede that 'the rudiments of what grew into Ionic science and history' are to be found in the poems of Hesiod, yet he remained clear that 'philosophy is not mythology'. It was an absolutely different kind of pursuit, one that depended on reason, and Thales exemplified it, in an embryonic way, whereas Hesiod did not. Recently Jean-Pierre Vernant has revived an old criticism of Burnet for implying that philosophy came into being at a definite date, namely in the lifetime of Thales, and has emphasized the merits of a different view advanced by F. M. Cornford, whom we have already met as a member of the 'Cambridge School' (see p. 15 f.).² In his first book, *From Religion to Philosophy*, published in 1912, Cornford used the sociological theories of Durkheim as a means of arguing that early Greek philosophy was as much affected by age-old social and religious attitudes as by the application of pure reason. He modified this approach later, but always disputed the supposedly scientific qualities of Thales and his Ionian successors, maintaining that the 'reason' they used was still heavily infected by mythical preconceptions and thought-patterns.

Vernant himself is more inclined to a Durkheimian view of Greek religion and myths than to the more pragmatic approach implied by Burnet and made explicit by Nilsson and Rose. His own assessment, nevertheless, is a kind of mediation between the two, and in general that is an attitude I myself would favour. He admits, for instance, that Cornford sometimes gave the impression that the only thing that matters in the study of emergent Greek philosophical thought is the identification of its ancient and irrational residues. Vernant is surely right in stressing that what we should be concerned with, rather, is to discover what is fundamentally *new* in philosophy itself. He defines this as, first, the rejection of the supernatural as a means of explaining the phenomenal world, and secondly the search for internal coherence in arguments.

Vernant sees the emergence of philosophy as the result of a kind of 'mental mutation' that took place between the seventh and the sixth centuries B.C. and affected all levels of Greek society. Like others, he lays stress on the probably liberating effects of political developments and economic advances like the invention of money. He has the great merit of avoiding the almost universal assumption (to which I shall return shortly) that there is such a thing as 'mythical thinking' that is displaced by 'philosophical thinking'. Yet he comes perilously close to confusion with his belief that 'philosophy ceases to be myth in order to become philosophy', which implies that philosophy is a kind of transmogrified myth, or that myth just needs something added to it, or subtracted from it, to turn it into philosophy.[3] Part of the trouble here is caused by his excessive devotion to Cornford, for whom the physical theories of Anaximander (in particular) were little more than a rationalization of certain mythical beliefs. Another part is Vernant's acceptance of 'myth' as a thing-in-itself, which might have been avoided by clinging (as I have tried to do) to the idea that there are *myths*, which are traditional tales of many different kinds and functions, but no such thing as 'myth'. Moreover by setting the main change between Hesiod and Anaximander he ignores the vital evidence of a rational expansion in myths at a much earlier date; and finally, in rejecting the excessively pragmatic approach of Burnet, Nilsson and Rose he tends to lean too far towards ideas (again, Cornfordian in tone) such as that the philosopher 'comes out of the Magus'.[4] Further examination of the relations between myths and philosophy in Greece is still needed.

It was seen in the first chapter that myths achieve their greatest prominence in traditional and non-literate societies. In most such societies traditional tales are an important means of argument, persuasion, consolation and communication. They are the primary form taken by generalized discussion of perennial topics. They are part of a way of life, but they are not usually consistent, still less philosophical. Philosophy tries to be consistently reasonable and to deal with general subjects of universal application; myths do not. In a non-traditional and literate society, on the other hand, individual views are encouraged, 'charters' are best done in writing, consistency becomes a virtue, the factual gains the upper hand over the fantastic and the poetic. Such a society is not necessarily philosophical, but it provides a background against which reasoning and generalization can develop. A traditional society does not. Even more important, by its very conservatism and traditionality, by its acceptance of myths as supplying all necessary answers, it is fundamentally opposed to change, whether in institutions and customs or in beliefs. The organic use of myths has to disappear before philosophy becomes even a remote possibility.

It is true that literacy in Greece became established as late as the period of Homer and Hesiod, roughly around 700 B.C. But we have seen already that this was not a typical case. Literacy entered the scene uniquely late in Greece in relation to the development of other cultural institutions. Pre-Homeric Greece was not a traditional society just because it was pre-literate; it had lost many aspects of traditionality not only long before Homer, but long before the Mycenaean age with its highly sophisticated political, social and economic organization. Myths retained unusual cultural significance down to and beyond the date of Homer, but must have already changed their emphasis and functions in society; furthermore they had been systematized to a degree without parallel in any truly traditional society. Indeed the oral heroic tradition in Greece, culminating in the *Iliad*, acquired many of the properties of literacy without being actually literate. In such ways as these Greece presents a unique case. Mesopotamia offers some parallel, but there literacy had begun as early as around 3000 B.C. In Greece, on the other hand, its prolonged absence (not counting the temporary and limited phenomenon of the Late Bronze Age linear scripts) allowed certain traditional attitudes to linger on in an environment that was otherwise progressive and even revolutionary. Myths were still important, but so was consistency: a rare and paradoxical state of affairs that may be partly responsible for the unique adventure in rational imagination that began in sixth-century Ionia.

Against this general background we can turn to consider that chimerical entity, 'mythical thought'. First the even more grandiose matter of 'mythopoeic thought' can be disposed of. It is a purely emotive phrase, usually brought on the scene when a writer becomes uneasily aware that the simpler 'mythical thought' is a suspicious character. The noun 'mythopoeia', on the other hand, is acceptable if unnecessary; it simply means 'making myths', *poieō* being the Greek for 'I make'. All that 'mythopoeic thought' can mean, therefore, is a kind of thought that leads to, or is expressed in, the making of myths. Anything that can be said for or against mythical thought will apply to the more complex expression, which can be dropped forthwith.

Thought either is, or presupposes, thinking, and it is helpful to inquire without delay whether there is such a thing as mythical *thinking*. (I shall not at this stage press the point that a myth is a traditional tale, although that is a relevant consideration.) Does the use of myths, then, whether through making or hearing them, entail a special kind of thinking? The answer was simple in the days when 'primitive mentality' was held to be the property of all tribal or savage societies; mythical thinking was assumed to be a manifestation, perhaps the primary one, of that kind of mentality. Yet we have already seen that the vision of non-thinking savages leading their lives in accordance with random impulses and mystical associations has failed to withstand the scrutiny of anthropologists. It has been specifically disproved by Lévi-Strauss's observation, nowhere seriously questioned, that members of simple societies, even if they wear no clothes, think systematically enough, although by different logics from that of Aristotle.

Classical scholars have been very free with 'mythical thinking', but have generally been reluctant to discuss what it might amount to. But here is Bruno Snell, a good Greek scholar and author of the influential book translated from German into English as *The Discovery of the Mind*: 'It is evident that mythical and logical thought are not co-extensive; many aspects of myth remain inaccessible to logic, and many truths discovered by logic were without precedent in myth ... They do not exclude each other completely; there is room, in mythical thought, for much that is logical, and vice versa, and the transition between the two is slow and gradual – in fact no transition is ever fully completed.'[5] This is admirable in its recognition that myths and logic are not absolute contradictories, that there is an area in which, in practice at least, they overlap. But it accepts the idea of mythical *thought* as almost axiomatic. Another passage shows that Snell had nothing very profound or precise in mind: 'Even before the so-called logical thinking came upon the scene men were able to speak in connected sentences, just as they did not wait for the arrival of rational thought before they began to feel the need for seeking out causes ... Mythical thought, too, is interested in aetiology ...'[6] The curious concession that pre-logical (pre-Aristotelian?) man actually used connected speech is presumably a riposte to Lévy-Bruhlian ideas about the strange behaviour of primitives; one notes, too, that pre-logical is equated with non-rational. The respect in which myths and reason overlap is now seen to be that they both offer explanations. Yet the concrete *aitia* of myths often rely on trivial or humorous resemblances and are hardly 'logical' at all, whereas mythical 'solutions' of more serious problems work in a quite different way from logical explanation and may be held to be exclusive of it.

Even more revealing, Snell draws the obvious comparison with dreams – obvious, that is, since Freud: 'Mythical thought is closely related to thinking in images and similes. Psychologically speaking, both differ from logical thought in that the latter searches and labours while the figures of myth and the images of the similes burst fully-shaped upon the imagination ... Logical thought is unimpaired wakefulness; mythical thinking borders upon the dream in which images and ideas float by without being controlled by the will.'[7] The images that are common to dreams and similes are evidently concrete visual images, it is they that 'burst . . . upon the imagination . . . without being controlled by the will'. For this view Snell must be partly indebted to Ernst Cassirer (see pp. 79–81), who simply asserted, with nothing in the way of supporting evidence, that myths leap into the mind rather in the manner of religious experiences. They are a response, by direct apprehension, to certain striking aspects of the outside world. It is indeed plausible that, whereas philosophical thought achieves its results by systematic reasoning, myths are created and apprehended more emotionally and directly. The story-teller, after all, is a very different creature from the logician. But the rest does not follow. Myths sometimes resemble dreams in a way; that is true, although not as it happens of most Greek myths as we know them. The resemblance depends on their striking oddity and inconsequentiality rather than on any visual quality as such. Admittedly myths are stories, and stories are made out of concrete situations which tend to be realized in as graphic a form as possible, but they do not consist of an apparently random sequence of images in the way dreams do. Nor does there seem to be any serious reason for believing that the figures of myth 'burst into the imagination' or that, having done so, they 'float by'. As for the images of similes, it is their symbolic rather than their visual quality that is often most remarkable, although the Homeric similes form an exception. Yet there is no reason to suppose that most myths are especially symbolic. Demeter and Persephone symbolize the fertility of the earth, and Enkidu symbolizes for Gilgamesh the death that overtakes all mankind; yet many myths have no such reference, and even those that are most mysterious, like the myth of the Labyrinth, need have no specifically symbolic meaning.

Snell's contention about myths and dreams, although suggestive in some respects, collapses at the points at which it engages with the idea of mythical thinking. Similar implications underlie Sir Maurice Bowra's assertion: 'Primitive myths are often hard to understand because they assume connections which mean nothing to us and operate by emotional or visual associations in which we see little coherence. They are not conceived in a rational spirit of explanation but appeal to half-conscious and unconscious elements in human nature.'[8] This comes from a book about primitive song, but the author held similar views about the nature of myths in Pindar. Like Snell, Bowra establishes a dichotomy between myths and reason. The spirit of Lévy-Bruhl is more in evidence than that of Cassirer, but with the sensible and almost Lévi-Straussian concession that visual and emotional associations can be valid even if *we* happen not to see the connection. Once more, however, there is the stress on the visual qualities of myths. But do they really have unique visual qualities? I have already cast doubt on this in general terms, but perhaps it is now worth considering a quite unusually imaginative myth of the primary and functional kind to see what its visual elements might amount to in practice.

The tale of Geriguiaguiatugo, told by the Bororo Indians of Brazil, is so central to the myths of this prolific culture that Lévi-Strauss took it as a point of departure for his whole investigation in *Mythologiques*.[9] Geriguiaguiatugo was a young man who followed his mother into the forest and raped her, which caused his father to try to destroy him by sending him on deadly quests. When they failed, through various magical devices, he stranded the boy up a cliff. Geriguiaguiatugo escaped to the summit with the help of a magic stick given him by his grandmother; there he killed some lizards for food and hung some of them round his belt as a reserve, then fell into an exhausted sleep. The lizards rotted and so attracted vultures, who devoured them and some of the young man's fundament as well. But they then conveyed him out of friendliness to the bottom of the cliff, where he found that he could take no nourishment because the food passed straight through him. He put a stop to this by modelling an artificial replacement out of a kind of mashed potato. Then he returned to his grandmother, whose fire was the only one to survive a great storm, and eventually killed both parents as well as his father's new wife.

I have omitted many details, including important references to cultural customs, for example that his mother had gone into the forest to collect leaves for a male initiation ceremony. The whole question of incest is being somehow related to the discovery of fire, and this, together with the vultures and the raw food that passes straight through the hero, are shown by Lévi-Strauss to be part of the raw–cooked, Nature–Culture polarity that underlies many of these South American myths. But what especially concerns us is the tale's visual quality. Is it really visual in some special way, so much so as to imply an exclusive mode of mythical thought or perception? Imaginative and fantastic, yes: there are graphic references to birds, animals, people and landscapes, as well as fantastic allusions to human physiology and social actions like incest and initiation. But in the end I suggest that, although strikingly imaginative in a visual way, it is little more so than many novels or poems, and that its visual qualities are those of vivid narrative and untrammelled imagination rather than of myths as embodying a special way of thinking.

Scholarship is a traditional activity in itself, and quite often a misconception survives just because it has been held by earlier generations. It is here, in my opinion, that an explanation is to be found for the ubiquitous modern belief that mythical 'thinking' depends on visual and figurative properties peculiar to myths. For this assumption, together with much concerning the dichotomy between mythical and rational thinking, appears to be based on a sporadic argument about the nature of being and knowledge that was conducted among German philosophers, especially Kant, Fichte, Schelling and Hegel, in the later part of the eighteenth century and the early years of the nineteenth. One of the main questions concerned the nature of judgements, and in particular the relation of perceiving to conceptualizing. Kant had maintained that all judgements (except exclusively analytical ones) involve both kinds of activity, in other words the combination of a particular observation or sense impression with a general concept.[10] Fichte and Schelling insisted that a kind of direct apprehension is possible in the case of aesthetic judgements. Gradually the idea arose of a kind of figurative thinking based on concrete images and excluding intellectual concepts. Furthermore Hegel's early book, *The Phenomenology of the Spirit*, had advanced the theory that the human spirit moves on from more rudimentary to more mature forms of thought and culture. That persuaded many nineteenth-century philosophers and historians, not least Eduard Zeller, the first systematic modern historian of Greek philosophy, that something akin to mythical thinking, based on the use of images, gradually gave way to philosophical thinking based on the use of concepts. In this largely schematic analysis there was no detailed examination of the myths themselves to see if they might actively support the theoretical distinction of two separate modes of thought.

If I am right, then, the belief in mythical *thinking* directed to visual and figurative objects is a hangover from the crude psychology of the late eighteenth century and the unworldly epistemology of the early nineteenth. Yet it still seems to be what another Greek scholar from Germany, W. Schadewaldt, has in mind when he writes of a 'capacity for concrete visual apprehension (*Schaukraft*) common to all Greeks . . . through which a notion so easily takes figurative form', and when he associates this 'visual apprehension' with 'prelogical thought'.[11] I have quoted mainly from German scholars not because they are unusual in making this kind of judgement, but because they express it more fluently and with fewer inhibitions than empirically-minded Anglo-Saxons. Many of the nineteenth-century attitudes to ancient Greece that spread from Germany in its greatest era of classical scholarship have been modified or replaced, but this somewhat bizarre idea about mythical thinking, together with the belief that irrational, mythical thought somehow flowered there into rational, philosophical thought, seems to have survived unscathed.

It would be foolish to argue that all these distinctions are completely false. Clearly the irrational is the contradictory of the rational; clearly there are periods and places where people make relatively more use of perception and relatively less of reason, and vice versa; clearly myths are strong in concrete, visual situations and weak in discursive arguments; clearly one may reasonably expect a general movement, at certain stages of cultural development, from more concrete to more abstract ways of thinking. Nevertheless the detailed understanding of myths and their possible relations to philosophy has been seriously distorted by those learned Hegelian speculations – as well, of course, as by the primitivism of Sir Edward Tylor and Lucien Lévy-Bruhl, the naïve comparatism of Sir James Frazer, the sociological exaggerations of Durkheim, Jane Harrison and the early Cornford, the ponderous neo-Kantian epistemology of Cassirer and the romantic functionalism of Lévi-Strauss. Deprived of support from dreams (not a form of thought) and primitive mentality (a chimaera), 'mythical thinking' can be clearly seen for what it is: the unnatural offspring of a psychological anachronism, an epistemological confusion and a historical red herring.

The dichotomy between myths and reason has done further damage by encouraging the belief that myths are completely irrational. Naturally they are nothing of the kind. The tale of Geriguiaguiatugo, which is stranger than most, is not untypical in this respect. Many of its hero's procedures presuppose a keen analysis of circumstances leading to reasonable decisions on his part. Tying the dead lizards round his belt was a rational thing to do, given that he would shortly wish to move on. The vultures devouring part of his posterior was presumably an unfortunate mistake on their part, but Geriguiaguiatugo's repair of the damage was seen by him to be necessary in order that he could take nourishment and therefore survive. This is a savage myth, in which inconsequentiality plays its part. Even so it is not wholly irrational, even at the most obvious level; and at a deeper one the apparent inconsequentialities lead to the formation of an attitude towards problems of culture and kinship that could be the object, in different circumstances, of deliberately rational procedures.

Greek myths are obviously more rational still, partly because in the form known to us they have been subjected to a long process of organizing and assimilation. Many critics, nevertheless, have assumed that the Homeric poems represent a pre-rational, indeed an irrational, stage of thought. Everything in the Homeric poems, according to W. K. C. Guthrie in his important *History of Greek Philosophy*, 'has a personal explanation', including 'external and physical phenomena like rain and tempest, thunder and sunshine, illness and death', and men view the world according to 'religious faith' which excludes the belief that 'the visible world conceals a rational and intelligible order'.[12] This is certainly exaggerated. Homeric gods and goddesses, as well as heroes, are constantly taking rational decisions. When Zeus wishes to weaken the Achaeans, in order to follow out his decision to help Thetis obtain redress for her son Achilles, he sends down his messenger Iris to direct Hector to a vulnerable part of the battlefield. The concept of a god using a rainbow to pass inaudible messages is not in itself rational, but everything else is. And, of course, the gods are often absent from the scene; to some extent, also, their activities had become a literary convention rather than a literal account of how men believe things to happen, and in any case divine motivation does not exclude reason. Odysseus has Athena to help and Poseidon to hinder him for part of his adventures, but with few exceptions he is represented as behaving extremely rationally, indeed as initiating complex processes of analysis and decision-making that would do credit to Bertrand Russell himself – in the circumstances.

It is true that most of Odysseus' rationality is on a practical level. Yet at times the *Odyssey* rises above this level, for example when at its very beginning Zeus complains that men blame the gods for all evils, but that in reality men are responsible, through their own folly, for much that happens to them. That is a generalization, a universal judgement, about important matters. Another well-known kind of epic generalization is the proverb, no doubt an age-old form of popular wisdom; for instance: 'Men's tongues can turn this way and that, and contain many sayings', or 'The rule of many is not good; let there be one ruler.'[13] Generalizing is even more remarkably combined with close observation and analysis in this short judgement on happy marriage in the sixth book of the *Odyssey*:

Nothing is better than this, when a man and a woman live together at home in harmony of mind – great grief to their enemies but joy to well-wishers, and they themselves know it best of all.[14]

For the most part this kind of generalizing and abstraction is directed to human behaviour (or quasi-human behaviour in the case of the gods). The range of rational decision and analysis is limited, and does not normally extend to the nature of the world as a whole – although it took in, as we saw just now, the problems of human responsibility and of evil. But enough has been said to show the idea of Homer as totally irrational is absurd, and the same can be said for those myths that happen to fall outside his restricted narrative range.

Instead of setting up wild oppositions between rational and irrational thinking and supposing that there are periods in which one or the other is completely dominant, instead of propagating the pallid notion that there is a special kind of mythical thinking that is the opposite, in some way, of philosophy, it would be better to look more closely first at what we mean by rational thought and philosophy, and second at the kinds of mental attitude that were actually involved in Greek myths.

First, the development of philosophy depends (I would suggest) not only on a *mode of thinking* – that is, both rational and systematic – but also on the *generality* of its objects – abstract rather than particular – as well as on a special kind of *attitude* on the part of the thinker, one of unrestricted and wide-ranging inquiry. Systematic rational thinking about the knee-joint of a gnat is not philosophy, for the objects of philosophy are general and abstract. Nor is thinking about all knee-joints, or the idea of a knee-joint, although it may be science (which differs from philosophy in being predictive, among other things), for the philosopher's interest is devoted to the world as a whole, even if it takes note of the parts. If that is roughly true, then it becomes plain that the emergence of philosophy in Greece cannot have depended simply on the rationalizing of myths, as is sometimes believed, and that even this process involves more than meets the eye. For the rejection of traditional and mythical accounts of the world entailed a radical change of attitude to what is interesting and important in the world, a further extension of thought from the particular to the general, and a desire to widen the range of systematic reasoning from the practical to the theoretical.

Secondly, it has not commonly been observed that Greek myths by the time of Homer had assumed a function that already had elements of both the particular and the general: they were now treated as paradigms or *exempla*, familiar and typical instances of certain kinds of situation and ways of reacting to them. This represented an extension of the primary functional use of myths as charters. In simple societies that was only one of the functions of myths, and did not cover all aspects of behaviour. In Mycenaean and post-Mycenaean Greece, on the other hand, the organizing of the myths may well have provided people with a new and more coherent world against which they could measure their own practical problems. Even in the Homeric poems it can be seen how exemplary myths were expected to determine a character's reactions. The well-known tale about what happened to Agamemnon on his return from Troy and the revenge taken by Orestes on Aegisthus and Clytaemnestra is constantly adduced as warning or encouragement to Odysseus (potentially in Agamemnon's situation) and Telemachus (already, in part, in Orestes'). In the context of the *Odyssey* this tale is seen as history, not myth, but other exemplary tales are more remote: for example that of Meleagros, who sulked because of a family quarrel but eventually gave in to his friends' entreaties. This is held up to Achilles, in the embassy scene in the ninth book of the *Iliad*, as an example of the kind of behaviour he, too, should adopt in order to avoid consequences visible in the Meleagros tale.

These instances occur within the action of the Homeric poems. Externally, however, these poems were themselves the source of hundreds of *exempla* for the post-Homeric era, and even before Homer the oral heroic tradition must for long have been a repository of instructive mythical cases. At the most popular level the *Iliad* and *Odyssey* remained as a familiar treasury of ancestral morality and even practical wisdom. People in the fifth century B.C. knew that the heroic age had utterly disappeared, yet they continued to take the reactions of Agamemnon, Diomedes, Achilles, Hector, Odysseus, Penelope, Telemachus, Eumaeus and others – not to speak of Heracles and the whole range of non-Homeric heroes – as a guide to the proper demeanour in analogous situations. On a more intellectual plane the great fifth-century dramatists took the traditional situations of myths, both Homeric and others, and subjected them to new kinds of assessment and interpretation. In other words, they used the myths as examples, but amended their implied situations and brought them up to date. Euripides tended to use them as examples of how *not* to behave.

In one sense, living in a Homer-dominated world was rather like living in a completely traditional society. Yet many aspects of social, political, economic and even religious life after 700 B.C. were not conservative, directed towards the reproduction of the past, but exploratory and evolutionary. It was mainly in the determination of personal behaviour that the myths made their effect, but this was an important area, with implications for society and human circumstances as a whole. In any case the tendency to use mythical exemplars had curiously contradictory effects. On the one hand it limited independent thought, and by concentrating on specific if idealized instances prevented men from developing general principles of conduct. On the other hand the assumption that particular situations could be classified as similar to or dissimilar from exemplary ones, and that these were typical or standard, entailed a promising degree of generalizing even if it stopped short of real abstraction. This was not a mode of thinking in itself, but rather, to use our earlier classification, it depended on an *attitude* to the past, and the inherited myths, that determined men's intellectual approach to life in general. Still less was it irrational. On the contrary, the whole exemplary use of myth was highly rational, particularly in this sophisticated sub-charter form; for one no longer had to believe that the mythical *exempla* were true, merely that they were appropriate. It is rather like people nowadays who claim to 'live *in*, or *by*, literature', who derive their values from situations in plays and novels, which they extract as exemplary for the situations of real life. The reasons for the modern attitude are entirely different, but the effects are not dissimilar: weird or mistaken, if you like, but not actually irrational.

This use of myths as *exempla* is one of the main distinguishing features of mental attitudes at the time of Homer and Hesiod. Another is the continuing acceptance of supernatural elements in myths. I have suggested that certain divine actions (for example Athena tugging Achilles' hair in the first book of the *Iliad* to stop him losing his temper with Agamemnon) may be little more than *façons de parler*; but much remains that cannot be discounted in that way. Should the acceptance of divine elements in myths be associated with a special kind of thought, precisely? At any rate it has nothing to do with an exclusive kind of 'mythical thinking', since what is entailed is clearly, if anything, *religious* thinking. Admittedly the divine apparatus of the myths often depends on personification and narrative development rather than anything specifically religious. Yet the acceptance of gods that can work at a distance and achieve miracles is more than a conventional attitude. If one believes that God works in wondrous ways, that is a belief that conditions one's whole mentality by drastically altering the limits of the possible. Greek myths were seen to contain much in the way of practical rationality, but they also clearly contain a degree of systematic irrationality. Yet even here – and this is the point I want to stress – religious thinking of the kind implicit in Homer is not the polar opposite of rational thinking. Rather it implies a different logic, a small number of shifts in the basic assumptions about cause and effect or, in more general terms, the nature of reality.

Beside religious thinking one could set a kind that is better termed poetic, the common quality of both modes being that each, while applying reason to some parts of its subject-matter, uses various looser metaphorical procedures for other parts. Myths in their primary forms may be held to involve something like poetical thinking, which proceeds by emotional as well as logical stages to achieve a quasi-intellectual end by impressionistic or inconsequential means. In the organized forms that Greek myths had assumed by the time of Homer and Hesiod this poetical mode had largely been suppressed, and only the religious variant, maintained by special forces, remained. Obviously this religious mode had to be abandoned, together with the quite different attitude to myths as *exempla*, before philosophy could make further progress. The former impeded the development of systematic rational thought, the latter the formation of a flexible approach to the world and to the proper objects of serious inquiry. And yet, as we shall see, the view of the cosmos that religion and the divine myths ultimately created made itself felt at a crucial stage in the development of Presocratic thought, even after the anthropomorphic figures of cult and myth had been for the most part discarded.

It is the common opinion, advanced for example by Cornford, that the emergence of philosophy in Greece was initiated by the rationalizing of the myths. That is an incomplete and misleading judgement, even if one takes into account that rationalizing in the broad sense began in the distant past and long before determinable figures like Thales, Hesiod or Homer. Rationalizing in the narrow sense really means no more than de-personifying, and far more than that was certainly involved. Personification, in any case, can take several different forms, with differing implications in respect of rationality and the reverse. Some of the gods, like Aphrodite, personify emotions; others, like Ouranos and Demeter, personify parts and functions of the natural world. It is worth observing that anthropomorphic gods can be created for other reasons than the reduction to human terms of important aspects of our experience. In any event most anthropomorphic gods are the product of social and religious beliefs rather than embodiments of embryonic views on physics or psychology. Mythically active gods are also much indebted to a lively narrative tradition; so too are the heroes, most of whom did not owe their existence to animistic or anthropomorphic procedures and could not, therefore, despite the speculative implications of a Heracles, be subjected to rationalizing in the sense of de-personifying. It is necessary to be clear on this point, because the process of 'rationalizing' to which Cornford and his followers refer is really restricted to the nature myths, and most of the gods implicated in these myths were never fully personified in the first place.

The nature myths in question are largely restricted to the cosmogonical myths described in Chapter 6. Their most conspicuous figures from the point of view of personification are Ouranos, Gaia and Okeanos, representing the sky, the earth and the freshwater river that surrounds the earth's flat surface. Hesiod depicts Gaia as giving birth to Pontos, the salt sea, as well, but at this point personification has virtually ceased. Pontos is barely a mythical person, and engages in no anthropomorphic action except for engendering the merman Nereus. Even Ouranos and Gaia are conceived as sky and earth no less than as persons; they are only partially and sporadically anthropomorphic. Unlike Mesopotamian nature gods such as Enlil and Enki, they did not acquire other functions or a variety of mythical actions, and Ouranos at least never became the recipient of an important cult. Since the succession myth seems to be Mesopotamian in origin (see p. 256), it seems probable that the whole conception of the Greek nature gods was affected by Anu, Ninhursag, Enki, Enlil and the rest. If so, then the latter's strongly anthropomorphic character as city gods and the like, a character already established by the middle of the third millennium B.C., was somehow rejected – either that, or the influence of their nature aspects was earlier still. In the first and more probable case, a kind of selectivity that is already rational and analytical in intention was being applied by 'Greeks' at a very early stage.

At this point it is helpful to pay special attention to the men who are commonly recognized as founders of Greek philosophy. The first group of these 'Presocratic' thinkers consists of Thales, Anaximander and Anaximenes, all of whom came from the Ionian city of Miletus, across the Aegean from metropolitan Greece, and whose lives spanned the sixth century B.C.[15] It was they who first consciously rejected the tradition of mythical explanations. They continued to be strongly affected by mythical preconceptions, but they do nevertheless, as Burnet insisted, represent the beginnings of a new direction of inquiry. 'Inquiry' was precisely what they claimed to be engaged in, and the same Greek word, from which our word 'history' is derived, was applied to his own very different activities by Herodotus. But the object of the Presocratics' inquiry was the world as a whole, and it was the nature and generality of their object, rather than the introduction of a new mode of thinking, that distinguished them from those who used myths. Even here, of course, the kind of organizing of myths exemplified by Hesiod, starting from the beginning of the world and only ending with the establishment of an ordered cosmos, provided the model. Yet the Milesian thinkers decided to reject the details of this model and to concentrate on trying to isolate some one material out of which the world, despite its variety, is constituted.

What was it that stimulated them to this fresh approach? Not simply the idea of de-personifying the nature myths, although the extension of that process was certainly involved. I suggest, rather, that the crucial factor was the *comparison* of Mesopotamian, Egyptian and Greek versions, which first became possible and probable at just about this time and place: namely in the late seventh and early sixth centuries in Ionia, especially Miletus. Mesopotamian Enki or Ea, Egyptian Nun and Greek Okeanos are all primordial gods, and each of them, even in mythical guise, plainly represents water. Thales believed, as it happens, that the world is somehow made out of water, that water is the unity which underlies apparent incoherence; but it was his assumed concentration on the rational common essence of Enki, Nun and Okeanos as an actual world constituent, rather than his choice of water as such, that was significant for the future. Anaximander went further.[16] He apparently objected to the idea of a single surviving constituent of our world being the originative material, and argued that the world arose out of an 'Indefinite' substance, which modern scholars have been tempted to relate to Hesiod's *chaos*. He also envisaged the natural world as dominated by the opposed powers of the different materials, such as fire and water, that emerged from the Indefinite. This idea of basic oppositions in nature had a more certainly mythical precedent than the Indefinite/*chaos* equation; yet even here there was already a strongly rational quality in Homer's connection of Aphrodite and Ares, Love and War, and even more so in Hesiod's reflections on Strife and Harmony – an opposition still maintained by maturer Presocratic thinkers, especially Heraclitus, Parmenides and Empedocles.

Such survivals are important, but probably the most crucial effect of myths on the early Presocratics was not the presentation of nature gods or love-and-strife figures to be even more completely de-personified, but the provision of an anthropomorphic model for their view of how the world maintains its unity. The Milesian thinkers are essentially cosmogonists, and their idea of cosmogony is plainly based on the theogonical model provided by the divine myths, or more generally by the genealogical undertone of all Greek myths in their organized forms. The Milesians seem to have unconsciously assumed that the development of the world is like that of a human or divine family. The kind of unity they sought in it was the kind conferred by an original ancestor or pair of ancestors, for instance Ouranos and Gaia. That is what I call the *genetic model*, and it is thoroughly anthropomorphic. That does not mean that it is necessarily mythical, or even necessarily false. Seeing things in genetic terms is a typically anthropocentric habit which need not depend on formal personification as in myths. Even so, I would guess that myths in this case provided the genetic model. Not only did the divine theogonies imply it, but even the heroic myths were based on the premise that the first information one needed to know about anyone was who his ancestors were and whether he was ultimately descended from a god. The Milesian thinkers evidently assumed, in much the same way, that the most revealing thing one could say about the world was *what single material it was ultimately derived from.*

By applying this inherited thought-pattern to the natural world, Thales, Anaximander and Anaximenes were able to carry out an inquiry into the physical material of the cosmos that was in some degree scientific. It was not completely so (and Aristotle when he called them 'physicists' only meant that they were concerned with *physis*, 'nature'), for the idea of experiment as necessary for verifying theories was only sporadically applied. But was this proto-science also a kind of proto-philosophy? In a loose sense, yes; but there are three reasons for caution. First, the thinking involved was still far from systematic, and still heavily infected by religious and poetical modes of thought. Even the Milesians' successor Heraclitus of Ephesus could write: 'One thing, the only truly wise, is both willing and unwilling to be called by the name of Zeus.'[17] What is significant here is not only the attempt to connect his individual world-view with the standards of conventional myths and religion, but also the deliberate ambiguity of 'both willing and unwilling'. It was the continuation of this kind of taste for paradox, for playing transformational games with predication, that culminated in Parmenides' disastrous conclusion that change from $x$ to not-$x$ is logically impossible. The second reason for caution is that the primary objects of thought were still too narrowly restricted to the concrete constituents of the material world; abstraction had made relatively little progress from the Hesiodic stage. Thirdly, the Milesians' general attitude to their inquiry was still anthropomorphic and mythical in fundamental respects. If we want to see how philosophy freed itself from myths, we must look further.

The next crucial move was made at the end of the sixth and beginning of the fifth centuries B.C. and is associated with Pythagoras (who was more than a geometer) and even more with Heraclitus, best known for his emphasis on the inevitability of physical change. It was Heraclitus who unequivocally rejected the genetic model, and this was the single most important act, it seems to me, in the emergence of Greek philosophy. 'This world-order,' he asserted, 'was made by no god or man, but always was and is and shall be.'[18] It still seemed important to Heraclitus to specify a single underlying material, in his case fire, but the crucial objective was to name, and explain the working of, a central *directive* constituent in nature. He called it '*logos*', meaning something like 'proportion' or 'measure', and it is in many respects identical with fire itself (which burns, and emits smoke and heat, proportionately to its consumption of fuel). In short, the unity sought by the Presocratics altered from a unity of material to a unity of process, of change and movement. Given the assumption that the world of our experience possesses some kind of underlying coherence – and it is an assumption few philosophers can escape – Heraclitus' formal unity was far less restricted in scope and potentiality than the material unity on which the Milesians had placed such emphasis. They, admittedly, were also concerned at times over the mode of change, but primarily as a means of defending their single material 'ancestor' and explaining its power of diversification. Once the coherence of the world had been established as explicitly dependent on a universal law of change, systematic rational thought was able to extend itself to all aspects of experience, including psychology and ethics, rather than being narrowly physical in scope.

What was it that persuaded Heraclitus to alter the emphasis of his inquiry in this highly productive manner? Was it merely his perception of difficulties and limitations in the methods of his Milesian neighbours and predecessors? If so, then his discoveries are barely relevant to the relation between myths and philosophy, since philosophy was already moving along its own path. But I do not believe this to have been the case. There is one last crucial intervention from the mythical past: I feel certain that what lay behind the Heraclitean *logos* was not only dissatisfaction with Milesian results, but also an essentially religious and mythical preconception. Men in the time of Hesiod (to look no further) had been in no doubt that the world was a unity, and that it was so under the direction of the gods, Zeus above all. Zeus in Homer and Hesiod rules men and Nature by virtue of *Dikē*, or Justice, which is a quasi-personified rule of regularity akin to the even more ancient figure of *Themis*, Custom or 'that which is laid down'. The Milesians had turned, rather, to the genetic model provided by theogonies of the Hesiodic type, beginning from the nature gods. The idea of Zeus ruling a completed world-order through the medium of *Dikē* sank, for them, into the background. And yet, as Hugh Lloyd-Jones puts it in *The Justice of Zeus*, 'The notion of a cosmos, of a universe regulated by causal laws, was a prerequisite of rational speculation about cosmology, science and metaphysics.'[19] In a sense, then, Heraclitus' innovation consisted in the tacit rejection of the genetic model and the revival of the model provided by Zeus and *Dikē*, in the substitution of an analytical and synchronic view of the world for a historical and diachronic one.

Yet this is, like most neat theories, an over-simplification. The Milesians had always been prepared to talk of their originative material as divine; Anaximander, for example, seems to have described his Indefinite both as steering all things and as immortal and free from old age.[20] Even with them, therefore, the religious notion of a world directed by a permanent being, or beings, was present. Yet their emphasis was undeniably on the nature of the material and its means of proliferation through cosmogony – in short, on a genealogical process – rather than on a permanent cohesive principle of our present and manifold world. Heraclitus, on the other hand, seems to have rejected mythical theogony altogether in order to concentrate on what begins to look like a de-personified version of the reign of Zeus. One cannot perhaps be absolutely sure that this is how his idea of the *logos* was consciously formed, even though the *logos* is akin to the wisdom that 'is willing and unwilling to be called by the name of Zeus'. Yet it is a reasonable conjecture that unconsciously, at least, he was affected by a belief in the divine control of the world that was actively held by many, perhaps most, Greeks and still comes out clearly in the plays of Aeschylus. If so, then this is one more critical stage in the long, almost leisurely interplay between myths and reason.

What I have been trying to show is that relations between philosophy and myths in ancient Greece were enormously complex. Existing reconstructions of the emergence of philosophy and the corresponding decline of the myths are still too simple, and set the emphases in the wrong places. There were not one, or two, but several critical steps in the evolution of that systematically rational and wide-ranging thought that we call philosophy. The argument by which I have sought to identify these steps has necessarily been rather dense, so perhaps I shall be forgiven for retracing its main outlines in the next two paragraphs.

One of the crucial observations is that philosophy has no monopoly of either rationality or speculative interest. Myths were subjected to careful arrangement and organization even by the time of Homer and Hesiod, and in a way which already reduced human experience to a kind of system. At some much earlier stage Greek myths, like most others, must have engaged in their own manner, quite distinct from that of philosophy, with social and personal dilemmas – in certain cases, as with the problem of death, more effectively than philosophy could do. Yet that stage had to disappear before the first steps leading to philosophy could be taken. It cannot be stated too clearly that the speculative functions of myths, although they may overlap some of the functions of philosophy, are intrinsically distinct: they *preclude* philosophy rather than facilitate its progress. Perhaps it was fortunate that, for reasons about which one can only remotely conjecture, the primary functions of myths were allowed to lapse at some prehistoric phase in the development of Greek culture, or were only maintained in rare cases. Whether this was the result or the cause of the long organizing process that ended in Hesiod, the systematic structure that appeared, complete with Olympian pantheon and a complex pattern of heroic myths, was an important element in the process that culminated in philosophy.

By Homer's time, too, myths had developed an exemplary role that is in one way an extreme application of primary charter functions. It stimulated, as we saw, a restricted kind of generalization, yet its main effect was conservative and highly discouraging to new ways of thought. Fortunately the pooling of knowledge about other cultures that took place in seventh- and sixth-century Ionia set off a new chain of inquiry, in which the common realistic substratum of foreign and Greek nature myths encouraged the final abandonment of loosely personified nature deities. In the Ionian developments that followed, two mythical models seem to have held sway in turn: first the genetic one, then the model of a permanent order under the rule of Zeus. The latter, which itself has a long history and is not so different from the polity established by the Sumerian and Akkadian gods, was by far the less constricting, even though the former has for obvious reasons most impressed modern scholars. It allowed Heraclitus to develop a systematic interpretation of the world that had many of the elements of philosophy – it only lacked systematic logic to be philosophical. Logic of that kind was gradually hammered out by Parmenides, the Sophists, Socrates, Plato and Aristotle; this stage in the process, in spite of reversions by both Parmenides and Socrates, was substantially free from the effects of myths.

And so it can be seen that the process by which Greek myths gave way to philosophy was far from a straightforward one. There was no simple and uninterrupted progress from the irrational to the rational, from dreams to logic, from the visual to the conceptual, from darkness to light. Some of the stages that seemed to represent an advance in logical terms, like the organizing of the myths, produced a retrogression in emotional terms, for example by encouraging the treatment of myths as traditional *exempla*. Other stages that seem at first sight retro-gressive, like the resurgence of the religious model that we posited for Heraclitus, opened up decisive new ways of advance. The development of philosophy in Greece was not the result of a sudden 'discovery of the mind', a dramatic unleashing of reason over five or six generations. It was closer to a spiritual and emotional Odyssey lasting for many hundreds of years, in which story-telling, social preoccupa-tion, migration, literacy, conservatism and religion all played their part.

Somewhere in all this (and one can say it with a sense of relief) a mysterious vacuum still remains, just as it must in any discursive description of the myths themselves. We cannot define precisely what it was that caused the Greeks of pre-historic times to start treating their myths in a new, more self-conscious and ultimately less serious way. The final result was the *system* of myths whose relics we enjoy and partly understand. By itself, it would have become sterile – did so, indeed, in its Hellenistic and post-classical developments. Fortunately, an enforced broadening of social and cultural horizons directed the rational impulse in which the myths had shared into new channels and led to a different way of looking at the world, no longer mythical, but analytical and phil sophical. Presumably, even in the light of the subsequent history of human rationality, the Greeks gained more than they had long since lost.

# SUGGESTIONS FOR
# FURTHER READING

Apollodorus, *The Library*, translated and edited by J. G. Frazer, Loeb Classical Library, 1921

Cassirer, E., *The Philosophy of Symbolic Forms*, Vol. II, New Haven, 1955 (Eng. trans.)

Dodds, E. R., *The Greeks and the Irrational*, Berkeley, 1951

Fontenrose, J., *Python: a Study of Delphic Myth*, Berkeley, 1959

Frankfort, H. and H. A. (eds.), *Before Philosophy*, Penguin Books, 1949

Grant, Michael, *The Myths of the Greeks and Romans*, London, 1962

Grimal, P., *Dictionnaire de la Mythologie grecque et romaine*, Paris, 1951

Guthrie, W. K. C., *The Greeks and their Gods*, London, 1950

Halliday, W. R., *Indo-European Folk-tales and Greek Legend*, Cambridge, 1933

Hesiod, *Theogony*, edited by M. L. West, Oxford, 1966

Hooke, S. H. (ed.), *Myth, Ritual and Kingship*, Oxford, 1958

Jung, C. G., and Kerényi, K., *Introduction to a Science of Mythology*, London, 1951, revised edn, 1963 (Eng. trans.)

Kirk, G. S., *Myth, its Meaning and Functions in Ancient and Other Cultures*, Berkeley and Cambridge, 1970; paperback, 1973

Kirk, G. S., and Raven, J. E., *The Presocratic Philosophers*, Cambridge, 1956; paperback, 1960

Kramer, S. N. (ed.), *Mythologies of the Ancient World*, Garden City, N.Y., 1961

Kramer, S. N., *Sumerian Mythology*, Second edn, N.Y., 1961

Lévi-Strauss, C., *Structural Anthropology*, N.Y., 1963; Penguin Books, 1972

Lévi-Strauss, C., *Mythologiques* (four vols.), Paris, 1964–72; the first two vols. available in English as *The Raw and the Cooked* and *From Honey to Ashes*, translated by J. and D. Weightman, London and New York, 1969 and 1973

Lloyd-Jones, H., *The Justice of Zeus*, Berkeley, 1971

Mair, Lucy, *An Introduction to Social Anthropology*, Oxford, 1965

Malinowski, B., *Magic, Science and Religion*, N.Y., 1948 (paperback)

Mylonas, G. E., *Eleusis and the Eleusinian Mysteries*, Princeton and London, 1961

Nilsson, M. P., *The Mycenaean Origin of Greek Mythology*, Berkeley, 1931

Oppenheim, A. L., *Ancient Mesopotamia*, Chicago, 1964

Otto, W. F., *The Homeric Gods*, London, 1955 (Eng. trans.)

Pausanias, *Guide to Greece*, translated by Peter Levi, Penguin Books, 1971

Pettazzoni, R., *The All-Knowing God*, London, 1956 (Eng. trans.)

Pinsent, John, *Greek Mythology*, London, 1969

Pritchard, J. B. (ed.), *Ancient Near Eastern Texts relating to the Old Testament*, second edn, Princeton, 1955; third edn (with same pagination and a supplement), Princeton, 1969

Reinhold, Meyer, *Past and Present*, Toronto, 1972

Ringgren, Helmer, *Religions of the Ancient Near East*, London, 1973 (Eng. trans.)

Rose, H. J., *A Handbook of Greek Mythology*, sixth edn, London, 1958

Rose, H. J., *Gods and Heroes of the Greeks*, London, 1957 (a much reduced version of the above)

Schefold, K., *Myth and Legend in Early Greek Art*, London, 1966

Sebeok, T. A. (ed.), *Myth: a Symposium*, Indiana, 1955

Snell, B., *The Discovery of the Mind*, Oxford, 1953 (Eng. trans.)

Walcot, P., *Hesiod and the Near East*, Cardiff, 1966

# ABBREVIATIONS USED IN
# THE REFERENCES

*ANET:*  J. B. Pritchard (ed.), *Ancient Near Eastern Texts relating to the Old Testament*, second edn, Princeton, 1955; third edn (with same pagination and a supplement), Princeton, 1969

*Myth:*  G. S. Kirk, *Myth, its Meaning and Functions in Ancient and Other Cultures*, Berkeley and Cambridge, 1970; paperback, 1973

*Mythologies:*  S. N. Kramer (ed.), *Mythologies of the Ancient World*, Garden City, N.Y., 1961

*Religions:*  Helmer Ringgren, *Religions of the Ancient Near East*, 1973 (Eng. trans.)

# REFERENCES

| page | note | |
|---|---|---|
| 17 | 1 | Andrew Lang, *Custom and Myth*, 1884; *Myth, Ritual and Religion*, 1887; *Modern Mythology*, 1897; cf. R. M. Dorson in T. Sebeok (ed.), *Myth, a Symposium*, Indiana, 1955, 25 ff. |
| | 2 | T. B. L. Webster, *Everyday Life in Classical Athens*, 1969, 97 |
| | 3 | H. R. Ellis Davidson, *Gods and Myths of Northern Europe*, Penguin Books, 1964, 9 |
| 30 | 1 | F. Boas, *Tsimshian Mythology*, Washington, D.C., 1916 |
| 31 | 2 | *Ibid.*, 880 |
| | 3 | *Encyclopaedia of the Social Sciences*, 1930–35, 11, 179 (s.v. Myth) |
| 32 | 4 | *Myth in Primitive Psychology*, 1926; reprinted in B. Malinowski, *Magic, Science and Religion*, Garden City, N.Y., 1954 |
| | 5 | *Op. cit.*, 14 |
| 33 | 6 | E. E. Evans-Pritchard, *The Zande Trickster*, Oxford, 1967, 15 |
| | 7 | Ruth Finnegan, *Limba Stories and Storytelling*, Oxford, 1967, 34 ff. |
| 37 | 8 | Jack Goody in *Antiquity* 45, 1971, 159 |
| 39 | 1 | Percy S. Cohen, 'Theories of Myth', *Man* 4, 1969, 337 ff. |
| 42 | 2 | See esp. L. Lévy-Bruhl, *Le Mentalité primitive*, Paris, 1922; Eng. trans., *Primitive Mentality*, 1923, *passim*. |
| | 3 | Paris, 1962; Eng. trans., *The Savage Mind*, 1966, ch. 1 |
| 46 | 4 | Hesiod, *Theogony*, 116 |
| 47 | 5 | Stesichorus, frag. 6, 1–4 (Diehl); Mimnermus, frag. 10 (Diehl) |
| | 6 | *Mythologies*, 96 f.; *Myth*, 99 f. |
| 48 | 7 | Plato, *Phaedrus*, 229 B–D |
| 52 | 8 | K. Meuli, 'Griechische Opferbräuche', *Phyllobolia* (Festschrift Peter Von der Mühll), Basel, 1946, 185–288 |
| 53 | 9 | See esp. the second work cited in n. 1 to p. 17. |

| 54 | 10 | See G. S. Kirk, 'Aetiology, Ritual, Charter', *Yale Classical Studies* 22, 1971, 83 ff. |
| 55 | 11 | R. M. and C. H. Berndt, *The World of the First Australians*, 1964, 334 f. |
| 56 | 12 | *Myth*, 50 ff., with references |
| | 13 | *Op. cit.* in n. 11 to p. 55, 336 |
| 57 | 14 | *ANET*, 101 f.; *Myth*, 122 ff.; *Religions*, 75 |
| 58 | 15 | [Homer], *Hymn to Apollo*, 493–6; M. P. Nilsson, *Geschichte der griechischen Religion* I, third edn, Munich, 1967, 554 f. |
| | 16 | Heraclitus, frag. 48 (Diels); Aeschylus, *Agamemnon*, 681 ff. (Helen), 1080 ff. (Apollo), *Supplices*, 584 f. (Zeus) |
| | 17 | *ANET*, 3 |
| 59 | 18 | *ANET*, 36 ff.; *Myth*, 91 ff.; *Religions*, 21 f. |
| | 19 | *Op. cit.* in n. 4 to p. 32, e.g. p. 101; cf. *op. cit.* in n. 10 to p. 54, 97 ff. |
| 60 | 20 | *Op. cit.* in n. 4 to p. 32, 100 |
| 61 | 21 | *Myth*, 21 f. |
| 63 | 22 | E. R. Leach, *Political Systems of Highland Burma*, 1954, 278 |
| | 23 | *Op. cit.* in n. 11 to p. 55, 223 |
| | 24 | E.g. *The Myth of the Eternal Return*, 1954; *Myths, Dreams, and Mysteries*, New York, 1961 |
| 64 | 25 | *Myths, Dreams, and Mysteries*, 33 |
| 67 | 26 | A. R. Radcliffe-Brown, *The Andaman Islanders*, Cambridge, 1922, 397 ff.; *Structure and Function in Primitive Society*, 1952, 178 ff. |
| | 27 | *Op. cit.* in n. 22 to p. 63, 13 |
| | 28 | *Op. cit.* in n. 11 to p. 55, 344 |
| 73 | 1 | 'The Relation of the Poet to Day-dreaming', 1908, *Collected Papers* IV, 1925, 182 |
| 75 | 2 | *Harvard Theological Review* 35, 1942, 45 ff. |
| 77 | 3 | The clearest exposition is by Jung in C. G. Jung (ed.), *Man and his Symbols*, 1964, ch. 1. |
| 78 | 4 | *Myth*, 275 ff. |
| 80 | 5 | E. Cassirer, *The Philosophy of Symbolic Forms* (Eng. trans.), New Haven, 1955, esp. Vol. II |
| | 6 | E. Cassirer, *Language and Myth*, New York, 1964, 33 |
| | 7 | *Op. cit.* in n. 5 to p. 80, 19 |

| 81 | 8 | Lévi-Strauss's theory is outlined in *Structural Anthropology*, 1963 (Penguin Books, 1972), ch. 11, and developed at length in the four volumes of *Mythologiques*, Paris, 1964–72. |

81 8 Lévi-Strauss's theory is outlined in *Structural Anthropology*, 1963 (Penguin Books, 1972), ch. 11, and developed at length in the four volumes of *Mythologiques*, Paris, 1964–72.

83 9 *Structural Anthropology*, 216

84 10 *Le Cru et le cuit*, Paris, 1964, 9

11 *Myth*, 73 ff.

89 12 *International Encyclopaedia of the Social Sciences* 10, 1968, 576 f. (s.vv. Myth and Symbol)

13 *Ibid.*, 577

90 14 *ANET*, 40 (Ninhursag), 97 f. (Gilgamesh and Enkidu)

91 15 *Op. cit.* in n. 11 to p. 55, 341

96 1 See e.g. my *Homer and the Epic*, Cambridge, 1965, chs. 1 and 2.

97 2 Herodotus II, 53

98 3 Xenophanes, frag. 11 (Diels)

99 4 Hesiod, *Theogony*, 116, cf. 700, 740

100 5 Simonides, frag. 38 (Page)

6 Sappho, frag. 44 (Lobel-Page)

102 7 Pindar, *Isthmians* 6, 20 f.; 5, 19 f.

107 8 Herodotus I, 34–45

9 Herodotus I, 107–113

109 10 *Iliad* 2, 558, in which Ajax is said to have stationed his (Salaminian) ships with the Athenians: interpolated according to several ancient sources.

112 11 For a very different approach emphasizing this point, see B. Vickers, *Towards Greek Tragedy*, 1973.

117 1 H. G. Güterbock in *Mythologies*, 155 ff.; *Myth*, 214 ff.

118 2 *ANET*, 60 ff.; *Mythologies*, 120 f.; *Religions*, 69–71

140 3 Pausanias 10: 4, 4

156 1 Pausanias 3: 18, 6 to 19, 5 (Amyclae); 5: 17, 5 to 19, 10 (Cypselus)

171 2 T. B. L. Webster, *from Mycenae to Homer*, 1958, p. 47 and fig. 9; cf. Mabel Lang, *The Palace of Nestor* II, Princeton, 1969, pl. 126.

172 3 I. M. Linforth, *The Arts of Orpheus*, Berkeley, 1941, 167 ff.

174 4 Pausanias 6: 6, 4 ff.

| | | |
|---|---|---|
| 179 | 1 | Herodotus II, 44 |
| 180 | 2 | F. Brommer, *Vasenlisten zur griechischen Herakles*, Münster/Köln, 1953; *Heldensage*, Marburg/Lahn, 1960 |
| 183 | 3 | L. R. Farnell, *Greek Hero Cults*, Oxford, 1921, 107 |
| 185 | 4 | R. Hampe, *Früher griechischen Sagenbilder*, Athens, 1936, pl. 8c |
| 186 | 5 | E.g. G. S. Kirk, *Homer and the Epic*, Cambridge, 1965, pl. 3 (b) |
| 187 | 6 | Euripides, *Heracles*, 380 ff.; Pindar, from 169, esp. vv. 20 ff. |
| | 7 | Apollodorus 2: 5, 8 |
| 188 | 8 | E.g. H. M. Lorimer, *Homer and the Monuments*, 1950, pl. IX, 1 |
| 190 | 9 | *Theogony*, 305–15 |
| 191 | 10 | J. H. Croon, *The Herdsman of the Dead*, Utrecht, 1952, *passim* |
| 195 | 11 | *Iliad* 1, 268 |
| 198 | 12 | Pindar, *Isthmians* 4, 52–5 |
| 202 | 13 | A. Brelich, *Gli eroi greci*, Rome, 1958, 373 ff.; (Psamathe), 253 |
| 211 | 14 | M. P. Nilsson, *The Mycenaean Origin of Greek Mythology*, Berkeley, 1932, 205 |
| 213 | 1 | *ANET*, 73 ff.; *Myth*, 132 ff. |
| 217 | 2 | M. P. Nilsson, *Geschichte der griechischen Religion* I, third edn, Munich, 1967, 378–84 |
| | 3 | For their distribution see e.g. C. Renfrew, *The Emergence of Civilisation*, 1972, fig. 4.2 on p. 48. |
| 225 | 1 | Pausanias 8: 25, 4–6 |
| 226 | 2 | *Political Systems of Highland Burma*, 1954, 13, cf. 264 |
| | 3 | *The Ritual Theory of Myth*, Berkeley, 1966, 54 |
| 227 | 4 | W. Burkert, *Homo Necans* (in German), Berlin and New York, 1972, 1–96, with refs.; cf. *Greek, Roman and Byzantine Studies* 7, 1966, 87 ff. |
| | 5 | L. Deubner, *Attische Feste*, Hildesheim and New York, 1932, reprinted 1969, 26, n. 2 |
| 228 | 6 | A convenient translation of Pausanias by Peter Levi is available in Penguin Classics (1971); also trans. by W. H. S. Jones, Loeb Classical Texts, Harvard, 1918–. |

| 230 | 7 | The scholiast on Lucian (Rabe, p. 28., 3 ff.) confuses the origin of the ritual with the myth of Icarius (*op. cit.* in n. 5 to p. 227, 61). |
|---|---|---|
| 234 | 8 | Aristophanes, *Clouds*, 985 |
| | 9 | Pausanias 1: 24, 4 |
| 238 | 10 | Origen, *c. Celsum* VI, 42; G. S. Kirk and J. E. Raven, *The Presocratic Philosophers*, Cambridge, 1957, 65 ff. |
| 240 | 11 | W. Burkert, *Homo Necans*, 1972, 103–7 |
| 245 | 12 | W. Burkert, *Classical Quarterly* 20, 1970, 7 |
| 247 | 13 | *ANET* 60 ff., cf. 332; *Myth*, 13 ff., with refs. |
| 248 | 14 | R. Benedict, *Patterns of Culture*, Boston, 1934, 174, 184–6 |
| 252 | 15 | Clement of Alexandria, *Protrepticus* 2, 12 |
| 256 | 1 | *ANET*, 120 f. (Kumarbi); 60 ff. (Apsu) |
| 257 | 2 | See e.g. W. K. C. Guthrie, *The Greeks and their Gods*, 1950, esp. chs. II and VII; M. P. Nilsson, *op. cit.* in n. 2 to p. 217, part III. |
| 259 | 3 | *ANET*, 1 |
| 260 | 4 | *ANET*, 52–7, 97–9, 106–10; *Religions*, 46–8, 121 f. |
| 263 | 5 | See esp. Sir M. Mallowan in *Cambridge Ancient History*, Vol. I pt. 1, third edn, Munich, 1970, pp. 353 f. |
| 265 | 6 | E.g. *ANET*, 37–9 (from 'Enki and Ninhursag'); *Religions*, 21 f.; S. N. Kramer in *Mythologies*, 102 f. |
| 266 | 7 | E.g. Sinclair Hood, *The Minoans*, 1971, pl. 60; M. P. Nilsson, *op. cit.* in n. 2 on p. 217, pl. 10, figs. 1 and 2 |
| 267 | 8 | *ANET*, 23–5 (Two Brothers); 15 (Horus and Seth) |
| | 9 | Clement of Alexandria, *Protrepticus* 2, 16–18 |
| 270 | 10 | *ANET*, 104–6; *Religions*, 74 |
| 271 | 11 | *ANET*, 11 |
| | 12 | *ANET*, 68, 69 |
| 274 | 13 | *The Justice of Zeus*, Berkeley, 1971, 33–5; *Hesiod and the Near East*, Cardiff, 1966, 62 ff. |
| 276 | 1 | John Burnet, *Greek Philosophy, Thales to Plato*, 1914, 18 |
| 277 | 2 | *Mythe et pensée chez les grecs*, 1965, 285 ff. |
| 278 | 3 | *Ibid.*, 290 |
| | 4 | *Ibid.*, 305 |
| 281 | 5 | Bruno Snell, *The Discovery of the Mind* (Eng. trans.), Oxford, 1960, 223 f. |
| | 6 | *Ibid.*, 213 |

7   *Ibid.*, 223 f.

283   8   Sir Maurice Bowra, *Primitive Song*, 1962, 234

9   C. Lévi-Strauss, *Le Cru et le cuit*, Paris, 1964, 43 ff.; cf. *Myth*, 63 ff.

285   10   'Thoughts without content are empty, perceptions without concepts are blind': Kant (from the introduction to the Transcendental Logic in *The Critique of Pure Reason*)

11   W. Schadewaldt, *Der Aufbau des Pindarischen Epinikion*, Halle, 1928, reprinted 1966, [49]

287   12   W. K. C. Guthrie, *A History of Greek Philosophy* I, Cambridge, 1962, 29

288   13   *Odyssey* 1, 32 ff. (Zeus' complaint); *Iliad* 20, 244 (men's tongues), 2, 204 (rule of many)

14   *Odyssey* 6, 182 ff.

295   15   See e.g. G. S. Kirk and J. E. Raven, *The Presocratic Philosophers*, Cambridge, 1957, 73 ff.

296   16   *Ibid.*, 104 ff.

297   17   Heraclitus, frag. 32 (Diels); *op. cit. supra*, 204 f.

18   Heraclitus, frag. 30 (Diels); *op. cit. supra*, 199 ff.

299   19   *The Justice of Zeus*, Berkeley, 1971, 162

20   *Op. cit.* in n. 15 to p. 295, 114; Aristotle, *Physics* III, 4, 203 b 7 ff.

# INDEX

Abraham, Karl 73, 87
Abdera 187
Acastus 35, 208
Achaeans 96, 106, 111, 121, 123, 155, 166, 219, 287
Achaia 238
Achilles (Achilleus) 23, 96, 102, 134, 143, 146, 163, 177, 198, 205, 208, 232, 242, 247, 256, 287, 290, 292
Acrisius 147, 149, 150, 165
Acropolis 122, 154, 196, 228 f.
Actaeon 157
Acusilaus 187
Adam and Eve 18, 273
Adapa 56 f., 138
Admetus 128, 170, 191, 205
Adonia, Adonis 234 f., 254
Adrastus 107, 225
Aeacus, Aeacidae 102, 134, 202
Aegae 48
Aegean 48, 95, 172, 179, 244, 255, 265, 268
Aegeus 152 f., 154
Aegina 101–3, 202
Aegisthus 165–7, 290
Aelian 147
Aeolus 111, 168, 217
Aerope 165
Aeschylus 46, 58, 97, 103 f., 105, 140, 143, 147, 165, 170, 300
Aethra 152
aetiology, aition 14, 19, 49, 53–9, 60 f., 65, 66, 79, 114 f., 125, 131, 138, 141, 144, 158, 163, 165, 189, 211, 214, 230, 231, 232, 233, 235, 236, 237, 241, 242, 246, 252, 281
Aetolia 204
Africa 33, 50, 125, 189, 204
Agamemnon 78, 96, 103, 105,

145, 146, 163, 165–7, 216, 290, 292
Agaue 157
Agenor 156
Aietes 160–62
Aigaion, Mt. 115
Aiora 231
air 59, 118
Aison 160 f.
*aither* 44, 86
Ajax 102, 205
Akkadians, Akkadian myths 45, 46, 47, 48, 56, 62, 66, 118, 138, 206, 213, 234, 247, 255, 258, 263, 267, 270 f., 301
Alcaeus 100, 183
Alcestis 191, 210
Alcmene 121, 136, 182
Alcyoneus 195
Alexandrian literature 127, 160
allegory 17, 43, 53, 59, 80, 91, 118, 120, 121, 141, 276
Aloadae 128
alphabet 159, 164, 268
Amazon
 (river) 27, 65, 68
 (female warrior) 35, 150, 154 f., 187 f., 204
Amerindian myths 44, 50, 55, 61, 64 f., 72, 83, 85, 91, 204, 209, 283 f.
 *see also* Indian myths
Amphitrite 154, 225
Amphitryon 178, 182, 185
Amyclae 128, 156, 192
Anath 258
Anaximander 278, 295–7, 299
Anaximenes 295, 297
Androgeos 153, 232
Andromache 96, 100, 188
Andromeda 149 f., 188, 223
animals 23, 27, 31, 50 f., 52, 64 f.,

# READ MORE IN PENGUIN

In every corner of the world, on every subject under the sun, Penguin represents quality and variety – the very best in publishing today.

For complete information about books available from Penguin – including Puffins, Penguin Classics and Arkana – and how to order them, write to us at the appropriate address below. Please note that for copyright reasons the selection of books varies from country to country.

**In the United Kingdom**: Please write to *Dept. EP, Penguin Books Ltd, Bath Road, Harmondsworth, West Drayton, Middlesex UB7 0DA*

**In the United States**: Please write to *Consumer Sales, Penguin USA, P.O. Box 999, Dept. 17109, Bergenfield, New Jersey 07621-0120.* VISA and MasterCard holders call 1-800-253-6476 to order Penguin titles

**In Canada**: Please write to *Penguin Books Canada Ltd, 10 Alcorn Avenue, Suite 300, Toronto, Ontario M4V 3B2*

**In Australia**: Please write to *Penguin Books Australia Ltd, P.O. Box 257, Ringwood, Victoria 3134*

**In New Zealand**: Please write to *Penguin Books (NZ) Ltd, Private Bag 102902, North Shore Mail Centre, Auckland 10*

**In India**: Please write to *Penguin Books India Pvt Ltd, 706 Eros Apartments, 56 Nehru Place, New Delhi 110 019*

**In the Netherlands**: Please write to *Penguin Books Netherlands bv, Postbus 3507, NL-1001 AH Amsterdam*

**In Germany**: Please write to *Penguin Books Deutschland GmbH, Metzlerstrasse 26, 60594 Frankfurt am Main*

**In Spain**: Please write to *Penguin Books S. A., Bravo Murillo 19, 1° B, 28015 Madrid*

**In Italy**: Please write to *Penguin Italia s.r.l., Via Felice Casati 20, I–20124 Milano*

**In France**: Please write to *Penguin France S. A., 17 rue Lejeune, F–31000 Toulouse*

**In Japan**: Please write to *Penguin Books Japan, Ishikiribashi Building, 2–5–4, Suido, Bunkyo-ku, Tokyo 112*

**In South Africa**: Please write to *Longman Penguin Southern Africa (Pty) Ltd, Private Bag X08, Bertsham 2013*

# READ MORE IN PENGUIN

## LITERARY CRITICISM

### The Penguin History of Literature

Published in ten volumes, *The Penguin History of Literature* is a superb critical survey of the English and American literature covering fourteen centuries, from the Anglo-Saxons to the present, and written by some of the most distinguished academics in their fields.

### Epistemology of the Closet   Eve Kosofsky Sedgwick

Through her brilliant interpretation of the readings of Henry James, Melville, Nietzsche, Proust and Oscar Wilde, Eve Kosofsky Sedgwick shows how questions of sexual definition are at the heart of every form of representation in this century. 'A signal event in the history of late-twentieth-century gay studies. I don't feel so remunerated, so challenged, so moved, by anything else I've read in the field' – Wayne Koestenbaum

### The Anatomy of Criticism   Northrop Frye

'Here is a book fundamental enough to be entitled *Principia Critica*', wrote one critic. Northrop Frye's seminal masterpiece was the first work to argue for the status of literary criticism as a science: a true discipline whose techniques and approaches could systematically – and beneficially – be evaluated, quantified and categorized.

### Slip-Shod Sibyls   Germaine Greer

'The premise of contemporary feminism has been a sentimental illusion from the start. Greer rightly turns her artillery against it, and from a startling new position: she maintains that ... it is coddling and condescending overpraise, not simple obstruction, that has done most damage to women poets' – *Observer*

### Dangerous Pilgrimages   Malcolm Bradbury

'This capacious book tracks Henry James from New England to Rye; Evelyn Waugh to a Hollywood as grotesque as he expected; Gertrude Stein to Spain to be mistaken for a bishop; Oscar Wilde to a rickety stage in Leadsville, Colorado ... The textbook on the the transatlantic theme' – *Guardian*

# READ MORE IN PENGUIN

## HISTORY

**Frauen**  Alison Owings

Nearly ten years in the making and based on interviews and original research, Alison Owings' remarkable book records the wartime experiences and thoughts of 'ordinary' German women from varying classes and backgrounds.

**Byzantium: The Decline and Fall**  John Julius Norwich

The final volume in the magnificent history of Byzantium. 'As we pass among the spectacularly varied scenes of war, intrigue, theological debate, martial kerfuffle, sacrifice, revenge, blazing ambition and lordly pride, our guide calms our passions with an infinity of curious asides and grace-notes ... Norwich's great trilogy has dispersed none of this magic' – *Independent*

**The Anglo-Saxons**  Edited by James Campbell

'For anyone who wishes to understand the broad sweep of English history, Anglo-Saxon society is an important and fascinating subject. And Campbell's is an important and fascinating book. It is also a finely produced and, at times, a very beautiful book' – *London Review of Books*

**Conditions of Liberty**  Ernest Gellner

'A lucid and brilliant analysis ... he gives excellent reasons for preferring civil society to democracy as the institutional key to modernization ... For Gellner, civil society is a remarkable concept. It is both an inspiring slogan and the reality at the heart of the modern world' – *The Times*

**The Habsburgs**  Andrew Wheatcroft

'Wheatcroft has ... a real feel for the heterogeneous geography of the Habsburg domains – I especially admired his feel for the Spanish Habsburgs. Time and again, he neatly links the monarchs with the specific monuments they constructed for themselves' – *Sunday Telegraph*

# READ MORE IN PENGUIN

## ARCHAEOLOGY

**Breaking the Maya Code**  Michael D. Coe

Over twenty years ago, no one could read the hieroglyphic texts carved on the magnificent Maya temples and palaces; today we can understand almost all of them. The inscriptions reveal a culture obsessed with warfare, dynastic rivalries and ritual blood-letting. 'An entertaining, enlightening and even humorous history of the great searchers after the meaning that lies in the Maya inscriptions' – *Observer*

**Ancient Iraq**  Georges Roux

Newly revised and now in its third edition, *Ancient Iraq* covers the political, cultural and socio-economic history of Mesopotamia from the days of prehistory to the Christian era and somewhat beyond.

**Schliemann of Troy**  David Traill

By uncovering what he claimed to be Homer's Troy and Mycenae, Heinrich Schliemann (1822–90) became one of the dominant personalities of his age. 'It is original, readable and gives a vivid portrait of this impossible man: belligerent, vulgar, egotistical, devious, grasping, generous, strangely impersonal and crackling with energy' – *Daily Telegraph*

**Lucy's Child**  Donald Johanson and James Shreeve

'Superb adventure ... *Lucy's Child* burns with the infectious excitement of hominid fever ... the tedium and the doubting, and the ultimate triumph of an expedition that unearths something wonderful about the origins of humanity' – *Chicago Tribune*

**Archaeology and Language**  Colin Renfrew
The Puzzle of Indo-European Origins

'The time-scale, the geographical spaces, the questions and methods of inquiry ... are vast ... But throughout this teeming study, Renfrew is pursuing a single, utterly fascinating puzzle: who are we Europeans, where do the languages we speak really stem from?' – *Sunday Times*